A HILLSIDE VIEW

OF INDUSTRIAL HISTORY

A

HILLSIDE VIEW

OF

INDUSTRIAL HISTORY

A STUDY OF INDUSTRIAL EVOLUTION
IN THE PENNINE HIGHLANDS
WITH SOME LOCAL RECORDS

BY

ABM. NEWELL

[1925]

REPRINTS OF ECONOMIC CLASSICS

AUGUSTUS M. KELLEY · PUBLISHERS
NEW YORK 1971

First Edition 1925

(Todmorden: Published by the Author, *At 5 Pickles Building, Longfield Road*, 1925)

REPRINTED 1971 BY
AUGUSTUS M. KELLEY · PUBLISHERS
REPRINTS OF ECONOMIC CLASSICS
New York New York 10001

. . . .

I S B N 0-678-00695-4
L C N 73-119540

. . . .

PRINTED IN THE UNITED STATES OF AMERICA
by SENTRY PRESS, NEW YORK, N. Y. 10019

Perennial flow of Energy (Frontispiece).   *Block kindly lent by Rev. A. W. Fox, M.A.*

A Hillside View of Industrial History.

A STUDY OF INDUSTRIAL EVOLUTION
IN THE PENNINE HIGHLANDS,
WITH SOME LOCAL
RECORDS

BY

ABM. NEWELL.

Published by the Author, at 5, Pickles Building, Longfield
Road, Todmorden, and Printed by J. Bentley & Sons,
Printers, Bookbinders, etc., Albion Works, Todmorden.

CONTENTS.

PREFACE.

AVING for the grester part of my life indulged the passion for making direct acquaintance with that portion of the Pennine Hills which surrounds my birthplace, and endeavoured to learn something of its past history, I now respond to numerous requests to place on record some account of what I have been able to learn of activities, interests and conditions which it appears to me are too little known. I can make no claim either to have exhausted the subject, or to have given literary finish to my treatment of it. My school-days were passed in the old dames' schools and a factory school such as existed before the passing of the Elementary Education Act. The reader will not fail to find evidence that the different parts of the work were not written continuously, but at intervals when opportunity occurred ; and as a result of this some ideas have obtruded themselves more than once.

The views set forth or suggested in the pages which follow can in some measure claim to be based upon personal touch and first-hand information. The materials upon which the work is based have nearly all been in hand some years. It was publicly outlined at the Summer meeting of the Sowerby Division Conference of Youth in the year 1915 ; but the work of developing and putting in shape suitable for publication has been frequently interfered with by other matters. Even when the work had taken its final form several long delays were experienced. The only importance that can attach to this statement lies in the relation of the present effort to that of other students who may have been engaged in the same or similar fields of research. In so far as there may be agreement or not in the results obtained, those conclusions have been reached by quite independent paths.

My indebtedness to others, both institutions and persons, is a great deal more than I can hope to adequately express. This production, whatever its merits, is one fruit of the University Extension Movement in its various forms ; public lectures with classes for students, and Summer meetings ; Ruskin College Correspondence classes ; and Tutorial classes. Without the opportunity for study and access to books which these organisations have afforded, this little effort would never have been possible. Then again there are the Public Libraries, especially the Reference Departments at Todmorden, Rochdale, Bradford and Leeds. These have provided me with the means of access to printed copies of original documents. To the various Staffs I would like to pay my tribute of thanks for the willing help which they have always given me. The several works which I have been enabled to consult are named in the text and footnotes. Another formative influence which I should mention is the classes held in connection with the Science and Art Department, South Kensington, long years ago.

I cannot omit to mention my indebtedness to several individuals. For more than twenty years the Rev. A. W. Fox, M.A., has been a most kindly helper, both in personal effort and the freedom with which he has placed his valuable library at my service, and when the manuscript was finished he very kindly read it through, and gave me the benefit of many useful suggestions and criticisms. My good friend Mr. H. P. Kendall has made me his great debtor by the unstinted help which he has given me. For many years I have enjoyed free access to his valuable library, notes, copies of original documents, and relics of early man in the district. To the late Professor Unwin, M.A., and Mr. A. N. Shimmin, M.A., my sincere thanks are due. It was the former's suggestion that I should write a history of my native heath which led me to hope that I might be able to produce something which would prove useful to students of history. Whether the result has taken the form which he had in mind, now, alas, will never be known. In any case, to both of these gentlemen I cannot do less than express my appreciation of the candid criticism and valuable suggestions with which they have favoured me. To those who have supplied me with photographs for the illustrations my grateful thanks are also due.

Since the work was in type I have had the privilege of reading Mr. Heaton's work on the Woollen Industry of Yorkshire, and have been agreeably surprised to find how, for the larger area, and worked out in fuller detail, my conclusions in that branch of the subject have been anticipated.

Finally, I cannot hope to have escaped mistakes and imperfections, and can only ask for charitable judgment. I shall be grateful for specific instances to be pointed out.

ABM. NEWELL.

TODMORDEN.
June, 1925.

INTRODUCTORY.

CHAPTER I.

SOME PRELIMINARY REFLECTIONS.

VERY local history must, by the very nature of the case, have a flavour which distinguishes it from most others of the like restricted range, no less than from the larger and more general national histories. Few, however, of the more limited works, are likely to be so far out of touch with those covering the wider field of human activities in the past as those, whose range of interest is confined to a portion of the Pennine uplands of the North of England. Similar differences between academic pronouncements and the results of local enquiry present themselves in relation to the lowlands of the North-west, except perhaps in a strip of territory adjoining the coast. Another defect not always absent from local histories, as well as from others of a more general character, which deal with those phases of national life which have attracted the attention of investigators in recent times, e.g., Industrial and the wider Social History—is their obvious effort to correlate themselves to the general historical tradition already established in a different field and derived from other sources of information. Hence a tradition was established before the ascendacny of the more critical habit of mind, which is the inevitable outcome of the modern scientific spirit. Briefly put, the endeavour has been made (largely unconsciously) to make research and its results in the new fields of historical study parellel to, and coincident with the old, both as applied to locality and subject. It has been imperfectly realised that there might be tracks and currents not strictly conforming with the conditions which were instrumental in framing the old conceptions.

3

The present work, based as it is, first upon a study of local conditions, then endeavouring to find confirmation or otherwise, for the facts and conclusions thus attained by reference to the more general studies, can modestly claim to approach the subject, in so far as it bears upon general problems, from a not very common point of view. Not having succeeded in finding that degree of agreement between local and generally accepted history which might have been expected, the main purpose before the writer's mind has been to use the materials derived from the investigation of a more limited and little known area, in order to present a new, or more correctly, a complimentary view-point of our national life and industry, as they disclose themselves in those records of the past centuries which are available.

Although the facts and inferences used in support of the main argument of this work are drawn mostly from a limited area, convenience of access to the sources of information being the only determining factor in the case, there are not wanting reasons for believing that an extension of the enquiry to the much larger upland of the north area, would result in the general confirmation of the conclusions hereinafter set forth. Indeed, in view of the great interest now taken in the economic basis of Society, and the relations of the different classes to each other, as they have grown out of the industrial life of the past, it is devoutly to be hoped that others better equipped for the task will undertake upon a much more thorough plan and for the whole of this neglected area a similar course of enquiry to that which is here imperfectly achieved. Moreover, in view of the present day attitude of many leading educationalists, that it is desirable to apply to the teaching of history the principle of proceeding from the known or familiar, to the unknown or unfamiliar, by approaching general history from its local manifestations, a valuable and useful piece of work might thus be accomplished. Not only might teachers be often able to fulfil a duty which to them is frequently altogether impossible, but they would always be better able correctly and confidently, to correlate these two and many other aspects of a very important subject.

4

The present limited enquiry, in so far as it has proceeded, does seem to point unerringly to the conclusion that if an adequate study were made of the local history of the hills and dales which constitute the Pennine Range, there would result a somewhat modified view, more particularly of industrial, social, and perhaps religious life and their developments, from those usually set forth by academic writers. Students of this kind, although they have very completely embraced the facts which have come within their range of observation, have nevertheless, been the victims of one rather serious defect. Their observations have been extended over a limited field, and their reasonings applied necessarily to the facts which that limited field has supplied. The prevalence of such a practice throughout past times has been responsible for the development of the tradition already referred to, namely, the attitude of mind, or habit if you will, of regarding the accustomed field of operations as embracing the whole territory, outside of which is little more than a desolate and unproductive waste. An apt illustration of this point is to be found in the work which has hitherto been done with a view of setting forth an account of past industrial life and developments. The evidence upon which that story has been based, has been drawn largely, if not entirely, from the records of trade and craft guilds, legislation, and royal or manorial orders affecting those organisations, which were largely in the nature of bargains with them. Anything in the nature of industrial activity in those regions where trade guilds did not function, seems to have been ignored, or perhaps, never conceived as possible.

Anyone familiar with the history of the north-central highlands of England, as reflected in the manners, customs social and industrial life, such as can be drawn from those more or less perfect and scattered local histories and documents, from the official records of the past contained in the MANOR COURT ROLLS, WILLS, SURVEYS, and other such public, private, and official documents, as have been made available to the average student, cannot fail to conclude that this very extensive area has largely escaped the cognisance of those responsible for our ordinary English historical works. After all, it is not so very wonderful, that in the centuries previous to the last two or three, these highland and remote districts should have escaped the notice, not only of the chroniclers of the time, but also of the records and observation of officials who have unconsciously provided the quarries from which historians have been in the habit of drawing material. But that later enquirers should have allowed themselves to be bound by the habit alluded to above and thus debarred themselves from excursions outside of the customary area, is indeed, passing strange.

It is hoped that some useful purpose will be served by dealing with a district situated in the heart of the Pennines, so as to bring into relief the way in which that area differs in the light which it throws upon the course of events in the past, and upon the development of national institutions, in comparison with more academic narratives and the philosophy of history. The study of local History has surely more than a local significance : at any rate, the case now receiving our attention, would seem to point to the need of considerable modification in some of the conclusions arrived at, in the productions presented to us as authoritative English history. Although many histories of this country have been written, some based upon original research, others simply attempts at popularising or making clearer, the stories of the more original treatises, no one will contend that the interpretation of the past has been fully represented, either in its various aspects, or in relation to different parts of our island. The object of the following pages is to indicate that there is one considerable portion of the land, which has scarcely entered into the purview of those who have undertaken the task of presenting to us the course of events in, and the lessons of, the past. Although the present writer cannot claim either by literary or other qualifications, or by peculiar historical gifts, a title to a special hearing ; yet some study of local history has forced upon his mind the definite conclusion that these upland territories, may in capable hands be made to shed new light upon our island's story and the lesson to be derived therefrom.

6

SOME REASONS FOR THE PAST AND PRESENT LIMITED OUTLOOK.

The reasons for so complete a neglect of the historical developments, of so large an area of this country are varied, and at least until we come to the more modern period of enlarged intercourse, are to some extent natural. The following attempt to indicate some of them makes no claim either to exhaustiveness, or necessarily their order of importance. Elsewhere (Chapters II. and III.), an attempt is made to portray the principal features of these difficult and rather inhospitable regions as they would be in more primitive times, and their isolation before the era of modern travel. They have afforded little of the weft and warp out of which are woven the web of conventional historical narrative. The district is especially unfitted for the operations of mediæval warfare, political intrigue, or constitutional developments. The land does not lend itself to that rich productivity looked for by early adventurers. Those in possession would have unique strategetic advantages over any attacking force. The obscure recesses of the deep valleys, the dizzy heights of abrupt hills with their rocky crests and crag-strewn slopes, made attack peculiarly difficult and hazardous. To win a position occupied by residents, conversant with every local resource, and all the devious paths, capable alike of utilisation for retreat or surprise, as circumstances might suggest, would need a force enormous relatively to similar operations on easier ground, and involve sacrifices out of all proportion to the gains expected or desired. No great territorial magnate could hope to find here an agreeable home or surroundings : nor does the land dispose itself suitably to the pageantry in which the ruling classes loved to display themselves. The available stage was too cramped for their ambitions, and too remote from the centre of political, personal, and social relations.

Consequently none of the favourite themes of writers— the presumed national questions arising out of the jealousies of great families or the strife of rival courtiers—had any part of their action worked out here. Politico-military-regal drama necessarily failed to flourish in so uncongenial a soil.

7

Few, if any, of the natives were concerned about the Wars of the Roses, or of the execution of Lady Jane Grey ; they were spared the degradation of becoming either the hirelings or partisans of such sordid and miserable adventures.   By the middle of the seventeenth century, however, this area had begun to emerge somewhat from its old-time isolation. Its people were profoundly affected religiously, industrially, and to some extent politically, by the Civil War.   There were of its sons who joined the forces on the one side or the other ; but few of their names have found their way into the pages of history.   Charles Townely, who fell at Marston Moor is in fact, the solitary exception to the general oblivion. Some years later Archbishop Tillotson, the son of a Sowerby clothier, having left the sect of his earlier years, and joined the Established Church, gained great distinction in religious annals.   Others might be mentioned in various walks of life who have acheived distinction, but failed to find recognition of their place of origin ; or whose position on the scroll of fame, has been less prominent than would otherwise have been the case.

Again the history of the books has been written from the point of view of the dominant classes, who established themselves in their positions by virtue of the strong arm, buttressed it may be by trickery, and other questionable methods.   Although party purposes and sectional ambitions, have pervaded the narratives by colouring and minimising facts and incidents, the writers, for all that, have largely belonged to the social class, which in the main acknowledged the age-long tradition of the greatness and superiority of classical England, as against the little known and despised out-lands. This tradition of superior rank, the last conqueror always reserved for himself and associates.   Hence it is of the very essence of the problem in trying to understand the northern upland character, to recognise that until a high degree of success in trade had established here and there one in a position of such riches that he became a local power and object of respect, the natives generally had seldom had ex- perience of any much above themselves in social status.

The agents of the higher outside powers, the representatives of the central government or local lords of the manor, who often only visited periodically and under the necessities of their office, were but little respected, and their demands acceded to grudgingly and with the worst possible grace. The social distinctions of rank in the old feudal sense never had a strong hold here.

The general history of the earlier centuries, as drawn from surviving evidence is largely an account of a series of struggles between the occupants of the fertile and genial low-land, and successive swarms of adventurers, whose desires were bent upon securing the rich heritage of the occupants. Those of the latter who declined to submit to, and escaped from, the ruthless demands of the conquerors made up the population of the elevated backwood regions. From the very nature of the case, the one being a dominant class in circumstances of comparative ease, the other beaten refugees in poverty and poor surroundings, such of the records of the times as have survived are deficient in their testimonies of the beaten party. Such accounts as we have from the unfortunate side are those of churchmen, who as we shall shortly see, were situated generally a long way from the harassed people, and the special objects of attack, at least by the Northmen, though after the tenth century, they became the aiders and abettors of the agressive Normans. Shut out by their secluded position from the advantages of culture, the refugees were at a great disadvantage both in making and preserving records. Such accounts therefore as have come down to us, we may fairly presume, are in the main one-sided and peculiarly imperfect, the temper dividing the two sections being such, that the one could never have justice done to them by the dominant party.

Had there been a demand for education, the physical conditions, to say nothing of universal prejudice, precluded the possibility of establishing in the social and political outlands of a seat of learning, in the least degree comparable with Oxford and Cambridge. Both of these ancient centres of thought and learning are situated within the richest and most accessible parts of classical England. They were controlled by, and catered for the requirements of that area, and probably to a large extent unconsciously, fostered and perpetuated that cultured ignorance of the benighted regions, which even to this day has not entirely disappeared. All along ecclesiastics were the only class who had any pretensions to education, the only people capable of filling many of the principal offices of state, or compiling chronicles and records. From the seventh century onwards, they were intimately associated with the Church of Rome, that most perfect and far-reaching organisation in existence. For the reasons stated in the very brief sketch of religious history (Chapter IV), the last fact would not strongly recommend them to the favourable judgment of the hillside man, and reciprocally, would not improve the clerical attitude towards his assumed inferior. Moreover, there is no need to rely solely upon assumption to support the opinion that personal and class interests largely influenced the policy of clerics, and the character of the evidence they have left behind them.

There is another feature of this question : the physical structure and surface conditions are such, that the area has never tempted the settlement within it of a religious house, the only source of such spiritual and cultured refinement as the middle ages afforded outside the two great centres of learning. Not even in their days of self-sacrificing hardship and devotion, did these zealous votaries of the softer and more refined sides of human life cast a look in this direction. Taking a straight line at right angles across almost the middle of the Pennines, we find it terminated by the two old-time institutions of Kirkstall and Whalley, both planted in the first genial and fertile spots to be found at the foot of the respective slopes, and these two by no means the earliest of their kind. This does not, however, affirm that the neglected people entirely escaped the attentions of ecclesiastical enterprise. It is quite probable that itinerant priests did visit at least, those portions of the population living along the main lines of communication. But in the more out-of-the-way places the most regular attention by religious institutions was paid by officials demanding contributions in the shape of tithes, rents, etc., in support of far distant establishments. To the natives, all this, especially the latter, was of a piece with the military and political overlordship of the conquering aliens, draining off their hard-won wealth for the benefit of unsympathetic institutions, filled with, or preyed upon, by what, to the native, would seem to be parasites and useless idlers.

Further, for many centuries, ecclesiastical authority asserted a firmer and more extensive grip upon all the phases of life within its reach. But over the backbone of England, where allegiance to the Celtic Church probably survived long after the synod of Whitby, that control was less paramount. Consequently chronicles and records whether of officials, local courts, or individual observers, are scarce, for the simple reason that they seldom existed, at any rate for the remoter parts. In the absence of important centres either of administration or pretensions to learning, coupled with the prevailing mutual prejudices, anything worth preserving was heavily handicapped against the possibility of survival. Ignorance of the value of such materials as may once have existed, or might in more favourable circumstances have been brought into being, was intensified amongst a people whose life was of necessity a hard one, and who were obliged to rely upon their mother-wit and determined efforts, to secure advantages more easily accessible to those living in more favoured localities. It is even probable that the use to which the officials who made their way into these parts put their own accomplishments, and such documentary evidence as they became possessed or aware of, may have prejudiced their victims against the acquirement or use of such resources. For the imposition of demands and obligations of an obnoxious character would be the most obvious guise in which clerical works would present themselves to the natives.

Again, it must be remembered that in the more national, literary, political, legislative, and administrative matters, the Norman tradition, the very antithesis of all hillside or outland sentiment, has been for nearly a thousand years paramount. Although it is usual to look upon the conquerors as

11

having become largely absorbed in, and adapting themselves to English ways and sympathies, this was only so to the extent to which it contributed to their own comfort as an upper class, and security as conquerors. The recognition of native ideals was more formal than real, and at all times directed towards ease and class domination. The absorption or adaptation was only to that section of the English, who by yielding and remaining in their original homes as subjects, had offered least effective resistance, and had finally submitted to the intruding authorities. This, again, is just what the refugees of the mountains would not do. On the other hand, the conquerors in constant touch with the rest of the world, besides being in league with the Vatican, had the advantage of obtaining and monopolising the world's ear, and of having recorded their doings, ambitions and sympathies. The parts where they settled or had influence, were emphatically the THE WORLD. Their lives and activities attracted the interest and secured the attention of scribes and chroniclers. Their version of events monopolised attention. The rest, that is the despised northerners and " wild " hillmen, were simply nowhere on the recognised stage, and of no moment. We have here again the common experience : that which has been able to assert itself and influence high quarters, has been what has passed into records and survived the wearing effect of time.

From such partial and incomplete sources we all have had to take our own material, and been too prone to accept as a sufficient reflection of national life, movements, and activities, during past time. That other territory, which was in continual potential revolt, or at least, grudging obedience and limited submission towards established authority, has been quite unable to have its actions faithfully recorded, or its ideas taken into account. To be in antipathy to " the powers that be," by those whose outlook is so widely different, is even yet regarded too much in the nature of a social crime. Allusion has already been made (pp. 3, 5, and 6), to the attitude of mind which has so largely dominated the historical field during past years. When the industrial developments which culminated in the revolution, which began during the latter half of the eighteenth century, forced into prominence these hinterlands, the old traditional methods of enquiry and generalisation manifested themselves.   The newly visible territory was treated rather as a recent creation, than as one which had all the time been coincident with the known, but had been the unfortunate victim of an oversight.   The resulting outlook was of this kind ; so little had apparently ever taken place there, that it could not be expected to yield anything worth looking for.

An interesting example of this attitude of mind and its results is afforded by the way in which even to-day writers and teachers treat the site of the battle of Brunanburh.   It is hardly necessary to point out that, though all agree that such an important struggle did take place in the year 937, the site where the sanguinary conflict actually was fought has slipped from all knowledge.   Various localities have been suggested as the scene of operations, on behalf of some of which the most that can be said is that they are more or less plausible or ingenious conjectures.   Most writers on Saxon history refer to one or more of these, giving guarded adhesion to one.   For more than fifty years they have had access to a printed paper read before the *Historical Society of Lancashire and Cheshire.* the author of which, the late T. T. Wilkinson, Esq., contended not without wealth of argument, for an entirely new site, namely, Saxifield on the slope of the Pennines dipping towards Burnley in Lancashire.   But judging from the scant attention it has received, one is almost tempted to say, that the position being within the area which the academic mind has been congenitally unable to bring within its grasp, has not received the attention which it otherwise might have done.   Be that as it may, few if any of the writers on the subject have bestowed upon the suggested site the barest reference.

The indifference thus manifested in learned circles has had its effects reflected in the mental outlook even of the most loyal inhabitants of the neglected area itself.   It reminds one of the somewhat misdirected education, which it would seem, has been a main reason for the German people's wide-spread support of that perverted nationalism which, in recent years has brought upon the world such an unparalleled calamity. Just in proportion as the old passion of exclusiveness has given way, and the northern people have submitted to the conventions of the larger and more dominant area, the prevailing education has been accepted with its traditional teachings. All unconsciously, the view has taken hold of the local mind that the area is one in which little worth attention ever did or could take place. Indeed the people who might justly be looked upon as being at least above the average in educational equipment, have habitually expressed astonishment when brought to see that the history of their own district was not limited to three or four centuries at the most, and, that beyond that time all was not a barren wilderness.

CHAPTER II.

PHYSICAL CONDITIONS OF A HILL COUNTRY DURING THE EARLY CENTURIES.

S a help to our understanding of the conditions prevailing in the back-wood territories during primitive and mediæval times, both as affecting the lives of the residents and their relation to the outside world, it is important that we should get as far as possible a conception of what those surroundings actually were. Without this we shall largely fail both to understand the local developments, and to appreciate the outlook of both scholastic and official outsiders, in relation to the peculiar problems here presented. We may also be enabled thereby to gain a better understanding of the mutual jealousies referred to in the fourth chapter, jealousies so deep-seated and extensive that even yet they have not yet quite passed away.

In these days of highly developed transit and intercourse, it is not easy to appreciate the remoteness and isolation of these rugged and elevated regions as they existed during the long preceding centuries. At the present day visitors to this district from more fertile and less varied parts of the country, are frequently amazed at the difficulties of communication and the barren aspect of some of the craggy hills. The upper portion of Calderdale, a principal pass between the eastern and western side of the Pennines, may serve to illustrate the character of the whole, at least in general outline and to a considerable extent in detail. About a hundred and forty years ago began the process of providing better means of communication, which had the effect of opening out to the natives opportunites of a fuller life, as well as occasional glimpses of the realities of hillside life to the self-appointed critics at large. First of all turn-pike roads, a generation

15

later, a canal linking up the natural water-ways which had always joined the feet of the hills with the two sea-boards, combined to put the secluded area into easier and more continuous touch with the world at large.

After another generation and a half, a main line of railway greatly increased these facilities. The electric telegraph and telephone followed in due course. It was only when these changes had been effected, that the area became really a part of the great world : but they are only of yesterday, compared with the twenty-fold longer period during which the older order prevailed with almost imperceptible changes. Of course, in the rest of the country the same kind of difficulties existed, but were less in dregee. Wherever there was a navigable river, or there remained in usable condition, either a Roman military or a monastic road, the difficulties of transport were thereby minimised. But apart from these two considerations, the difficulites of maintaining good roads, were much greater where steep hills were everywhere, where the wash of the rainfall was greater, and official interest more difficult to obtain.

Let us now try to picture one wide-spread scene, as it unfolded itself in a pass which is not far from the centre of the great Pennine range of hills. In the higher third of its course, the Yorkshire Calder and its many rushing tributaries, flow through dales which are narrow and deep. In some places the width of the valley is barely sufficient to accommodate the stream of undefined age, and its triple transit arteries of modern date. It attains a depth of a thousand feet in a width of three miles, a feature still more accentuated at many points where the steep sides rise more than half of their height without receding more than half-a-mile. Still more impressive does this feature become, when we reflect that in recent geological times the valley-bottom has certainly been more than sixty, and probably ninety feet lower relatively to the hill tops than it now is. This is further accentuated if allowance be made for the wearing down of the exposed summits, which must have been considerable during the intervening long course of time, during which the silting up of the bottom has been effected. Exactly how long is the lapse of years since this greater distance between hill, summit, and valley bottom existed, there is no means of saying. It is probable that the uplift of the British Isles during the Glacial period is responsible for its existence, and that a depression of the same area which ocurred at the close of or subsequent to the Ice age, is ultimately responsible for the silt-up of a series of lakes which came into being through the blocking of the valley at one or more points. It is well-known that on both the east and west sides of England, old river-valleys are filled to a depth of ninety or a hundred feet with typical glacial drift.

In our interior part of the country, however, the glacial character of the silted-up material is not so obvious. From about Whiteley Arches, Hebden Bridge, to above Scaitcliffe in the Burnley Valley, and to an equal extent in the Walsden Valley, the bottom contains a thick deposit of blue-grey loam, and at many places river gravel has been seen under or interbedding the loam. Where the valleys widen out somewhat, as at Hollins Bottom in Walsden, and about Adamroyd Mill, and Toad Carr in the Burnley Valley, beneath the topcrust there is a bed of peat. At the last named place it was cut through during the making of the Corporation main sewer in the year 1906. At Gandy Bridge, there was found to be a layer four feet thick of brown peat and peaty soil. Growing thinner westwards it finally disappeared at Tantam (the modern Spring Bank). It would appear that the peat extended some distance up the hillside ; for when building operations were in progress at Harley Bank during the seventies of last century, several feet thick of it were cut through. So, too, during the year 1921, when the municipal housing site was being prepared, excavations near the western limit just behind Ferney Lee, disclosed a bed of peat six feet thick in some parts. At both places great trunks of bog-oak were found. It would thus seem that during the later stages of the silting-up, where water had the chance of spreading out, or bog conditions prevailed, marsh-plants grew, died, and their remains accumulated for a long number

17

of years, during which this deposit was laid down. At Crow-Carr Ings during boring operations, in search for water at a depth of sixty-two feet, one pebble was found which was probably ice-borne.

These facts, however, taken in conjunction with others to be given later (pp. 24-5), make it probable, that the greater depth of valleys detailed above existed previous to man's presence here, at any rate as a settled resident. All along, the sides of the valley are precipitous, often craggy and rock-strewn. At a height varying from six to nine hundred feet above the bed of the stream the bluff terminates in a thick bed of grit-stone, whose non-yielding character is responsible for the preservation of the prominent crests, and the varying resistance to erosive agents of these several grit-stones and underlying shales has determined the width and abruptness of the valley-sides. Another factor which has helped to determine some of these physical details is the faults, or crust-dislocations, which have in many places disturbed the original continuity of the beds. The principal one of all these, the great Pennine Fault, which extends along the whole range, passes through the district, where a vertical displacement of nearly a thousand feet shows itself. The rocks on the south side of Burnley Valley are that distance chronologically higher than those of the north side. The line of displacement shows itself superficially as follows. Coming from Blackstone Edge to Waterstalls, it is revealed by powerful and little varying springs of water both there and at Knowl. Behind Waterside Mill the Yoredale Shales of the east may be seen abutting on the Mill-stone grits of the west. Crossing the valley it cuts through the Ridge near to the chimney, and traverses the Burnley Valley obliquely. It is evidenced on the northern summit of the valley by the sudden termination of the Kinder Scout grits of the Stansfield moorlands above Shore, and by another powerful spring in the neighbourhood of Hawkstones.

The particular resistent bed which is responsible for the abruptness of the lower and greater portion of the valley varies from place to place. About Hebden Bridge it is the

Kinder Scout grit. From Eastwood to about Whirlaw, it is a bed of very coarse grit which comes in the higher por- tion of the Yoredale series. At this point, we come definitely within the influence of the great dislocation, Whirlaw Stones itself, being a piece of Kinder which has slipped down two hundred feet. Further west, until we come to Orkan, the breakage brings in an element of confusion. Along the probable line of the fault the lower shelf is not so prominent ; but at Orkan and Knotts Naze, the crest is again in evidence but determined by the Middle grits. On the south side of the Burnley valley, the middle grits command the whole sit- uation. This statement of present geological knowledge, may have to be modified somewhat when the results of a recent official survey are published. From the irregular line of this crest, on all sides the slope up to the summit is more gentle, being terminated at the central ridge, which is generally on the east-side of the fault-line, by Kinder Scout grit. There are grand exposures of this at many places from Derbyshire northwards. Locally much romantic rock scenery may be found at Robin Hood's Bed on Blackstone Edge, Lang- field and Erringden Moors, and most notable of all that fine and time-honoured outcrop on Stansfield heights known as· Bride Stones. On the extreme heights of Heptonstall and Wadsworth, other impressive examples are to be seen. At similar heights to the west of Walsden, and the north-west of Todmorden and adjoining Cliviger, the lower coal-mea- sures cap the hills.

As we ascend the course of this Yorkshire stream, we find that contact with the rival county of Lancaster involves its splitting into two portions, each of which originally con- tinued for some distance to separate the two territories. But the making of the canal at one point, and the railway over another considerable length, more still in the lower part of the Burnley valley and about Lydgate, private enterprise involved the diversion of the stream to such an extent, as to introduce confusion in the delimitation both of county and townships, which not one per cent of the present population could unravel. One of these branches of the river taking a north-westerly direction originally bounded the sister-counties for a distance of a good two-and-a-half miles. At the present time from the foregoing reasons, it does not do so for more than two-thirds of the distance. Beyond that point it, at Redwater Foot, plunges into the western county for a distance of a mile and threequarters, where we find the head waters on the south side of the Lancashire and Yorkshire Railway at Cross i' t' Deyn. At this point was formerly a swamp which received the drainage from the adjoining hillsides and supplied the head waters both of the Lancashire and Yorkshire Calders. When the turnpike road was made, this swamp was interfered with, and was more completely drained when the railway was constructed.

The sources of these two rivers although quite near to one another are now more separated than formerly : superficial observers still maintain the old tradition, making a pond on the west side of the summit into the source of both, which is quite impossible for the eastern one. The other branch of the river bends southwards, at the present day alternately cutting and bounding the counties for half-a-mile, then for another stretch bounding them up to Swineshead Clough, which makes the whole distance close upon a mile. Thence it becomes wholly a Lancastrian subject for nearly three miles of its infant course to the neighbourhood of Summit. These upper reaches until quite modern times were rather out of the way, and the uncertainty of their geographical relations involved an even greater neglect, both by historians and others. than has been the fate of the larger outside areas. Each outside local scribe has agreed with the other, in assigning whatever there might be of interest in this tiny buffer state to the province and care of another. The inevitable result has been that the district has been almost entirely neglected. Wherever outside writers have deigned to notice it, their allusions have served rather to show the limits of their knowledge than anything else, which both of the locality and its people has been even greater than the paucity of their writings would lead us to infer.

Another feature of the district which marks the difference in its appearance and character during earlier centuries
from those prevailing to-day, is the almost universally wooded
growth which covered the whole.   Place-names all over the
district, and the remains of trees which are still to be found
at many places such as Calderbrook, Langfield Moor, Harley
Bank, Blackshawhead, and Widdop, in all which places, roots,
trunks, bark and nuts have been found, leave little room for
doubting that in primitive times and for centuries later the
whole countryside was covered with trees and undergrowth,
except perhaps the cliffs and rocky scars which afforded
no hold for roots, and the highest summits which might be
too bleak and exposed.   The disappearance of woods needs
no change of climatic or other conditions to explain it.   Ever
since man came here he has been busy cutting down timber
for fuel, buildings, utensils, furniture and other purposes.
In the earlier times wood was the universal fuel : until the
seventeenth century, or possibly later, buildings were mainly
made of wood, and for centuries it was in large demand by
woolcombers for charcoal, and only to a less extent for iron-
working.   Little, if any, attention was given to the planting
and protection of this valuable product.   What planting
has been done in recent years has been very limited in extent,
and inspired more by the desire of ornamenting the surroundings of a private residence than for utility.   A litttle attention
given to these matters during past centuries, we can now see,
would have yielded great benefits to us in the present.   Had
the banks of the canal, for instance, been planted with alder,
the existing scarcity of wood for clog soles would have been
minimised, besides bringing a harvest to the owners as a
result of of judicious planting.   In addition we might have
been spared the sight of a few ugly scars, which now spoil
an otherwise admirable landscape.

This part of the " backbone of England " provides
two passes between the east and the west slopes, where are to
be found the sources of four streams each known from time
immemorial as the Calder.   Two of these streams have
already been spoken of.   From Cross i' t' Deyne or there-

21

abouts issue the head waters of the west or Lancashire Calder, and from the same point north-east Lancashire opens out. From Summit at the head of the southerly branch of the main Yorkshire Calder stretches the district of south-east Lancashire and the fourth Calder also rises. Perhaps the name for the stream flowing in that direction is not generally recognised at the present day ; but there does not seem to be much doubt that that really was the old name. In its earliest course it washes the foot of the slope on which the village of Calderbrook stands ; then it flows by Calder Moor. These facts, the repetition of the name, and the features of the land through which its waters pass, probably afford a clue to the origin of the name itself ; namely Col, a narrow opening or passage through the hills, and the Celtic Dwr or Der—water, that is, the water issuing from a narrow gorge of the hill. Another tributary of the east Calder is known in its upper portion as Colden.

Until comparatively recent times the people lived mainly, and in the earliest times almost certainly entirely, on the higher grounds, though probably not on the summits. It has often been urged that the reason for this was that " the fear of the enemy was ever before them." This may have been one factor in the choice, but another more potent was the fact that the valley bottoms were originally swampy and flooded without any attempt to minimise or control the waters. Moreover, it is highly probable that they were filled with a tangled mass of rank vegetation, which would present insuperable obstacles to primitive tools and methods of cultivation. Such enemies as beasts of the forest, would here present themselves more numeroulsy than on the higher grounds. Evidence is not wanting that, during the late middle ages destructive beasts were still to be encountered. In the Wakefield Court Rolls from the year 1274 onwards, there are numerous references to deer in various parts of the upper Calder Valley (Yorkshire) : but it would also appear that they were preserved for hunting, the district being a royal forest. Erringden was a park said to have been stocked with " wild and savage beasts, as stags, bucks, does, wild boars and other beasts of venerie " (v. *Watson's History of Halifax*), from sometime in the twelfth century to the year 1449, when it was dispaled.   In the year 1297, Alan, son of Richard Talvas, was imprisoned for taking from William del Hirst, six sheaves of oats against his will, alleging that William owed him the same for preserving his corn in the night from the beasts of the wood.

On the north-east Lancashire side there is more conclusive evidence.   The Earl of Lincoln had there about forty cattle breeding stations, some of them containing sixty or seventy beasts.   Exact accounts were rendered yearly by the keepers and fequently there was such an entry as this :— " Roscyndale.   ' 1 calf strangled by wolf.'   ' William Dynley, 1 cow strangled by the wolf '."

Several of the vaccaries were situated at a high altitude on the western slope of the dividing ridge, and therefore only a few miles from the Yorkshire watershed.   These facts are also, perhaps, indirect evidence that the Norman owners looked upon these exposed hill-slopes as ill-fitted for anything but the simplest type of agriculture.   The Earl of Warren had also a few like stations of somewhat smaller dimensions in the graveship of Sowerby.   We know of Saltonstall, Hathershelf, Withens, Rattonstall, Cruttonstall, and Ferneyside, wherever this last may be.   There are, however, no existing accounts available relating to these.   But for the De Lacy territory there are detailed accounts of their Lancashire and Cheshire Manors for the years 1297 and 1306, from which brief extracts have been given above.   Hence it is that side of the ridge upon which we have to rely for documentary evidence on such points as the one immediately before us. Capable authorities upon place-names, suggest that such designations as Boars-greave, Wolfenden and Walvreden are probably derived from the uneviable association of the places with these animals during the early settlement of mankind in the surrounding localities.

Returning to the question of man's occupation of the upper slopes of the valleys during the former centuries, we find that the south slope of the main valley, and in most of the side valleys one or both, are so steep in their first rise, as to defy all attempts at cultivation or even safe pasturage for cattle. Consequently for centuries before tools and implements were available, which enabled them to tackle the swamps and dense growth of the lower part of the valleys, the pioneers' efforts were perforce confined to the occasional sheltered recesses of the first slope, such as Ashenhurst and Cross Lee, and the more gently sloping land above the first crest and below the storm swept summits. The northern and sunnier slope occasionally presents like features, but on the whole rises less abruptly than the southern one. It presents, however, even to-day an irregularity and unevenness of surface, which two thousand years of work directed to improvement have only succeeded in smoothing out to a minor degree.

This imperfect sketch of the topographical and other natural features of the north central highlands, suggests that the estimates of the wealth and population of the English counties, which are usually given by writers on English Industrial History, are somewhat misleading in their implications. The northern counties which figure so low in the lists, generally have within them large areas of barren crag and desolate exposed moorland, which are quite impossible for utilisation either for agriculture of the most primitive kind, or for mere residence by a population engaged in any possible industry which could be carried on apart from intimate association with the land. This was a contingency which in those times was only possible to a limited extent in towns small as compared with ours, and with a large area of rich agricultural land in close proximity to them. A more truly instructive comparison would be one based upon wealth and population per acre of the land capable of occupation, and of supplying the necessaries of life for the population in each county.

EVIDENCES OF GLACIAL ACTION. This is perhaps the most convenient place to put on record the present state of our knowledge respecting the evidences of glacial action in the upper reaches of the east Calder, as during recent years the knowledge at our disposal has been somewhat amplified.

24

Forty years ago students of this branch of nature knowledge, were puzzled by the fact that up to that time no traces of that great geo-climatic eruption had been found between Hawks-clough and the two summits of the drainage area, although abundant evidence of its presence existed below the point named, and beyond the water-parting all around. True, in the year 1871, the elder Abraham Stansfield had stated before the Todmorden Botanical Society this fact :—" Many years ago, whilst making some excavations at Lydgate. at fifteen feet below the bottom of the valley, we came upon a few rounded pebbles of encrinal limestone." But this isolated fact could not by itself be taken as disposing of the difficulty. Some fanciful theorising was suggested by this enigma, as nearly always happens in similar cases. One theory suggested that the valleys became filled with stationary ice, presumably the local waters frozen in their native home, and the northern ice-sheet slid over the top without either marking the subjacent rocks, or depositing the usual travelled rock material. During the immediately succeeding years, however, evidence accumulated which made it impossible to doubt any longer that the glacial period treated this district much in the same way as the surrounding area.

In addition to Mr. Stansfield's record mentioned above, about 1880, the late Mr. Robert Law, F.G.S., found a small patch of drift on the hill-side just to the west of Nip Square, Walsden. Then in the spring of 1895, a large patch was struck during the excavations for a gas-holder at Millwood. This spot is near the middle of the area which was formerly thought to be quite bare. During the earliest years of the present century a very thin but unmistakeable deposit was found about Fair View in Langfield. The ground stretching from the west end of Wellfield Terrace right across Davy Wood (now Crossley Street), towards Baltimore is strewn with pebbles, both local and derived from a foreign source, like those at Millwood. Similarly at the southerly end of Dobroyd railway cutting, pebbles of quartzite have been found. In the writer's possession is a piece of fine grained sandstone found in Beater Clough (the modern

Green's Clough) during the late seventies of the last century. A peculiar feature about it, is that it contains casts of bivalve shells, a thing which is very uncommon in sandstone. Twenty years later the specimen was shown to Professor Boyd Dawkins who pronounced it to be Silurian grit, and originally somewhat calcareous, but exposure to water containing acid had washed out the lime. This pronouncement classes the pebble as foreign to the locality ; indeed the only way in which its presence in this locality can be explained, is by assuming it to be ice-borne. These facts seem to establish the presence of glaciers in this district, the scantiness of its usual remains being accounted for by the comparatively high rate of denudation, resulting from a high rainfall on the steep slopes of the land, and by the circumstance, that the area was the meeting place of, or rather between, the east and west ice-sheets.

THE WEATHER OF FORMER TIMES. As to the weather conditions which prevailed in the mountainous districts during the bygone centuries, for accurate and reliable facts we are in much the same position as the rest of the world. Notes by chroniclers and occasional references by scribes in various capacities are all the guidance we get in relation to the weather which prevailed generally, using that word in its widest sense. Such scraps of information as we do derive from the sources named, would seem to suggest that in this respect at least, man has always been a most pessimistic creature and not often satisfied. It may be here noted that the climatic conditions have a close association with the height above the sea level, and the relative positions of land and water, so that there cannot have been any great variation thereof during historical times. In these northern hill regions rainfall (and snow) is greater and more continuous than that which is found to prevail over the lower-lying lands, especially those of the southern and eastern portion of our island. Guided by analogy we should infer that for at least a thousand years this has always been the case. As far as regards the collection of accurate facts, northerners will feel a thrill of satisfaction in the knowledge that the earliest known rainfall observations in Great Britain were taken at Towneley near

Source of Two Calders (pp. 20-4).

Photo. by H. Hardaker.

Burnley, which is situated near the foot of the western Pennine slope where it joins the Lancashire plain.   In his *Rainfall of the British Isles,* Mr. Carl Salter has alluded to this fact, and the Meteorological Office which he superintends has provided me with information which shows that during twenty-two of the years which occur between 1676 and 1704, the rainfall at that place was approximately the same as would be shown by a modern similar period.   Not only is the distribution through the months of the year about the same, but the oscillations of the annual totals differ little from what we find to be the case in more recent times.

CHAPTER III.

RELIGIOUS INFLUENCES OPERATING DURING THE EARLY TIMES.

THE scheme of the present work does not include an exhaustive account of the religious movements which helped to mould the character, and to determine the activities of the hillside people during former times. But in attempting to relate something of the course of events and the lives of the people who have lived in the part of the country under review, we cannot altogether ignore this generally diffused formative influence, but must give some indication of such activities as there is good reason to think have prevailed. This is the more necessary at this point, as the next section will be devoted to an estimate and criticism of those personal characteristics of the northerners, which have always been regarded as offering a striking contrast with those of the people occupying the rest of the island. The documentary evidence available for such a purpose is scanty indeed ; especially so must it be regarded in the light of the very preponderating share which churchmen took for centuries in all works of a clerical kind. Relics of a more solid and enduring kind, in a more or less perfect state of preservation are, however, still to be found here and there along the country road. Others there probably were once, whose memory now only survives in the verbal testimony of old people who are now almost all beyond the reach of further enquiry ; in legend and tradition. Besides helping in the fulfilment of the object stated above, a detailed account of the known existing, or recently existing, objects of this kind may serve the purpose of placing on record and rescuing from oblivion, some of the objects and their associated ideas, which during long bygone centuries played a much larger part in the lives of our ancestors than they do in ours. Unsatisfactory as the available evidence is in relation to definite times, purposes, and the originators of these relics, there is sufficient testimony afforded by the finding of flint and bronze implements at various points, to the fact that the district was visited, if not definitely occupied, by mankind long before Christianity was introduced.

The unconventional character and circumstances of the early inhabitants of these parts, and their relations to the official and governing classes suggest that in this phase of life also they may have been possessed of an unusual outlook. It is unnecessary now-a-days to labour the point, that the landing of Augustine and his train of monks on the shores of Kent in the year of grace 597 does not mark the introduction of christianity into these islands, as at one time was generally stated and is still popularly believed. That episode rather marks the conversion of the ruler of one of the small kingdoms, into which the island was then divided, and the making of that event into an opportunity of linking up the scattered and unorganised western Church with the more completely organised Roman hierarchy. How far Ethelbert and Bertha were animated by political ambition, and the courting of continental favours is a fine point outside the scope of our present purpose. It will be sufficient for us at this juncture to note that for many years previous to Augustine's entry upon the shores of southeast England the Celtic Church had been conducting a zealous missionary campaign, and that considerable success had ensued, perhaps most of all in the north and west. Further, it may help us to a more sound judgment, if we bear in mind that historical accounts of the prevailing practices and beliefs both social and religious, are a reflex of those supposed to be held by the Court and governing classes. Although it was an accepted tradition that the people took their religion from their official superiors, it would not be a very improbable assumption that there were sometimes bodies of dissentients, who however, might find it judicious to remain on the whole rather obscure. Indeed the very essence of the present contention is, that the people whose lives and affairs we are now considering, were largely out of touch with, and in a state of chronic revolt against the practices and assumptions of the conventional historian's England.

The central highlands were well within the western missionaries' sphere of operations, and there are not wanting reasons for the presumption that for a considerable time after Augustine's arrival in Kent, the natives were quite uninfluenced by the southern and eastern districts' submission to Rome. Indeed evidence of a more general character will be submitted elsewhere (Chapter IV.), pointing very conclusively to a justification of the northerners' strong distrust of anything sought to be imposed upon him from without. Moreover, the new religious authority sought to impose a ritual and discipline, which were, and always have been to a large extent since, repellent to native traditions of personal freedom and independent judgment. It has always been a charge against the northern people by those of the south, who with a fine presumption of self-superiority and arrogant " culture " set themselves up as unquestioned judges, that the former has always been " behind " in all human accomplishments. This assumed backwardness has in reality, been nothing more than a refusal to accept and adopt new conventions at the bidding of those, who as we have elsewhere indicated, have over a long series of centuries made themselves obnoxious to the very people whom they have looked upon as suitable objects for the imposition of unfamiliar usages or patronising care.

The SYNOD OF WHITBY (664) alike by its very necessity, by the turn which the discussions took, and the place of meeting, indicated that in the north of England generally the Romish communion was far from being universally accepted, although its chances were probably best in the extreme east, where the meeting took place. Rome did, however, secure a technical victory, and very probably something more, wherever there was a disposition to rely upon royal and other official leading strings : but that fact does not necessarily imply complete submission everywhere. Neither will it be profitless to notice that it was not until the latter half of the seventh century that the southern part of Cumbria, including roughly the whole of the present West Riding area, was brought into subjection to the English Northumbria. It is no unwarrantable assumption that the rivalries of the two Churches played a part in the long drawn out struggle, nor one which can safely be ignored entirely in estimating the influences which were all the time at work helping to develope a political union. Nor would the older communion be immediately discarded by all who had hitherto shared its hopes and enjoyed its consolations, and who knew no other. It is on record,[1] that fifty-six years after the Synod, a place of such dignity and importance as Scone still adhered to the discipline of the Celtic Church. Indeed there is abundant room for the suspicion that it is this recognition of the Celtic Church in preference to the more official organisation, coupled with the stubborn refusal to acknowledge the feudalism which the Normans introduced later, rather than the paucity of the population which accounts for the absence of Churches during former centuries in this benighted area. Until the middle of the thirteenth century there was no church building between Halifax and Burnley, although one of the main routes of communication from west to east, passed through a fairly numerous (for those times) body of inhabitants.

After these more general observations, we may now pass on to a statement of the evidence remaining to us of religious influences operating amongst our primitive and mediæval forbears in that part of the great hill country with which the writer is more intimately acquainted. Although the remains which still survive are by no means abundant, we need not confine ourselves exclusively to those bearing the impress of Christianity. There are a few which can with some degree of certainty be assigned to pre-Christian times, which we will first enumerate. Brevity is enforced both by their fewness and the little that is known about them. First may be mentioned, as being within the area under discussion, two natural and one obviously artificial objects, which have been credited by local tradition or reputed scholarly interpretations

1 Rhy's *Celtic Britain*, p. 173.

of their folk-names with what we, in our latter-day wisdom, call superstitious rites, practised at a date which although certainly in the remote past is undefined. The Norland Lad Stone and Orkan (fifteenth century spelling Orkynd) Rocks in Stansfield both by their conspicuous position and their old-time popular names have had conferred upon them an association with ancient sacrificial ceremonies. They are both undoubtedly naturally produced rocks, which according to the theory were utilised as being convenient for the grim purposes of our benighted ancestors. They are still intact ; and until about the middle of last century there was only a few hundred yards away from the last-named another smaller group of rocks known as the little Orkan. The Two Lads situated on Erringden Moor consists of two artificial piles of stones a few yards apart, standing in the midst of a great area of high moorland given over to grouse, heather, bilberry, cotton-grass, and other coarse herbage. The traditional story of two lads having been sent on an errand, who, as they crossed this solitary waste, were overtaken by a snow-storm and perished at this spot, whilst bearing traces of modifications to fit obvious circumstances, does also suggest the probability of a double tragedy having taken place here at some time. The date or nature of this tragedy there does not appear to be any evidence available for fixing with any precision. In the wider area of the highlands generally, there are others about which similar traditions are related, or learned conjectures made, though the details of the stories may vary.

Readers of Mr. Holden's *History of Todmorden* and the local newspapers for the last twenty years, will be aware of the Bronze Age circular barrow, which was found on Black Heath behind Butt Stones. The first attempt at investigation was made by the late Alderman Abraham Crossley in company with Mr. Robert Law, F.G.S., Mr. Tattersall Wilkinson, and others. Subsequently Dr. Russell undertook a thorough exploration, and was assisted, I believe, by some of the Geological Staff of the Manchester Museum. Dr. Russell gave the results of his investigations to the Society of Antiquaries in London, and to the Manchester Literary and

Philosophical Society on December 13th, 1899. His paper giving full details was included in Mr. Ling Roth's *Old Halifax*. The objects recovered by Dr. Russell are now on exhibition in the Museum at Centre Vale, Todmorden. Many of them are figured in the book just referred to. I have heard of a few articles, flints, etc., picked up on the site which are retained in private hands. During the making of the Walshaw Dean middle reservoir in the year 1902, there was found a circle of nine upright stones and one missing, similar to many others which are figured and described in works upon prehistoric monuments. The evidence points to the use of these circles for the burial places of distinguished persons, and almost certainly in some cases at any rate as centres of religious devotion. In the case of the Walshaw Dean circle no urns or any other prehistoric remains were found ; but the diggers found evidence that the soil near the centre, where an urn is usually discovered if any remain at all, had been recently disturbed. If anything ever was found at this place, it is still in concealment.[1]

Other urns have been found, some in circles, others without any obvious traces of anything like barrows, at Thievley near Holmes Chapel in Cliviger, at Cliviger Laith on the hill above Barcroft, on Worsthorne Moor, in Hell Clough, and other places in the neighbourhood of Burnley. There is some reason to believe that what is known as the " old " Stoodley Pike was built upon the site of a cairn, i.e., the burial place of one whose life and deeds had impressed themselves upon the people with whom he lived, and after death had his memory preserved by his admiring followers. Maybe in after years these devotees showed their respect by bringing and piling stones over the tomb, until sometimes quite large mounds accumulated. In the year 1814, when the preparations for building the Peninsular War Memorial were begun, the clearing of the ground from an accumulation of stones revealed a quantity of bones. Whether the bones were human or not was never definitely ascertained ; but legends of the locality lend colour to the view that the place was the site of

1 *Halifax Guardian*, July 26th, 1902.

a human burial or tragedy.[1]   If these bones did really represent a human burial, it must be assigned to a different and probably later date than that of those whose bones had been cremated and placed in urns.

The next group of monuments which attracts our attention is that of the MENHIRS, or single large upright stones, set up by our early ancestors to mark the site of some striking event, some great deed, or to keep in memory the work of some venerated person.   They are generally roughly hewn into shape, both the shape and position being obviously artificial, and without inscriptions that will enable us to get a clue to their date and meaning.   The most imposing example in this upper Calder Valley district is the one which stands in a field behind Stones, Todmorden, a few yards to the north of the old highway leading from Gauxholme by Sourhall and Flow(er) Scar into Rossendale.   It stands nearly four yards in height and is about twenty inches square. Nothing whatever seems to be known of its origin, date, or the purpose which first called for its erection.   During the latter end of the year 1898, and the beginning of 1899, there was some correspondence in the local newspapers relative to this object and some others to be mentioned.   The late Mr. John Travis wrote :—" Over forty years since they found the stone *much as it is now*—the italics are the present writer's—there was not much dressing beyond what a scapling hammer would effect.   Sam Greenwood (the owner) saw it, and said he would have it set up where they found it.   After Mr. Green-wood's death, Mr. Wm. Robinson his nephew, architect and land surveyor, was appointed as land steward."   A week later over the signature of " One interested " the following appear-ed :—" In 1889 I was informed by ' one of the oldest in-habitants,' that on one of his visits to Stones the late Mr. Wm. Greenwood of Stones, and the late Mr. Wm. Robinson took him into the field where the stoop is erected, and told him that it was put up to commemorate the Battle of Water-loo."   There is no need to comment upon the transparent inconsistencies between these two statements.   They are

1 See the writer's paper on " Stoodley," Halifax Antiquarian Society.

Menhir at Stones (pp. 34-36).   *Photo. by H. Hardaker.*

perhaps not more than may be expected, where each speaker depended entirely upon the memory of a verbal statement which they had heard many years previously : but in neither case was the information derived from the original party to the incident. There is also the possibility of some confusion existing in the minds of one or more of the persons concerned.

A score or two yards away, in the top corner of the same field is another tall stone post, obviously much more recent, which until a few years ago bore a weather-cock. It may be noted that one of the Greenwoods mentioned above was keenly interested in physical science and had a wooden observatory in the garden above the house. The present writer can vouch for the existence of the weather-cock in the year 1862 or earlier. But after all, one important fact does seem to emerge, that the principal stone was found " much as it is now," and was " set up where they had found it." There can be little doubt that this obviously artificially-shaped object had been in use before, in or about the same place. The surrounding ground had up to that date been in its natural state, and it is not an unlikely assumption that the stone had previously been on end for some memorial purpose, especially as the lower end still bears evidence of having been shaped to fit into a socketed base-stone. There is no means of telling how long it has stood a silent witness of some primitive man's memorable deed or event, which was finally forgotten. Nor can we estimate how long it lay prone and unnoticed after the storms of centuries had laid it low.

Another similar object, though somewhat less in size, stands on the hill immediately behind Stansfield Hall in a field bearing the curious name of Nont Hill. It is placed on a hillock or mound which bears a strong resemblance to a sepulchral mound of the kind known as the " long barrow," some of which support a post, though in this case the post is at the wrong end. Some years ago the writer was permitted to bare a portion of the buried base at one side. Finding the newly exposed part black like the above ground portion, he came to the conclusion either that the ground had been raised somewhat around the post at a later date than the original fixing, or that the post itself had possibly been re-set or brought from some other place. Mr. Travis writing at the date previously mentioned says :— " John Shackleton of Durn, near Cross Stone, told me long ago that he was one of those that helped to put it there, Mr. John Sutcliffe, the owner of the land being present giving directions at the time." Again the definiteness in one way of the statement is balanced by an equally irritating vagueness. Nothing is said as to the motive of the undertaking, though in both cases the gentle-man proprietor was sufficiently interested in the work to be present and give it his personal supervision, a fact which in itself places the incident out of the common. Neither is anything said as to where the stone had been before, a cir-cumstance of importance, for like the one at Stones the slab bears evidence of a very long weathering, much more indeed than other stones whose history is limited to a century or two. It may also be noted that Stones and Stansfield Hall are amongst the earliest of our local principal homesteads. In contrast with Mr. Travis's statement another gentleman, who was born in the near locality in the year 1818, told the present writer that the Stansfield Hall post was in its present position as long ago as he could remember.

If for no other reason, limitations of space prevent the question of the age of these memorials of the past from being fully discussed. The following quotation from *Beowulf* may, however, be given, partaking as it does of the nature of docu-mentary evidence. It is generally agreed that the composit on took its present form about the end of the seventh or beginning of the eigth century A.D. :—

Have the battle heroes
Build a mound, gleaming after burning,
On a cliff by the shore, it shall a memorial
To my people tower high on Hrones-naes,
So that sea-farers seeing call it Beowulf's mount.
Who drive afar their keels o'er the mists of the floods.

There are other isolated posts at various places in the locality. Some of these are very obviously boundary marks, such as those on the moor separating Langfield from Walsden, on the one hand, and the same township from Erringden (originally Sowerby) on the other. Similarly there is one standing in the middle of the great pasture known as Olympus behind Harbour in Stansfield, which defined the limits at that point of the Higher and Middle Thirds of Stansfield. In former years, the division of this great township into three for local administrative purposes was of much more significance than it is at present, it being now of little value. Once more, there has been suffered to remain in the middle of a meadow to the east of Hippin's farm-house in Blackshaw, a heavy stumpy block of grit-stone which does not lie upon its natural bed. Further north on the top of Brown Hill in Blackshaw, there is a rather slender stone pillar about a yard and a half high, which bears no particular relation to exisiting fences and roads. What they were originally intended for there is no certain knowledge ; but there is reason to suspect that they mark the boundary on that side of the old Manor of Rattonstall, and probably also the division between the Middle and Lower Thirds of Stansfield.[1] There are others again which do not appear to have any relation to boundaries either of a public or private kind. Neither can the shallow and short-sighted " rubbing stoop " theory be made to fit some of them, as for instance the two next to be mentioned. Two or three hundred yards to the west of Higher Winsley farm-house is one, and about the same distance to the west of the Harbour is another. They are certainly not more than two feet above the ground to the top. Like all the rest described above, they are undoubtedly of human origin ; but what their purpose was or when they were placed seems to be a complete mystery. There are several others rudely shaped, and standing four or five feet high in the land of the two Rough Farms, near Bride Stones, and below Fast Ends. Some forty or fifty years ago the fences of these fields were somewhat re-arranged, and possibly some of the posts may have formed the gaps in the old fences ; but there are two or three which certainly have no such relation. Like all the

1 See paper on " Rattonstall," Halifax Antiquarian Society, 1917.

rest mentioned above, they bear no evidence of having ever supported either stangs or gates.

EARLY CHRISTIAN REMAINS. Here as elsewhere the introduction of Christianity made a difference in the character of the monuments that were set up. The early missionaries and the Church authorities right on to the period of the Reformation were in this respect zealous in their work, and had a high opinion of the value of symbolism. Consequently their influence was responsible for the fact that all memorials, landmarks, guides, or other permanent objects set up to be seen by the people, in all cases took the form of a cross ; either in the shape of the stone or incised upon one or more of the surfaces. In their anxiety to bring the people to a sense of the greatness and importance of the new faith, the missionaries went to the length of compromising with the people's devotion to the older memorials, by converting in many cases the pagan into a Christian symbol. The Christian symbols in their turn became the objects of much reverential devotion, possibly even superstition, as is the case to-day in some Roman Catholic countries. So much was this the case, that when the Puritan manifestation of Chistianity became strong and assertive, much of its misdirected zeal was devoted to the destruction of these so-called emblems of idolatry. The quality of a beautiful and elaborate work of art was no protection against the hand of the spoiler. It is estimated that through the influence of that misguided spirit throughout England, thousands of these early religious statues, some of them exquisite works of art, were destroyed. Many have disappeared, fallen, or crumbled away as the result of centuries of neglect and forgetfulness, others again became the victims of ignorant utilitarianism or wanton destructive vandalism. Often the name is now the only remaining trace of their former existence ; and where we have a place-name in which the word cross occurs, there is a strong presumption that it is derived from a one-time existing Christian symbol. Where one of these objects is now found, if it be not obviously of the more tolerant and broad-minded recent period, it is almost safe to fix its date as at least pre-Reformation.

LOCAL CROSSES.   After these general observations we can the better proceed to a detailed description of what is known concerning the ancient crosses now to be found, or which once existed, in the neighbourhood of the higher reaches of the Yorkshire Calder.   We have still scattered about the hill country a considerable number, especially if considered in the light of the generally presumed sparse population during primitive and mediæval times, and the very strong Puritanic temper which has for centuries leavened local thought.   Incidentally it may be worth noting, that a principal factor in determining the hill country's passion for nonconformity, has been the religious manifestation of that antipathy, born of age-long experience, to the control of distant outside rigidly disciplined authority.   In the earlier centuries it was directed against the Church of Rome.   After the Reformation, the rigid discipline and authority of the Protestant English Church has come to share the distrust of the people.   Besides this, and perhaps partly caused by the mutual misunderstanding, there has operated in these highland expanses a neglect on the part of the Established Church, of the needs of the people.   The nature of the ground and climatic conditions, as explained in a previous chapter, as well as the character of the industries in which the people were engaged (to be explained later), necessitated their being scattered widely over the country-side.   The churches were often several miles apart, in a country where both roads and weather were difficult and trying during a considerable part of the year.   The old Parish of Heptonstall for instance had an area of nearly 20,000 acres ; and until about the year 1536 there does not appear to have existed a building in which services could be held, besides the Parish Church itself, and that was situated rather at one side of that widespread field of influence.   There are known to have been two private chapels ; but both of these were comparatively near to the Parish Church, and could not have had much influence over the people generally.   The presence of families sufficiently wealthy to uphold a private chapel, implies the existence also of a fairly numerous population. Thus a feeling of neglect was generated amongst the people, and opportunity provided for unofficial activities in the mere provision of religious conveniences, over and above the questions of theological differences or the personal touch of official ministers and direct association with regular services and church government. It will be found upon investigation, that the great majority of the early dissenting conventicles are situated in the midst of what were at the time of their origin, little communities of people between, and miles away from any legally authorised place of meeting.

Returning to the immediate task. Cross Stone is probably the principal, and cetainly the best known position where a cross once stood in the higher reaches of Calderdale. Unfortunately there is now no known fragment of the object in existence ; even its exact position can no longer be identified with certainty. The Ordnance Survey makes no attempt to mark it. One old native when appealed to on the point, said that he had always understood from his forbears, that the site of the cross is covered by the tower of the present church. Another stated that the situation was close by Butcher Laithe at the top of the first rise of the road from the west end of the churchyard, and that there the priest formerly met all funerals. The allusion to priests and funerals adds a touch of circumstantiality to the latter statement, and the place is a likely one. It is the junction of four old roads and more conspicuous from all directions, than would be any object placed in the first named situation, which is concealed under the hill. Watson in his *History of Halifax*, speaking of Cross Stone says it " takes its name from an ancient stone cross, the top of which is now destroyed and the bottom is made into a seat, from whence is a good prospect of the country." The Rev. T. Fawcett, M.A., speaks in 1849 of the base and socket being " still visible." These statements confirm the Butcher Laithe site, as the present church had, at the date named, been built, and also directly implies that even in the eighteenth century the cross was very old indeed. The form of the name itself

(Cross Stone) not the syllable cross preceded by another identification supports the same view.   Except when designating a particular body or structure upon which a cross stands, as in this case and others like Crosshills, the symbolic portion of the name always comes last, as Stiperden Cross, Stump Cross and many others.   The name Cross Stone had certainly been in use centuries before Watson's time, and had been derived not so much from the cross as from the dilapidated remains.   There is the greatest probability that the little hamlet grew up about the traffic junction and the cross which had been placed at this spot by the priests from Heptonstall or Halifax, as a guide for travellers and a convenient place for worshippers from the outlying townships of Stansfield and Langfield.   Thus it is very probable that the name which came to designate the little hamlet, and later the ecclesiastical parish, had its origin in the stone remains of a disappeared cross.   Possibly also from the fact of the original and its later fragments being widely known, both as a guide to travellers and a meeting place for religious and other purposes, it may have been the means of superseding an older place-name, or of originating one where no specific one had previously existed.   It is now established that there was a chapel at this place in the year 1536, and both it and the parish took their name from the older existing cross.   The correct form of the second word is stone, not stones as it is fequently given by those who are not natives.   This point has some importance from the fact that the plural form of the word might be taken to imply that the name might have been derived from the rocks or stones which abound all around, and were probably at one time still more prominent.   A native-born person never by any chance makes the mistake just pointed out.

Next in importance from the standpoint of situation and what is known of it, we may make allusion to Mankinholes Cross.   Watson states that it is mentioned in a deed of the year 1519.   Whether it is meant that the reference is to the original object, or only to something else in its neighbourhood is not quite clear.   There do, however, survive to this day a Cross Hill and a Cross Farm, so that we may take it that there was once at the place, a symbolic figure which served the purpose of a preaching station and general meeting-place, possibly also of a guide to travellers on the road. The last idea is suggested by the fact that the two places whose names have just been given, are quite outside the " town " itself, and beyond the " Towngate." They are, however, close by one of the old highways. The situation scarcely lends support to a local tradition that Mankinholes was once a market-town, in which case the trading would be done around the cross ; unless indeed the market were really a cattle and sheep fair, and the mediæval authorities were in advance of their contemporaries and put the crowding, dirt, and confusion outside the narrow places of the town itself. A few years ago a T-shaped stone about 2 feet 6 inches high and broad, which had once been found near Cross Farm, and for some years been kept in the grounds at Shaw, was placed on the top of a stone post which stood in the field to the north of the highway. On the top of this again was fitted a small stone, thus completing the form of a Latin Cross. There is fairly clear evidence that the post just mentioned had previously been one side of a gap in the stone fence which had at one time run across and divided the present field into two. About the T-shaped piece there is not much certainty, but some probability of its being part of the original cross. That the present situation of the relic is the original one is doubtful, somewhere near the present farm-house being more likely its true home.

Passing through Mankinholes up the Long Causeway by the Long Stoop, and forward over the moor, there will be found just through Withens Gate a short thick stone fixed firmly in the ground. On the south side of it is a neatly incised Latin Cross, and on the east a rather rudely inscribed " Te deum Laudamus." The first two of these words are used by many people to designate the object. On the other side are the two letters I.D. What these mean or indicate is by no means certain. Possibly they have at one time been the initials of adjoining landowners, although this is discounted by the fact that the west side is common land. Possibly they may stand for Jevu Devs. There does not appear to

Catholes Cross (pp. 42-46).   *Photo. by W. Quayle.*   Withens Cross.   *Photo. by Rev. A. W. Fox, M.A.*

be anything known about this stone ; but the situation and the inscription together suggest something. The road by which it stands is the old pack-horse road from Todmorden and beyond to Sowerby Town ; and the point is where Langfield and Erringden (the latter, at one time included in Sowerby) townships join. It is therefore highly probable that we have in this case a boundary cross both between the townships, and the old ecclesiastical parishes of Heptonstall and Sowerby ; and also, if as is quite likely the stone was once taller, it may have served as a guide over the desolate and lonely moorland.

At about a mile north-west of the centre of Todmorden, in the township of Stansfield, is the ancient tiny hamlet of Cross Lee. There is no positive evidence that there ever was a monolith of any kind here. But the name is suggestive, and the fact that the old pack-horse road from Rossendale to Heptonstall and Halifax passes through the group of houses, renders it probable that the name is derived from a cross, which once stood hereabouts, serving as a guide for travellers, and a meeting-place of the natives for religious and other purposes. Rodwell End, a mile and a half below Todmorden, or Rodhill as it is often written in ancient documents, may be a name derived from a monolith of some kind which once stood on the hill ; for the word rod or rood is an older word designating the same thing.

Taking a trail over the hills nearly due northwards, a distance of three-and-a-half miles, right across Stansfield, we come to Reap's Cross on Heptonstall Moor, locally known as " t' Long Stoop." It is a tall, slender, graceful one of its kind. Both arms are broken off, and some years ago the shaft was broken and lay some distance away. Two or three gentlemen were responsible for its restoration, the shaft being fastened together with iron cramps. What the original motive was which led to its placing in this lonely and exposed situation, cannot now be definitely decided. A story has been told of its marking the spot where two noted characters had a great fight. If this be true, it must indeed have been an encounter which excited considerable and widespread interest ; and one of the combatants very likely fell.   Nothing less than this can account for the erection of such a monument. On the other hand, an existing landmark on an open and public space may have served as the choice for the scene of a widely known contest.   It is also of interest to note that close to the spot is an ancient footpath along the hills, and the suggestion that the cross was a pilgrim cross, to guide the wayfarer bound for Whalley Abbey may have some relation to fact.   At any rate it does serve a useful purpose as a landmark for travellers whose destination is more local and purpose more general.

Two-and-a-half miles further north-west, on the Wadsworth side of Widdop Gap, the Ordnance Survey has marked the site of Widdop Cross.   It survives only in name, and being exactly on the boundary which divided Lancashire from Yorkshire, may be set down as a boundary cross.   The road connecting the two counties does not now pass close by the Ordnance Survey's site of the cross, but it is a short distance to the south-west.   Whether in the remote past, the track and the boundary mark were in closer touch cannot now be said ; but whether or not, the cross would be able to be seen from a considerable distance, and its sight would be welcomed by wayfarers over the lonely expanse of moorland.   This cross stood at the highest altitude of any that we now know of for many miles around.   From the place a wide range of country may be seen, ridge beyond ridge, wild, bleak, and grand. Just below on the Yorkshire side is the narrow rugged Widdop Valley, where Wesley on his journeys from Colne to Heptonstall and Todmorden, sometimes halted to preach to the simple and hardy hill-folk, who congregated from every farm-house and cottage far and near, though the date on " Wesley's Rock " (1766) is not confirmed by the great evangelist's Journal.

Descending from this high place to the heart of Wadsworth, the double memorial near Abel Cote, overlooking the beautiful Crimsworth Valley, may be seen.   Two stone posts, each standing in the socket of a stone base, which was originally one, have each an incised cross upon the two sides.   Some years ago they narrowly escaped destruction, an act of grossly ignorant vandalism being stopped by the late Wm. Lipscombe,

44

Esq. Nothing definite is known of the time and purpose in view when they were set up. The unusual circumstance of two memorials within a couple of yards from each other, the name, and the situation, taken both separately and together, do however, suggest much. Take the negative side of the problem first. The field path near which they stand, is of the most local kind, leading only from a more important road to the farm-house, Abel Cote. The objects cannot be considered either as defining a boundary, as guiding to anywhere or indicating a meeting place of any kind. A single object would have served quite as well for any of these purposes. The two in such close association suggest something extraordinary ; and this brings us to the positive aspect. The most likely suggestion that has been made or can be thought of, is the purpose of commemorating a double sacrifice or subject for lamentation, something analogous to the Cain and Abel story of the OLD TESTAMENT. The name Abel does most certainly strongly support such a supposition, whilst a single monolith would have met the needs of an individual tragedy quite as well as two. It is extremely likely that the farm took its name from the memorial, and not the other way about. Remembering the importance of the event which the two imply and their extreme plainness though substantial character, it is very probable that the crosses are of great antiquity. The possible time of their erection has been put as far back as the eighth century. Retracing our steps and coming back to Heptonstall itself, we find at the top end of the town the elevated point known as Cross Hill. It is a most likely place for a cross to answer several purposes. As a guide for travellers along the adjoining ancient highway between Halifax and Burnley, and also to Colne, as a preaching and general meeting place before the building of the Church in the thirteenth century, it would serve equally well. This is another case in which the name alone remains to us.

In the little romantic glen of Catholes in the Burnley Valley, about two hundred yards or thereabouts above the reservoir of that name, there is on an upright exposed face of a grit-stone block an incised Greek Cross with double curved terminals, and across it the legend JESV DEVS DOMINUS MONTIUM. The cutting has been done in keeping with the rough natural surface of the rock. Whilst not delicately carved the letters are uniformly sized and spaced, and of an old-world style. Altogether they suggest that the cutter knew what he was about, and was possessed of something above the average education. The work is no product of an irresponsible wanderer let loose with a hammer and chisel and whiling away an idle hour. Possibly at some time a zealous and impressionable admirer of nature, perhaps an old-time monk moved by the romance and grandeur of the scene around him, might be stirred to give vent to his feelings of admiration and gratitude towards his God, as Maker and Controller of the universe, and left his message indelibly inscribed for the benefit of his fellows both present and future. The registers of Cross Stone Church prove that a hundred years or more ago, there was at least one family living close by this spot. But if we were to assume that such a one was responsible for the task, seeing that they were but humble cotters, the feat, considered from the educational point of view suggested above, is more wonderful still.

Some old maps mark a cross at Cross i' t' Deyne near the source of the Calder in Cliviger. An old inhabitant who knew nothing about maps, has pointed out to the writer where tradition fixed it. It is a likely place where the monks of Whalley might have set one before a church could be built for the locality. The old pack-horse road is said to have crossed the valley at this point also. Above the village of Shore in the Burnley Valley, there is a cross which ranks in importance second only to Cross Stone. It stands in a field attached to Lower Mount Farm to the north of Stoney Lane, and about one hundred and fifty yards from where the latter joins Mount Lane. It is the most artistic of the whole series of local ancient monuments. The cross itself is still entire, but narrowly escaped destruction during the summer of 1898, when a frolicsome youth jumping on the leaning object threw it down, and the fall broke the shaft just under the arms. Fortunately it was repaired with copper dowels, and it now stands as perfect as ever, except that as a result of thoughtless vandalism just referred to, it is in two pieces instead of one. Another point to be mentioned is that the portion buried underground is shouldered on all four sides as if intended to fit into the socket of a base-stone.   But no such fixture is known to exist.   The question arises—how and why came the base-stone to disappear ? Where is it now ? Or has the cross been at some time hurriedly removed for safety from some other situation to its present site ? Or again, was it originally prepared, and then before the substantial fixing could be got ready, did a suddenly arising emergency neces-sitate a temporary setting up of the sacred object ?   After which as it appeared to stand well, was the original intention delayed and finally forgotten ? There is little evidence avail-able to help us to answer these questions.   Speed's map published in 1610 does, however, indicate the existence of a cross about this place, as nearly as a small scale map can do. The name Stiperden, which he gives to it, is almost certainly a mistake ; but a statement of the reasons for holding that view would take up too much space to justify its being entered upon here.   Confusion has been helped by the habit of the local folk, who invariably refer to it as " th' idol God at t' Mount," thus pushing into obscurity any designation other than Mount, which it might at one time have had.   From that phrase too, comes out the strong Puritanism of the locality.

As to the purpose for which this comparatively fine piece of work was originally set up, we can only judge from its general character, position, and scanty tradition.   It is very similar in design and size to the Godley Lane Cross at Burnley, which again is connected by some authorities with one or more at Whalley, and by some (e.g., T. T. Wilkinson) with the one at Dewsbury.   On the strength of this, some writers, accepting the Paulinus and Whalley tradition, have classed it as a Paulinus Cross.   Its situation overlooking an early human settlement, near the meeting of the roads leading to different parts of that settlement, points to its being intended to serve as a preaching cross, or more correctly a Field Kirk.

Old natives tell us that it was set up by the Romans, who used to worship it. Giving a religious interpretation to the word Roman, the legend becomes quite intelligible, and umnistake-ably reflects the local Puritan attitude towards the earlier ecclesiastical symbolism. The association with Whalley is not quite so strange as might at first sight appear to us to-day, who are accustomed to the connection of the district with Halifax Parish. In spite of local industrial connections and West Riding administrative authority, the relative near-ness to Burnley, has always attracted this people to the western slope of the Pennines. Before county and ecclesiastical boun-daries were exactly defined, the social ties of the district would link it naturally with the Lancashire side. The persistence of Cumbrian political authority as far eastwards as Leeds until late in the seventh century, and popular sympathy still longer surviving in outlying districts, bespeak a western association not very easy to realise in these days.

Then something must be said as to the time when the cross originated. Here again we have no certain evidence to go upon. The Paulinus connection suggested above would place its date very early, but does not necessarily imply actual personal touch, possibly only the missionary's influence, which might have extended many years beyond his death. An old lady, a life-long resident in the immediate locality, told the writer that she had heard it stated, that the cross marked the burial place of a noted outlaw who had been refused Christian burial. But why a finely wrought christian symbol should have been erected in memory of an excommun-icated person does not serve to make one any wiser. Surely if ecclesiastical authority could deny the offices of the Church to this supposed recalcitrant individual, its powers would have been sufficient to prevent the erection, or at any rate the continuance of the sacred emblem as a memorial. The story may, however, rest upon a basis of truth, but in the application of it, details may have been somewhat per-verted. That is by no means an uncommon thing with respect to details conveyed through a series of lips inspired by untrained minds. Certainly the style and workmanship

48

of the cross denote the attachment of some importance to the original purpose of its making, and it's very existence—if it be assumed that there is any solid foundation at all in the legend—indicates that at the time of its setting up there must have been a Christian organisation functioning here, other than the more generally recognised one. No adequate explanation of the apparent circumstances suggests itself without going back towards the time of Synod of Whitby, which met in the year 664. It cannot be expected that the decision there come to would result in an immediate and complete cessation of the activities of the Celtic Church. Districts such as this, remote from the seat of official authority, and where the feeling against the new outside interference was particulay acute, would hold out long against what to them might seem an uncalled for change (see p.p. 30-1). The " outlaw " must have been an ecclesiatical one, and the victim's offence defiance of the new ecclesiastical allegiance. Hence we may have here the last tribute of a loyal and devoted, though possibly mistaken flock, to the memory of a zealous and trusted dignitary of that older Church, on behalf of whose authority both pastor and people were taking their best if unavailing stand, local feeling being strong enough to withstand for a time the powers of the new authority. Thus we come to the conclusion that Mount Cross dates back to the time of the British Church, not necessarily so far back as the year 664, but not a very long number of years afterwards. In later times its existence may have been taken advantage of by the then official church representatives as a convenient site for the observance of religious offices for the benefit of the neighbouring people, just as they did of pagan relics still older. Stansfield's *History of the Stansfield Family* (pp. 76-7) says, " A rude stone, cut as a Calvary Cross, was found in a field next below the road, under Bride Stone." This can hardly refer to Mount Cross, although Bride Stones do extend along the crest of the hill above Mount ; but a short distance higher up another and more important road, soon to be considered, extends eastwards to Kebcote, its whole length passing just under this portion of the Bride Stones range. No further information about this cross seems available : possibly it may have been a hitherto unrecognised member of the series about to be described.

The road just referred to can scarcely be identified with any existing one, unless it be the very old line of communication between the West Riding of Yorkshire and northeast Lancashire. It has probably been for two thousand years the principal route for traffic, until the making of canals turnpike roads and railways superseded it for most purposes. From Halifax its line passes through Warley across Luddenden valley by Midgley and Wadsworth to Hebden Bridge. Then mounting the Buttress, or running by Hanging Royd, Lee Wood and North Gate, it goes through Heptonstall, crosses the Colden Valley and Jack Bridge to Blackshawhead, thence passing Kebcote and Stiperden over the Long Causeway, and dropping down to Mereclough and on to Burnley, etc. At one time there was a piece of doggerel describing a journey from the last mentioned place to the first, which runs :—

> Burnley for ready money,
> Mereclough nooa trust ;
> Yo' takken a peep at Stiperden,
> But call at Kebs yo' must.
> Blacksha' yed for travellers,
> An' Hep'nstall for trust ;
> Heptin Brig for lan' ladies,
> An' Midgley by the moor.
> Luddenden's a warm shop,
> Royle's yed 's varry cold ;
> An' if yo' git to Halifax,
> Yo' mun be varry bold.

From what we know of monoliths generally we are led to expect that we should find numerous examples along such an old and important thoroughfare. Many may have disappeared altogether and been forgotten ; but at Halifax we have memories of former ones at Stump Cross and King Cross. At Heptonstall there is a Cross Hill, and the one mentioned by Stansfield may have been to the west of Kebcote. When we enter the Long Causeway portion of the road we find it unusually prolific in these emblems. At the top of the hill to the west of Stiperden there was once a Stiperden Cross. Several old inhabitants have been consulted about its site ; for the doubts referred to when dealing with Mount Cross seemed to leave the matter in uncertainty. But all unhesitatingly declared for the position just given. Proceeding westward along the road we pass successively the sites of Duke's Cross, Maiden Cross, Robin Cross Hill, and Stump Cross. The position of Duke's Cross cannot now be exactly defined ; but it was somewhere about half-a-mile to the west of Stiperden Hill just mentioned. The present writer has been shown stones in the roadside wall, which were alleged to have been parts of the old Cross. Maiden Cross and Stump Cross both still survive although in a much mutilated condition. The former stands about thirty-five yards distant from its Ordnance Survey position close to the delivery station of the long abandoned Moss Pit or Maiden Cross Colliery, where it serves the utilitarian purpose of a gate post. Robin Cross Farm and Robin Cross Hill are only about a quarter of a mile distant from Stump Cross. " Stump " is obviously not the original designation ; after mutilation like some others it would come to be referred to as the stump of a cross, which usage would soon wear down to " Stump Cross," Probably this is the original Robin Cross, and the adjoining hill and farm acquired their names from it.

With regard to the origin and purpose of the whole five, their serving as guides along this lonely bleak road before it was definitely marked out with stone walls, seems to be the most likely suggestion. Tradition has associated them with the monks of Whalley : that, however, would place their date as being later than the end of the thirteenth century. In order that the guidance might be complete, that is that one cross could be seen from another, there would need to be two or three others along this undulating road. Some of the crosses mentioned above are dealt with in the *Halifax Naturalist* for 1896, in the *Proceedings of Burnley Literary and Scientific Club*, vol. 1., and the *Halifax Antiquarian Society* 1911.

RELIGIOUS INFLUENCES AS REFLECTED IN AVAILABLE DOCUMENTS. The survival of these relics of the past, which we have just enumerated, is a fortunate circumstance for us when we try to estimate the probable influences which operated upon the people in the past, in moulding the character which has been transmitted to the present. In their absence the evidence would have been meagre indeed. With the advent of more definitely expressed testimony in the shape of Manor Court Rolls, Ecclesiastical Orders, Poll Tax Returns, and later of Wills, some faint glimmers of light do begin to break through the otherwise dense pall which hides the past from the present. Yet the real enlightenment which we get is very small, when we consider the comparative monopoly which the clerical order had in dealing with most public affairs, and the greater range of their powers over the ordinary business of life. Little of the personal touch or direct influence of the priesthood in teaching or other religious activities reveals itself. Such records as we have access to, relate to a period when the Whitby decision had asserted itself fully at least amongst the officially recognised clergy, and this received much of its impetus from the increasing sway of the Norman authority. We can hardly expect that that combination would assert itself very vigorously to benefit an injured and rebellious people who had always been a thorn in its side.

Viewed from our immediate standpoint, the Manor Court Rolls are a record of the more material affairs of everyday life, and when we do get from them a glimpse of the activities of churchmen, it is a revelation of their more sordid interests. Thus :—At a TOURN held at Halifax on July 7th, 1277, it is reported that, " The Vicar levied a new custom on the whole of the parish ; for whereas they were accustomed to give one calf as tithe on seven calves, he now makes the whole parish give (one) of six, and they may no wise count till they come to ten, as they used to do in the time of his predecessors ; and the parson of the church deals in the same way with the lambs ; they can get no remedy except through the Earl's bailiffs." We can conceive something of the effect which would be produced amongst the parishioners by this proceeding, even if the locality were a normal one where the ecclesiastical authority had been accepted without question.   But given some surviving memories of the older, and to these people more agreeable authority, these evil effects would be considerably aggravated.   Twenty years later another aspect of the same spirit is illustrated.   At Wakefield Court held on March 25th, 1297, the Earl's Forester in Sowerbyshire is justified for having bribed the Vicar of Rochdale with a hart, " with a view to his drawing the malefactors of that neighbourhood away from the Earl's chase, so that they should not enter to do wrong there."   To say the least of it this was putting the priestly office on a low mercantile basis.

So far as is known, there was no building devoted to religious purposes in the tract of country stretching between Halifax and Burnley before the middle of the thirteenth century.   There was a chapel at Heptonstall in 1260 ; St. Mary's, Todmorden, was founded in the latter part of the fifteenth century, and the Chapel of Cross Stone was in existence in the year 1536.   We may reasonably infer that each of these cases implies the presence of a priest devoting his energies to the service of the people amongst whom he lived. Of the exact nature of these activities the evidence at our command is still distressingly vague.   That the clergy performed the recognised and formal rites and ceremonies we may take for granted ; but how far they came into direct touch with the general body of the people, bringing to bear upon them influences that would direct them to a well regulated life, apart from what the recognition of set ordinances might do, we have little evidence indeed.   That the possibilities in this direction were here as elsewhere limited by the demands made upon them by the civil authorites and ecclesiastics' own claim for domination in regions of the social sphere which are now given over to the secular courts, may be taken for granted.   An early instance of the secular duties imposed upon church officials is afforded by the following.   At a court held at Halifax on the 20th of July, 1286, " Master Peter, proctor of Halifax, alleged on behalf of the men of the church of the same place that they are not bound to lead thieves to York. Therefore that case is respited until the coming of the Earl." On the other side, namely that of the Church's jurisdiction on matters now placed beyond its pale, the *Act Book* of Whalley gives some interesting information. Up to the time of the Reformation an ecclesiastical Court sat periodically at Whalley Church for the purpose of dealing with cases in which arose matters affecting marriage, divorce, sexual relations generally, and probate affairs. The district affected thereby included that large portion of north-east Lancashire and some of what is now south-east, as, for instance, Rochdale parish, which made up the old parish of Whalley.

Incidentally it may be mentioned that the document just cited reveals to us what became of a Mankinholes family, which from 1275 onwards fequently appeared in the Manor Court Rolls, but does not appear in the Poll Tax Returns for 1379, and thus gives an indication of the migrations which were then possible. They appear to have passed from the original scene of their activities altogether : but this was not because the family had died out, as might be inferred from the absence of further information. What happened was, that the whole body of them transferred their allegiance to other quarters. One hundred-and-fifty years later we find persons who are presumably their descendants appearing in the Whalley Courts, sometimes involved in cases, at other times acting as jurors. They hail from such places as Crawshawbooth, Barley Booth and Pendle. Other sources of information extend our knowledge of the migrations of this family. At later dates we find them at Bury, Burnley, Padiham, Colne, Blackburn, and Newchurch-in-Rossendale.

The Christian symbols already described (pp. 40 et seqq.), most of which were probably in existence before the chapels named, imply at least periodical visitations at some of the places by representatvies of the Church ; possibly at more populous centres there was a resident priest. Occasionally we may extract from the more material affairs dealt with in the Manor Courts an allusion to a priest, either as involved in a suit, or more commonly as surety for one of the parties.

At Wakefield on the Friday after the Octave of Easter, 1316, William de Heptonstall, clerk, became pledge for John, son of Ivo Smith, who farms Ferneshide dairy. Eight years earlier one John, the clerk, is involved in a plea of debt with Thomas de Langfield and others. Neither of these is named in the " List of Chaplains, Vicars, etc " in Mr. Arthur Odgen's paper read before the Halifax Antiquarian Society at one of the meetings during the year 1909. That list is the most complete one of the priests associated with Heptonstall which has hitherto been published. The Court Rolls also mention Simon the Chaplain of Heptonstall, who was fined 2d. for some offence ; also on May 6th, 1371, the Court finds that Sir Simon Chaplain owes to Thomas de Helilee of Sowerby 6s. 8d. for one mare sold to him. In the Langfield Poll Tax Returns there are the two names Hugo and Wilelmus Clerkson, a surname which was probably derived from an ancestor, possibly more than one generation back, whose occupation was that of clerk. In the year 1250 there is mention of William, the clerk de Langfield. Whether all of these individuals were in Holy Orders or not, we cannot be certain ; probably in the case of those simply designated " clerk " the balance is on the negative side. But we may fairly assume that they were more closely associated with the ecclesiastical officials than a more modern meaning of the word clerk might lead us to expect. The name Henricus Prest in the Sowerby list of Poll Tax-payers may put us on surer ground, seeing that that township, next to Halifax, was the most important one in upper Calderdale. There is, however, the difficulty that churchmen were exempt from the tax. Such names as Presteley and Kirkeshagh appearing in the Court Rolls, and the latter in the Poll Tax Returns for Sowerby and Langfield respectively, may have been derived from lands devoted to the maintenance of the Church or its servants. That there were people who were influenced by deep religious convictions, or who at least gave their adherence to the presscribed formularies, we have some evidence. At a Wakefield Court held on January 25th, 1307, we find under the heading of " Sourby," " The dispute between Beatrice Kay, plaintiff, and Nicholas de Bateley, defendant, for trespass, is respited until she returns from Rome." Thus it would appear that even in the early part of the fourteenth century a pilgrimage to the Holy City was not too big an undertaking for a woman living in these remote highlands.

When we come to examine the wills by which deceased persons have disposed of their former belongings, we find more positive evidence of how at least the latter days of many of the socially leading people were influenced by their spiritual advisers. In the cases of persons who had lived in the Parish of Heptonstall, which may be taken as a typical example, the earliest of which date from the fifteenth century, it most frequently happens that one of the clergy often indeed two of them sign the wills as witnesses. In a large portion of them bequests to the Vicar and the Church and other religious institutions much farther afield, testify to the testators having had some affection for, and some desire to further the work for which the Church stood. Other bequests in aid of such works as the building of " Heptin Brig " and " Coldenstock Brig " may have in them a combined element of charity and practical business ; but the fact cannot be ignored that at that time the provision and repair of roads and bridges to facilitate travel, were held up before the faithful as pious duties.

When the Reformation came, it found in these upland regions a soil not altogether unprepared to receive and nourish the new seed. Possibly the causes of any predisposition in that direction which existed, were not exactly the same as those which prevailed in other parts of the country. Although its imposition came from without, an order from London, especially as many native born sons had now intimate business relations with the capital, was less repugnant to local prejudices than distant and overbearing Rome could be. By the Middle of the seventeenth century Quakerism, Independency and Presbyterianism were well established amongst even the remote hills and dales of the north. Possibly the sect then known as Anabaptists was not not quite so early in the field ; but in a list of places licensed for worship, which is given in a *History of Halifax* dated 1789 we find :—

" Amongst other places of worship of Halifax Parish in 1758. Licensed under the Act of Toleration, Presbyterian Meeting houses—Eastwood Chapel in Stansfield. Quakers—Shoebroad in Langfield. Anabaptists (as they are called)— Rodhill End in Stansfield, Slack in Heptonstall, Wainsgate in Wadsworth." There are others which can establish a good claim to existence before the last quarter of the eighteenth century was far advanced, but do not appear to have been licensed. Their meetings in private houses, the remoteness of their situations from the seats of authority, together with the fact that they did not flaunt their illegal practices before the world so long as they were permitted to worship in their own way undisturbed, and probably a certain amount of official winking, enabled them to pursue the even tenor of their way and establish the various causes upon a firm footing. The Anabaptist cause at Rodwell End (as the place is now called) for some reason or other did not survive. But during the earlier part and far on into the nineteenth century there was a Wesleyan Methodist Chapel there, which during the seventies removed its operations to Springside.

Wadsworth has been a very fertile field for Anabaptist enterprise. There would appear to have been earlier centres elsewhere, notably the neighbouring Stone Slack and further off Rossendale ; but Wainsgate was apparently the earliest local organisation. From here went out quite a number of pioneer preachers, and many chapels in Yorkshire, Lancashire and further afield, trace their origin to the inspiration caught up on the Wadsworth hillside, carrying it abroad from thence with burning enthusiasm and courageous zeal. It was here also that the revolt from the original stern Calvinism through the influence of Wesley received if not its first conception amongst the Baptists, at least a powerful impulse. The Rev. Dan Taylor is credited with being the prime mover in the establishment of the General Baptist Connexion. He organised the Church now known as Birchcliffe in the year 1763. Many others followed including Shore in Stansfield, the first building of which was begun in 1777. These were succeeded by many more both far and near ; and wherever Baptism as an essential rite of an organised religious community exists, especially of the non-Calvanistic type, it owes much to the genius and inspiration which have flowed from the hills and dales around the centre now known as Hebden Bridge.

Nowhere did the evangelical mission of Wesley and his co-adjutors prove more fruitful than on the slopes, and in the recesses of the Pennine Range ; and the new movement was established upon a large scale, which has retained its relative strength unimpaired ever since. True the somewhat auto-cratic system of Church government which John Wesley set up, was hardly consonant with hillside sentiment ; but the fervour combined with a consistency of profession and practice as compared with more conventional forms of Christianity, appealed so sufficiently to the native temperament as to obscure the defects of formal organisation. When, how-ever, the political reform agitation became an effective force, it had nowhere a stronger backing than in the districts bordering upon and spreading up to these central highlands. Wherever their sons had established themselves, the same spirit spread, reinforced by the passion for consistency, into the realm of religion, and a break away from the " Old Body " resulted in the formation of several new organisations, including the Wesleyan Association and the Wesleyan Reformers. During the course of years some of these came together and formed the United Methodist Free Church. A further merging of forces resulted in the launching of the United Methodist Church in the year 1907. In all these religious movements, as well as in political and social activities, the spirit which has always animated the life of this part of the country and the influence which it has shed upon the outside world, cannot fully be realised, unless it be understood how the passion for democ-racy brought over by our Anglo-Saxon forefathers from the continent to this country, thus draining the larger area, survived in these parts with greater force and more persistent energy than where Norman domination contrived to establish itself more thoroughly.

CHAPTER IV.

RELATIONS OF THE TWO PEOPLES OF ENGLAND. PERSONAL CHARACTERISTICS OF THE NORTH-ERNER AS CONCEIVED BY THE SOUTHERNER.

THE north countryman displays personal character-istics, which mark him off from the southerner and native of the lowlands generally. For this reason he has been made the butt of much gratuitous depreciation by self-appointed critics of the academic and conventional literary school. That there was in former times a great gulf fixed between the two peoples—the northern highlanders and the southern lowlanders—needs no emphasis, and if the facts were understood would cause no surprise. The growth of the modern omnivorous spirit has somewhat narrowed and shallowed the opening ; but a very real differ-ence still exists, which our legislators and administrators might with advantage both to themselves and the people with whom they have to deal, take into consideration more than they are habitually accustomed to do. This constitutes another phase of the general subject to which we cannot avoid giving some little attention, one of those aspects of historical development the neglect of which in the past affords some justification for the present work. But to estimate justly and judge fairly the differences in character and temperament between the descendants of refugees who were for centuries in a state of chronic rebellion against what they conceived to be the robbers and oppressors of their people on the one hand, and powerful intruding autocrats and their tools and hire-lings on the other, must be to anyone an exceedingly difficult task. This is doubly the case with one bred and born of the hills, reared and trained amidst their rugged strength, and inspired by the storms which have swept over and moulded their serrated grit-stone crests. Yet the duty cannot be entirely ignored.

All of us are familiar with the usual statement of the northerner's uncouth rough habits and tastes, his invincibly harsh, reserved and suspicious manner towards strangers. Such a view has been unquestionably accepted by the educated classes in obedience to the decrees of the fashionable world. Any other opinion has been almost outside of accepted literary traditions. The hillman's statement of his own case, or his views upon the character, customs, and temperament of his critics has never been put forth, partly because all who have had the qualifications to speak and command a hearing, have been educated under and largely accepted, the dominant academic traditions. Moreover, had anyone presumed to do so, there is grave reason to believe that the statement would have been received with amused contempt, or held up as confirmation of a benighted inferiority by the social and literary wise-acres, who, tied to traditional Latin standards, maintain their self-appointed national ideals and usages.

The nearest approach to anything of the kind issuing from the pen of one generally accepted as invested with powers and standing sufficient to be regarded as an authority, is that of Dr. Whitaker the historian. The place in which he made his home is situated on the western slope of one of the principal passes of the Pennines, just at the point where these rugged hills decline rapidly into the plain, which was for centuries dominated by the Norman De Lacys and the Romish Abbey of Whalley, whose monks were their dependants, patrons and successors. These facts of themselves postulate a richer fertility of the soil, and a more conventional kind of political, ecclesiastical and social usages. Although by descent a native, but not born here, the young Whitaker's parents came to live at Holme during his earliest days, But there is reason to believe that his younger days did not give him much close acquaintance with the native hillman ; nay even during his thirty years residence amongst them his impressions of the psychology of his neighbours were coloured by the spectacles of his academic training in one of the older universities. Hence we cannot look upon his estimate of the northern character as being by any means free from bias and consequent perversion.   Indeed his life and work at Holme brought him into rather close relations with some of the more objectionable aspects of the new industrialism, at that time blindly groping its way towards crudely conceived possibilities. His finely sensitive soul revolted from the ugliness and squalor of it all, and led him into uncritical and unbalanced judgments, which are powerful antidotes to our acceptance of him as an unprejudiced observer.   But side by side with this he had a large experience of the world ;   hence he presented the usual mentality of classical England without altogether losing his knowledge and appreciation of the character of his own people.

The learned Doctor tells us in relation to the subject now in hand :—[1] " Then again, forests when enclosed, are usually granted out in small parcels, and are colonised with a race of inferior yoemen at most ; these, in situations like the forest of Hardwicke, partly from the stubborn genius of their soil and climate, and partly from sweets of commercial gain, naturally decline into manufactures ; hence a spirit of equality and republican independence become universal ;   they have no superior to court, no civilities to practise.   A sour and sturdy humour is the consequence, so that a stranger is shocked by a tone of defiance in every voice, and an air of fierceness in every countenance."   In this statement there is much truth, but a pure native would see in it, particularly in the last sentence, something of a caricature.   The origin and causes of the prevailing character as given are partly false and partly inadequate.   No colonising in the sense implied by the writer ever took place.   Evidence of many kinds points conclusively to the fact that the territory has been occupied continuously by man ever since late Palaeolithic times.   This evidence may be briefly summarised as follows.   Flint implements and tools of the later Old Stone Age and the New Stone Age have been found scattered over the moors.   Others of the succeeding Bronze Age have also occasionally turned up under similar conditions.   Both of these in conjunction with pottery and ornaments of bone, jet, and glass are commonly associated with sepulchral monuments.   Relics of the Romano-British

[1] *Loidis and Elmete* (pp. 370-1).

period are not entirely wanting. The native place-names and folk-speech are compounded very largely of elements derived from Anglo-Saxon, Scandinavian and British sources, in relative proportions indicated by the order in which they are here given. Although, of course, not quite absent, Norman influence in these directions shows itself much less clearly than is found to be the case in the major portion of England. There is also reason to think—were this the place to pursue the matter—that the same conclusion would be reached by a study of the phonetics and grammar of the native speech, which was prevalent throughout these mountain recesses prior to their modern invasion by books and newspapers, bringing with them the more classical forms associated with Norman domination and the later classical revival, both of which were embodied in the only education which had ever been available to anybody. Such an education involved the discarding of all distinctively northern sympathies and the cultivation of an alien political and social outlook.

The exposed and rugged character of the hills together with a lean soil makes it highly probable that before the district had been considerably developed, very few, least of all those who had been accustomed to the more kindly physical conditions of southern and eastern England, ever settled here voluntarily. As has already been said, they came here a succession of refugees driven or elbowed out of more fertile lands, where they could only have remained as inferiors subject to the tyranny of alien masters. These relations between the two peoples did most to originate and develope the northern character. Dr. Whitaker's judgment of the connection between personal bearing and social conditions, although in some measure true as applying to the Pennine hillman, would have applied just as effectively to any strictly industrial community with a similar age-long experience of life, which obviously it never has done, except to this region.

In the second chapter of her *Life of Charlotte Bronte*, Mrs. Gaskell, has given us a typically conventional literary picture of the northern character. In these impressions gathered from her intercourse and associations with the famous moorland parish, the lady is obviously trying her best to be perfectly fair and just.   But so thorough a south-erner is she, and steeped in all the cultured traditions of classical England, that it was impossible for her to avoid drawing a picture that would strike the models she sought to portray as a distorted exaggeration.   As is so commonly the case with educated people, and especially with those of a social grade above the lowest and least educated, she failed to realise the difficulties of her subjects.   They, nearly always uncultured and illiterate, and consequently unable to grasp the essential bearings of the questions put to them, in any case knowing nothing of the literary side of the Bronte's lives, who themselves were exceedingly shy and retiring, at the same time realised somewhat of their own imperfections and inability to appreciate the unfamiliar mentality of their ques-tioners.   Of this conscious failure to understand the motives of inquirers or satisfy the curiosity of their questioners was born a personal reserve or cautious silence, when escape from harassing inquirers was impossible.   Such a reserve has often been interpreted as jealous or unsociable rudeness. Moreover, allowance must be made of the natives' own feeling of wearied contempt, generated frequently by pestering questions upon subjects about which they knew or cared little, or looked upon as matters interesting only to leisured triflers, but outside of their own practical every-day lives. Besides, the questions addressed to them related to persons who certainly had lived about them, but were never of them, whose manner of life however unconsciously, must have engendered the conviction that they considered themselves better than or above their neighbours : that is a most serious defect in the eyes of a " northerner," and a sure guarantee of silence unless some other great merits could be easily dis-cerned, which might be turned into an effective set-off against those defects.

At that time too political and religious differences of outlook were prone to manifest themselves in social an-tipathies, and in these matters the Bronte's were completely out

of harmony with their neighbours.   The attitude of mind
displayed by the writers already quoted is not confined to
the older generation.   Even a twentieth century author [1] of
some distinction, referring to books written for children
during the latter half of the eighteenth century, can say,
" though perhaps his publications did not yet penetrate to
the *wilds of Yorkshire.*"   Coming to the more average type
of person, the following incident which took place in a small
mountain-girt town may be thought by some to be an extreme
case which exaggerates the prevailing outlook of the nothern
and southern peoples respectively : but it strictly represents
what actually happened at a time when the twentieth century
could fairly be said to have passed its infancy, and is a fair
sample of what has happened more than once.   A district
superintendent nurse wearing the badge of Queen Alexandra's
Nursing Institution, was visiting a sick man.   During an
ordinary conversation, which happened to drift into the
relative merits of north and south (where the nurse came from),
the man asked her what led her to take an appointment in the
north.   " Oh ! " she said, " I'm come to teach the A——
people ; they're so ignorant ! "   To which the sick man
instantly replied, " Well, d—— thee, go back.   Happen A—
folk can teych thee sommat ! "

A NOTHERNER'S VIEW OF THE SOUTHERN CHARACTER.
In trying to set forth briefly the complementary judgment,
i.e., the northern hillman's judgments of the personal traits of
his lowland kinsman, it may be questioned whether an unmixed
advantage will result, whether in fact another misjudgment
equal to the older one will not be furnished, which may be
utilised as an intellectual weapon for throwing at the heads
of hereditary rivals.   But one thing at least can be said in
its favour : in estimating the character of the Englishman
as a whole it will serve as a foil to the time-honoured lob-
sided pronouncement to which we have been long accustomed.
The dominant section may perhaps in some measure be
brought to realise that neither their assumed unquestioned
superiority and perfection of themselves, nor the equally

[1] Elizabeth Godfrey, *English Children in the Olden Times* (p. 275).

assumed undoubted social and intellectual inferiority of their patron rough, are necessarilly so patent as has been hitherto taken for granted.   As has already been seen, the one victim of such misjudgments has long sustained the consequences of the shafts of his rival without the sorry consolation to be derived from a return of the compliment.

Whilst the southerner is apt to look upon the northerner as uncouth, self-opinionated, reserved and distrustful towards strangers, besides being aggressively jealous of his own rights and privileges, the northerner is equally convinced that his rival is a weak and submissive creature of unfortunate circum-stances, to which, however, he and his ancestors have largely contributed by meekly bowing their heads to escape temporary hardships and momentary discomforts, effects which might at least have been minimised had they at first been met by resistence to the ambitious claims and unscrupulous im-positions of ruthless adventurers.   Furthermore, he is prone to abject servility towards not over fine-principled " superiors," while his basely chosen freedom from struggle against wrong has made him effeminate and the slave of cultured form and ceremony passing for good manners, but wanting in sterling reality.   Once more the northerner holds that a debased success in life born mainly of easier physical surroundings, accompanied by the interested patronage of those who have imposed upon him (the southerner) a mean servitude, has generated in him a conceited view of his own superiority. Still more the hillman looks down upon his weak-kneed rival of the lowlands as being deficient in independence both in judgment and economic position, but obediently accepting his social superior's flattering assertion of mutual higher standing than the despised northerner.

CAUSES WHICH ORIGINATED AND DEVELOPED THE TWO TYPES OF PEOPLE.   To rightly understand the northerner's character and his relation to the rest of the community, we must try to understand the experiences which have been his almost continuous lot until comparatively recent times. When this has been done we may cease to wonder at the widely

65

different outlook upon social relationships, and in some respects political aspirations to be found amongst the hills. On the other hand we may come to see that he is just what he is simply because circumstances have made him so, and that little short of superhuman attributes could have resulted in his being anything else. Indeed towards those circumstances his self-satisfied critic has contributed much, and placed under like circumstances would have been the same. Some indication has already been given (pp.7, 61-2 also et seqq.66-8) of the probable way in which these primitive inhospitable backwood regions first came to be inhabited, with reasons for assuming that that occupation has been continuous. The very nature of the surroundings as described (Chapter II.) suggests the strong probability that settlers in such remote and difficult lands would be comparatively free from intrusion, except under abnomal pressure acting upon those without, against whose intrusion they would enjoy valuable strategic advantage in defence. The Romans for instance, those world conquerors, apparently were never able to secure an appreciable domination here. They would seem to have had to content themselves with here and there a minor station with connecting roads, and with the driving of one of their principal east and west lines of communication over the high ridge of Blackstone Edge. But all these left untouched great areas into which the natives could retreat and enjoy comparative security. The Anglo-Saxons very probably came here in order to escape the depredations of the Scandinavians, thus supplementing or superseding earlier settlements of British tribes. Lastly hosts of both of these intruders fled to these hill-retreats in order to escape from the succeeding onslaught of the Normans. It is quite probable that William's harrying of the north, which followed the revolt of 1068, had much to do with establishing amongst these central hills and valleys the Saxon and Scandinavian preponderance which shows itself in these localities.

It is now generally agreed amongst historical students that in none of the successive struggles between invading hosts and native occupiers did there ensue that annihilation of the latter, which at one time was thought to have been the case. Massacres there probably were, but there would be numbers to whom neither that fate nor the playing of the part of serfs amid the scenes of their former liberty and plenty, would be acceptable. To such the mountain recesses would be a safer refuge than the more westerly lowlands, which might expose them again to similar attacks from the opposite shore. Indeed we may take it that some of the raids of the Northmen and probably of others did come from that side. It took the powerful and persistent Normans several centuries to establish themselves in anything like secure domination in this outlying barrier to their triumphant advance. Beyond it lies that north-western area, whose absence from the *Doomsday* survey suggests the failure of the Norman endeavour.

The township of Heptonstall is a portion of that eleventh century unknown land, which intrudes itself between two recorded border territories—Wadsworth and Stansfield. That could not be on account either of its existence as a separate inhabitated entity, or its name being unknown. The main road between the West Riding of Yorkshire and what is now known as north-east Lancashire passed through it. Less than two centuries later, when it was found desirable to divide the great parish of Halifax, Heptonstall became both the seat of a chapel and gave its name to the much wider parish which included adjoining townships already recognised in the great document. The most probable reason for the omission of Heptonstall from the Norman survey was the fact that its unique strategetic position enabled its inhabitants to make a successful resistence against the entry into their town of the ruthless and inquisitive enemy. A glance at the map and a knowledge of the high town's contours bring this fact of strategetic advantage vividly before the mind. Its plan is roughly triangular running west by north-west from the apex, where the town itself has always stood, from which there is a very rapid descent into three valleys five hundred feet deep. Behind the town the land widens out and rises another seven hundred feet to the Pennine axis five miles away, passing on its course into boggy moorland altogether impraticable to a mediæval cavalcade. Approach would be impossible from anywhere near the populated parts but the narrow end of the township. Here the situation could easily be held by a comparatively small force provided with primitive ammunition against very great odds. Some greater prize than anything we can now conceive would need to be aspired after in order to justify the overwhelming force required, and the great sacrifices that would have inevitably been incurred before the objective could have been attained. It seems probable that the Conqueror's agents were never able to gain access to the town, and therefore could report nothing of its resources. Thus we may find a satisfactory explanation for the omission of Heptonstall from the great survey.

The native dis-union which elsewhere afforded the opportunity for success to the well organised Norman phalanx, was in these parts less obvious, and the advantage thus accruing, reinforced by native stubbornness and a still more formidable natural advantage for the weaker side, made up for their deficiencies in military training and equipment, especially in the strength afforded by position. The contour, structure, and constitution of the ground were quite unfitted for the successful operations of closely ranked, impetuous, heavily armed warriors. To these conditions the unyielding native hillman owed somewhat of a respite from even a minor defeat at the hands of the otherwise all-conquering hosts. We are told [1] that, " Before the close of the eleventh century the De Lacy family settled at Clitheroe Castle . . . . and it was not until then that Lancashire began to fully realise the effects of the Northern Conquest." It can easily be understood that the adventuring hosts, possessed as they were of the official ear, would not delay recording, nor fail to make the most of even a precarious and uncertain footing, encouraged therein by the readier and apparantly permanent victory elsewhere. Moreover although Clitheroe is but a few miles distant from the Pennine hill-retreats, it is nevertheless within that richer land and more favourable ground for Norman military op-

[1] Lt.-Col. Fishwicke, *History of the Parish of Rochdale* (p. 31).

erations, which are always to be found where their earlier successes were obtained. More than one line of approach to Clitheroe might be suggested without the hosts needing to touch the Pennines, as for instance from Chester.

The superior organisation and staying power of the Norman adventurers, however, eventually told against native obduracy : but the struggle was a long and grim one, nor did the ultimate victor ever at any time achieve what might fairly be called a marked triumph. Herein may be found a reason for the fact that the conditions imposed upon the local manorial tenants were much less exacting than those which were general where the conquest had been more easily achieved and consequently the new dispensation more rigorously enforced. This may be seen in different parts of the Manor of Wakefield which was held by Earl Warrenne and Surrey. The money rents paid by tenants in the hill regions are about the same as those which obtained both in the rest of this manor and in other parts of England, namely sixpence an acre for new land and fourpence for the rest. Thus there is the Grave-ship of Hipperholme just where the Calder Valley has cast off much of its bleak and rugged outlines, and ceased to afford shelter for unruly natives, and where it opens out into the broad and fertile lands of central Yorkshire. In addition to the money payments mentioned above the tenants here were called upon for the following services and dues :—
" all those twelve men who hold the said thirteen oxgangs of land ought to mend, repair and renew the mill dam at Wake-field as often as shall be necessary . . . . And there are there tenants formerly of Sir Hugh de Eland, of John de Stansfield, and the tenants of Richard of Hiperum, who will give towards the custom of ploughing 4d. for a ploughing if they have ploughs, and for a half-ploughing 2d., and for a fourth part 1d. All the tenants as well free as natives (serfs) ought to do suit at the mill of Rastrick and will give mulcture, to wit—one vessel in sixteen." Again :—" All the tenants shall pay and give each year for their pigs 2d. each and for piglings (hoggets) 1d. But if they buy pigs to sell they shall give for a pig 3d. and for a pigling 2d., whether they shall be

feeding on acorns or they shall not. All the natives shall give aid at the Lord's mill, and the free tenants shall give aid in proportion to their holdings. All the natives shall give marchet for their daughters at the Lord's mill, and also pay lecherwyte. And every widow shall marry herself by the Lord the Earl's licence." [1]

The Graveship of Sowerby embraces the upper portion of the Calder Valley as far as the Lancashire border. Besides being more remote from the manorial headquarters, practically its whole area consists of high hills, deep valley-recesses such as have already been referred to (Chapter II), and favourable retreats for refugees, where it would be difficult to enforce an unwelcome authority. Here dues and services are limited thus :—" to [2] grind at the mills of the Lord all their corn growing within their holdings, and to give mulcture of the 20th vessel, and they have to grind malt, and they say that they owe no other service to the Lord unless the Lord wish to make his eldest son a Knight or to marry his eldest daughter, then they ought to give aid to the Lord according to the size of their holdings." The obligation to grind at the Lord's mill " their corn growing within their holdings " might even be less burdensome than appears at first sight, because as we shall see (p. 93) these people may not have depended altogether upon home grown corn.

The contrast between these two is striking enough if nothing be said of their ease in both cases as compared with the terms imposed in many southern manors, where in addition to the above, payments in kind, some periodical, others imperfectly defined, had to be met. Possibly some of the difference is accounted for by the relative profusion and niggardliness of the soil, or convenience of access to official centres for the contribution of goods or services. But such difficulties as the latter could have been got over by the substitution of cash payments, had such terms in either form

[1] and [2] Extent (or Survey) of the Graveships of Rastrick, Hipperholme and Sowerby, 1309. Halifax Antiquarian Society Record Series, Vol. II.

ever been possible of application. There are also some dues found in the lower graveship and not in the higher, which in themselves are just as applicable in the one case as the other. Pigs for instance were just as necessary, equally general, and as easy to breed and feed in one place as in the other. The grinding of corn was intrinsically just as valuable in one case as the other. It is difficult to see how the customs of " marchet " and " lecherwyte " can have any relation either to geographical position or fertility of soil. The allusions and distinctions drawn between " tenants as well free as natives (serfs) " in the Hipperholme extract, and the total absence of any reference to them in the Sowerby document is significant. Are we to infer that none but " natives " or their equals from neighbouring outlands could be induced to take up holdings in that bleak and socially and politically unsettled area, and were they as a body thus able to drive a better bargain, when the Lord's slowly advancing authority began to threaten the stability of old-time freedom and isolation. ?

It may be well, however, to point out in this latter connection that there is in the Court Rolls one entry relating to the outlying township of Stansfield, which may seem to suggest that there was in existence something akin to serfdom even in that remote district at an earlier date than the one cited above (1309). In the year 1275 a Jury sitting at Halifax said, " that John the Smith of Staynesfeud is the Earl's villien and holds free land in Staynesfeud. He is to be distrained to answer how and wherefore he went out of villenage to freedom." Nothing further, however, is recorded of the case, so that we cannot know whether or not the Earl's claim was sustained. But such omissions are not rare ; even some serious charges, including the high misdemeanour of poaching, are apparently left undecided. Whether such omissions arose merely from imperfectly kept records, or the difficulty of obtaining testimony from reluctant adherents to the law living in the locality concerned, it is now impossible to say. A solitary case like this, left in that vague way, can, however, be scarcely regarded as definitely establishing a custom, the only other evidence for which is rather negative than otherwise. Perhaps the appearance at all of this particular case may be explained in one or other of the following ways. (a) Possibly it was an attempt on behalf of the Lord of the Manor to assert a power over these parts which he had hitherto been unable to win. (b) It may have been that the township had had a vacancy for such a skilled craftsman, for which no local candidate was available, and he had been brought from some other demesne and given the position on condition that he acknowledged bondage to the Lord. (c) If the Earl's claim to the bondage of John was a good one, perhaps his services were due in some other locality, from which he had fled without permission. In this way it seems fairly clear that the new feudalism found it increasingly difficult to establish itself, as it advanced towards the "backbone of England," a metaphor containing a wider significance than was thought of in its original material setting.

Let us now examine some of the facts, and the consequences which naturally followed from even the limited application of the new order set down above. Nor must we forget the peculiar local atmosphere which age-long experiences had already created. The central government only concerned itself with these parts so far as to collect such taxes as it could extort from a people, who in addition to the ordinary antipathy to taxes and tax-gatherers, regarded it as an alien authority, and the proceeds of taxation as destined to be spent upon ambitious schemes of conquest, the maintenance of a useless foreign connection, or the support of hated royal favourites. All such undertakings to these natives were as remote and useless as a proposed expedition to the moon would now be universally regarded. The Lord of the Manor sought to impose laws which were especially galling to a people who had hitherto maintained an independence and unyielding attitude towards all outside authorities, as compared with other parts of the country, where the Norman element was stronger and the subjects had more completely submitted to the new order of things. Rents and fines on accession and succession were collected from such as considered themselves or their ancestors to be the victims of a gigantic spoilation, and had not even the meagre satisfaction of occasionally feasting their eyes upon the sight of the great man and his associates who was theoretically their protector ; much less of sharing in the bounty or profits accruing from a resident feudal establishment. Moreover they were harassed by regulations and restrictions over beasts of the chase and fish in the waters in a manner quite strange to them, and all for the benefit of privileged and unwelcome outsiders. The great tithes of the Parish of Halifax were collected and straightway carted off to the distant Priory of Lewes in Sussex. Even in the case of other ecclesiastical dues, if we take into consideration the distance apart of the churches and the persons put in charge of them, who were generally outsiders educated and trained in the southern convention and attitude of mind towards the northerner, we can see how their imposition must have tended to generate and foster a feeling of being taxed for the benefit of alien institutions and unsympathetic officials. So long too as any lingering tradition of the Celtic Church remained, that feeling would be accentuated.

This essential difference in the foundation of character and economic relations between the Northerner and Southerner has not yet entirely passed away. The latter is even yet to a greater extent than the normal relations of worker and director may imply, a sort of parasite upon the former. With the exception of better results in agriculture, due to a kindlier climate and a more generous soil in the lowlands, the one is the producer, the other the manipulator of the tokens of wealth. These tokens, moreover, are so managed that a portion of them shall still remain in the hands of the operators. The old-time conception, that the more desirable objects of life are a creation designed more particularly for the gratification of the senses of a privileged class, still holds sway amonst the descendants of a long bygone generation of adventurers and their docile victims.

Furthermore there is another consideration. The common failing of the ruling classes the world over, who have established themselves and maintained their position by superior brute force and its complementaries solely in furtherance of their own personal ambitions and luxuries, has operated here in an exteme degree with a subject race peculiarly unfitted for anything approaching a satisfactory application of its methods. It is only in recent times, and then imperfectly, that it has been realised that in order to win the confidence of a people it is first necessary to understand them, to know something of their history and perceive their outlook. Before that the policy has always been to compel them into obedience, or if that were impossible, to ignore their existence as far as possible. With the northern people herein under consideration the inevitable consequence of all these factors has been to implant a feeling that the persistent policy of all outsiders towards the natives has always been either to levy tribute or impose upon them some hardship or injustice. In all the relations between the two peoples of this island the one has approached the other in the spirit of the conqueror and masterful director of affairs, divinely appointed for that function, and against whom there could not possibly be the suggestion of a questioning of their infallible authority and judgment. Political and social movements have been in the past largely, and still are to some extent, dominated by and have received their inspiration from a few fashionable clubs and drawing rooms.

Success in government has been measured by the extent to which subject territories have lent themselves to material exploitation and the adoption of the conventions and social usages which the dominant power sought to impose. All influences, official, educational and conventional, have been directed to the end of imposing entirely the southern outlook and practices upon the north without regard to local conditions. All parties, sets and cliques are equally subject to this influence, even including the fondly imagined ultra-democratic Labour Party. The London Labourist just as unconsciuosly, just as persistently, just as gratuitously and innocently as all the rest of the parties, expects that his supremely artificial conception of life, his centuries-old assumption of self-superiority to all the rest of creation and especially to the antiquated dull-headed simpletons and boors of the north, expects that all should as a matter of course take their cue in everything from the specially created genius who resides amidst the bustle, the worry, the fog and make-belief of what is in reality the greatest perversion of the natural conditions of healthy social existence that the world has ever produced, or will ever tolerate. So far are London and the south out of touch with the psychology of the north, and consequently so harassing to the activities of the latter, that there has grown up in some northern quarters a feeling that it would be a mutual advantage and stimulant to real progress, if the centre of political, social, educational, and financial government and administration were to be shifted to some northern centre.

In those varied, subtle and often intangible forces which make general social relationships work smoothly and sympathetically, it has never been realised by the south that when two peoples widely differing in their outlook upon the world and its affairs are fated or intended to come together and mingle, mutual concessions and forbearance, or at least the recognition that neither possesses either all the virtues or all the faults, are the only avenues through which agreeable relationship can be approached and jarring notes avoided. Unfortunately the nearly continuous experience in this case has been that in all those movements in the past towards amalgamation and a better understanding, the two processes of *give* and *take* which the best understanding would make mutual, have separated and ranged themselves preponderatingly in isolation. Whilst the north for centuries has been absorbing the education, customs and generally responding to the demands of the south—although the latter has looked upon these movements as very slow at best—the reciprocal motion has been practically nil.

What has already been said relative to the causes of hill-country exclusiveness does not exhaust that phase of the subject. There has been another important influence at work. The wars with Scotland and the raids of Scottish freebooters upon the more fertile valleys of north, north-east and north-west England must have provided a theme upon which the passion for the spectacular and romantic has not failed to dilate in the histories with which we have hitherto been provided. The two purposes of thrilling the reader and gratifying the pride of the writer have been fulfilled to a degree out of all proportion to the importance of the subject, so far as the incidents recorded disclosed the more intimate and immediate effects upon the lives and personal characters of the peoples concerned. Momentary national prejudices and literary genius animated by the southern spirit of adventure and domination have unduly obtruded themselves through the floods of eloquent rhetoric. The relations subsisting between the two countries of Scotland and the English governing authorities were, of course, of a piece with the general martial spirit always cultivated towards foreigners. It should, however, be borne in mind that the England which was engaged in these adventures, was rather that dominating power which had always been out of sympathy with the inhabitants of the Pennine Hills, supplemented by such adventurers as could be drawn in from the last-named area, especially the border portion, than the entire English land itself. Whilst the raiding Scots were animated by the same military hunger for spoil and tribute, augmented by a rude sense of justice which mainfested itself in seeking compensation for the injuries they had suffered at the hands of the aggressive southerner.

Between these two were the people of that area with which we are especially concerned in the present work, who there is much reason to believe had no affection for their northern neighbours, and certainly quite the contrary for those of the south. Indeed it is highly probable that the raiding expeditions did not always miss entirely the retreats of the innocent neutrals. If we may take the current accounts of the Scottish forays at their face value, may we not conclude that again in this case those inhabitants of the marauded districts who were attracted by a settled and peaceable life, even if it involved some sacrifice of immediate comfort, would flee to the more retired and secure uplands penetrated by deep valley-recesses, where still safer retreats were to be found, and there settle ? This in addition to the already fixed conviction that the conditions which had brought about their relations with the southern intruders, and possibly a consciousness that any attempts at reprisals or to secure satisfaction for wrongs endured could only result in still further aggravating the misfortune already suffered, or at least could produce no beneficial results, conspired to make them satisfied to remain secluded in and make the best of their remote and thus less disturbed home-lands. Ground between the lower mill-stone of southern aggression and the upper one of Scottish retaliation, the intermediate victim was driven to that exclusive retirement and distrust, the very obedience to which has militated against their recognition as factors in the development of the country, at least in that conventional outlook which is the pervading spirit of our national history. Their moral uprightness and economic independence have led to the ignoring of these people and the obscuring of their existence by a cloud of politico-social adventure and romantic military glory.

SOME OF THE FRUITS OF AGE-LONG ISOLATION AND MISUNDERSTANDING. It has been unfortunate for both parties to this long-standing feud that the exclusive bearing and jealous attitude of all primitive peoples to strangers has been fostered and perpetuated in the north to an unusual extent, and its reaction in the south has set up an air of superior arrogance and patronage. The treatment which the former have received from new-comers and outsiders for at least a thousand years, soon converted natural distrust into a rankling sense of injustice, and national authority came to be looked upon as a meddlesome interference solely in the interests of those who acquired power by the success of a purely selfish adventure. Their rugged independence and blunt primitive speech, combined with an absence of deference towards hereditary vanity, have been interpreted as ignorant barbarism ; whereas it is in reality merely a difference of convention born of hard unyielding circumstances and long-endured wrongs and neglect. The Normans, the last and most complete of the many conquerors, were never able entirely to impose their will upon this stubborn-willed people, and repaid their loyalty to native ideals and spurning of tyranny by diligently cultivating towards them an interested adverse judgment amongst the rest of the world.

Apart from the traditional hostility between themselves and the people inhabiting the rest of the island, the very topography, climate and remote situation until recent times, have conspired to beget an absence of respect for, or willingness to submit to, the classes who have sought to impose conditions of life unsuited to native conditions, however they might fit the easier circumstances of more fertile and genial lowlands. Moreover the inhabitants of these backwoods could never come in touch with, or even become remotely cognisant of, the ceremonial usages and dignified symbolism of the dominant classes and their associates, as had been the case elsewhere. Centuries of seclusion and isolation have only accentuated and crystalised their primitive disposition and natural reserve. The strifes, jealousies and animosities of early times added to an inherent difference of temperament, created, devloped and sustained a difference of feeling and provincial jealousy which the mingling of later and happier times has failed to eradicate entirely. Again a good deal of prejudice on the part of lowland towns against the northern hill-country folk has been born of the inability of the latter to organise their craftsmen and dealers on the lines of the trade guilds, together with their passion for free enterprise and their refusal to recognise the authority of those who sought to monopolise industry for the exclusive benefit of a select class. It had also the effect of limiting the means of contact or association between the peoples, whether tradesmen or craftsmen, of the two regions.

In connection with this phase of the industrial life of the nation is to be noted one striking difference between the hill-folk and the lowlanders. The higher ranks of the former have never looked with that contempt upon trade, which

78

with the latter has undoubtedly grown out of their passion for military glory, political adventure and social domination. From this naturally grew up amongst the official classes an intensification of the theory of social grades, with themselves of course as supreme heads, which still holds much of its old force over the rural peoples attached to the domains of territorial magnates. It has always been gratuitously assumed that the northerner was of an inferior race, to be kept in order, instructed, and if he proved himself sufficiently submissive, to be graciously patronised. Herein we have just the attitude of mind and bearing towards others, which it has been frequently alleged has made Englishmen obnoxious when amongst foreigners generally. With his age-long experience of " foreigners " any attempt at the imposition upon him of such terms of association was always hotly resented by the pariah of the north. Few of the north-central land-owners but have had their wealth founded upon trade, and it has only been when the sons of the rich traders have been " educated " that the infection of trade degradation has seized them.

UNRECOGNISED VIRTUES OF THE NORTHERNER. There remains another aspect of the secluded one's character which has received but a partial acknowledgment, to be touched upon briefly. Confined to a narrow world, where the national resources—before the era of machinery made coal the basis of manufacture—were of the minor degree, and his intercourse with the outside world limited by the unsatisfactory relations which had been his continual experience, he has been driven back upon his own resources. In order to achieve a fair degree of comfort his energies have always had to be directed to the task of making the most of difficult circumstances and un-responsive materials. Isolation has begotten a need for re-liance upon his own energies, and the making of the very utmost of such opportunities as were available. Confine-ment of living areas and cultivable soils to comparative strips along the hill-sides, or during later centuries the bottoms of the valleys, has restricted profitable operations to long and scattered portions. In the administration of public affairs the same conditions have produced costly working ; either large areas made up of small and scattered units, or small ones with heavy burdens upon them have tended to exclusive and jealous rivalry. Operating through the centuries these circumstances have devloped a character in which initiative, self-reliant thrift, scorn of dependence upon either private or public charity, combined with mutual help in times of need, have seldom been equalled and never surpassed. Whether we compare the rates of pauperism in the northern upland unions with those of the south and lowlands, or the houses, furniture, dress and probably the savings and other provisions against calamity, the same conclusion is borne upon us. A common jest amongst the inhabitants of some of the towns in this area is,:—" Everybody in A—— lives in their own house ; and in B—— everybody owns their own house and the next door." Such qualities as these have been important factors in moulding the national character, and the extent to which they have flowed from highland valleys to lowland plains, fertilising, invigorating and revivifying the human organism which they have impregnated, has been but imperfectly recognised by writers and thinkers generally.

Despite the restraining influences operating against free intercourse with the outer world, pressure of local economic and social conditions, combined with the spirit of adventure which adverse conditions were unable to crush out, some of the more active and spiritied natives whilst still retaining the old association with the home-land, established and maintained regular trading relations with London and other distant centres. Others again went boldly forth, establishing themselves in distant places where in many cases they acquired both fame and fortune. Although at some disadvantage educationally, the northern area has contributed more to a comprehensive national life than the prevailing judgments would lead us to infer. Most of the interests which contribute to the making of a full and rich human life have had their ambitions stimulated and their activities helpfully impelled along the highway of endeavour by northern influences. This conclusion will be abundantly justified when the origins of the controlling and directing forces of British life in its many-sided interests have been traced to their source. It is surely not too much to expect that those who have fared forth abroad with their strong characters and sturdy endeavours have not failed to influence their new neighbours. Although the England of conventional outlook and academic thought may have imagined that theirs has been a constantly outflowing current of civilising forces from which the north has most benefitted, its leaders may at length be brought to realise that a converse current has unobtrusively pervaded them, for which they have some cause for thankfulness.

AN OLD-STANDING MISJUDGMENT. In the endeavour to justify the ordinarily accepted attitude of the south to the north, and as evidence of the brutality of the hill-man's personal character, much has been made of the long-continuance of the Halifax Gibbet after that mode of punishment had been superseded elsewhere, as a means of correcting minor offences. The following evidence given by Mr. Ling Roth [1] tends to show that in this matter we have not a case of unmitigated brutality, but that where this gibbet-law operated longest, the spirit behind it was in one respect at least centuries ahead of those who presumed to take upon themselves the function of a critic. At a Manor Court held at Halifax during the year 1360, " It was found by inquest, ' that if any tenant of the Lordship shall have been beheaded for theft or other cause, the said tenant ought not to lose his inheritance, notwithstanding any lease made, the meantime, by the steward.' According to the law of the realm, felonies were punishable by loss of lands not entailed, and of goods and chattels real and personal. Thus it would appear that the custom of our own country leaned to the side of mercy in this respect, though such mercy, one would think, would have been to the prejudice, rather than otherwise of the Lady of the Manor." Thus we have northern hard-heartedness reduced to a refusal on the part of the guardians of the law

[1] *Yorkshire Coiners and Old Halifax* (p. 131).

and order to impoverish the children for the legal lapses of their parents.

The alleged defect may thus be considered as having somewhat less reproach left in it than has been assumed, and there is no need to labour the point much farther : but there are other circumstances suggested by the isolated fact upon which the charge is based, that may profitably have a brief reference given to them.   May not the persistence of this primitve legal machine with its worn-out terrorism be an indication of the weakness and incapacity of the central government, and its inability to command the respect and overcome the antipathy to itself of these northern hill-folks ? Certainly an Act of Parliament passed during the reign of Queen Mary relating to the wool trade of Halifax—to be quoted at a later stage of this work (p. 181-2)—does not display the legislators of that day as possessed of either a very high appreciation of the social status of the people, or an extensive knowledge of the physical features of these parts.   As already shown (Chapter II), the district was one lending itself to safe refuge for outlaws, with the consequent difficulty of tracking and securing law-breakers.   The general industry was one in which a valuable product in universal demand and therefore easily disposed of, had in the later stages of its preparation to be exposed for lengthy periods including the night in the open air, thereby offering both great temptations and easy opportunities of escape for wrong-doers.   Besides this the central government was apparently weak in authority everywhere and especially in this area.   Here was a special need for strong protection against idlers and evil-doers ; but instead of receiving it from the source where above all others lay the responsibility of supply, the people were thrown back upon their own resources and left to make the best they could of an awkward situation.   Possibly the more advanced and far-seeing of the natives had realised that the old isolation must sooner or later succumb to a wider nationalism, in which local customs must become merged into a general legal code, so that a system already effete and discredited had its existence prolonged in the hope that government would at no distant time realise its duties and rise to its opportunities. In accounting for an imperfectly understood phenomenon the old-time habit of mind on the part of the conventional critic has seized upon a custom which was never half so bad as assumed—since a greatly redeeming feature of it has been ignored—and worked it up to accord with a foregone conclusion of the moral depravity of the victim.

CHAPTER V.

INDUSTRIAL HISTORY OUTSIDE OF THE ACADEMIC AREA : PASTORAL MANIFESTATIONS.

RURAL ECONOMY DURING PAST CENTURIES. Until quite recent times a close connection with pastoral pursuits on the part of the great majority of the people everywhere was a necessary condition of obtaining the most ordinary materials for sustaining life. Even had the relations between different groups of people been of the most agreeable character, difficulties of transport in all direction caused the production of perishable goods, such as food stuffs, and heavy and cumbrous ones like building materials, and much of the raw materials of manufactures, to be made necessarily near the seat of consumption.

Not until the latter half of the eighteenth century had in some measure accomplished its improved ways of communication, did it become possible for the application of a strict division of labour to be made between the two main departments of industry—the pastoral and the manufacturing. The physical difficulties combined with the social exclusiveness already indicated (Chapters ii and iv), intensified and prolonged those primitive conditions in the mountainous regions of the north midlands and further north. Even when the Industrial Revolution as applied to manufactures had established itself, up to a time reaching well into the third quarter of the nineteenth century, practically the whole of the master manufacturers, professional men, retired people and landowners worked a fairly large dairy farm, in order to provide their own families and at least a portion of their workpeople and dependants with the more urgent necessaries of life. Milk, butter, bacon, eggs, fowls, cheese, oat-meal, malt and in the case of some of the larger men, beef and mutton also, were largely provided from this source. So too it was not uncommon for cottagers to have a pig-stye, a poultry-place, and a garden-patch, from which their economic resources were augmented. Cheese, being both the most durable and difficult to produce, and the easiest to store and transport, was the first of these home-produced foods to succumb to the specialisation of an outside world. Corn yielded to the inevitable consequences of the repeal of the Corn Laws ; home-produced butter, bacon, eggs and fowls have at the present time only partially allowed their one-time domination to be shared by imports, a concession due to the necessities arising from an increasing population and a decreasing area of pastoral land, rather than from satisfaction with the new order of things. The phrases " fresh farmer's," " home-fed " and " new laid " still possess a magic charm which drives with eagerness the thrifty house-wife's fingers deeper into her purse, even though that purse may be but a small one.

Any inquiry into the social conditions of an early people necessarily brings us into an investigation of agricultural interests and practices. In the essential needs for maintaining life, the people of the north and south portions of England were in the main identical ; but the means adopted in the northerly area to secure that end and the apparent motives behind some of the practices do not agree very closely with those which we are given to understand prevailed in those parts of the country from which the recognised authorities have drawn their materials. The differences are not in the main such as would arise from the variations of soil and climate prevailing in the two areas. Something may be due to the influences exerted in several respects by the social and political forces which became dominant after each conquest, and especially the last one, upon those respectively who came immediately and wholly under that power, and upon those who succumbed more tardily and less completely. Something has already been said upon this point in a previous chapter. But the chief source of this disparity between the alleged customs of the south and the surviving evidence and practice in the north would seem to lie in a misunderstanding of some of the facts, possibly due to their interpreter's limited acquaintance with surviving circumstances as they relate to the records of the past, and an over emphasis upon changes introduced or more extensively adopted at that time, when eager advocates exceeded discretion in proclaiming the virtues of a new thing.

AGRICULTURAL LIFE AND PRACTICES OF THE PENNINE AREA. The deficiencies of general history which present themselves to the mind of the student who approaches the subject from the point of view of the north-central uplands, are intensified when attention is directed to the industrial development of that area. The conditions both past and present existing over this large region, seem to be little if at all understood. There is something lacking in the usual story, which is based entirely upon a different kind of material, drawn from regions where widely varying practices seem to have prevailed. Hence the generalisations are misleading, inasmuch as they ignore the facts relating to the northern district. Not only has existing documentary evidence of the past been overlooked, but practices still surviving on a large scale have not been taken into account. Some of these evidences would probably have shed new light upon some of those facts, which have been responsible for the deductions with which we are familiar, and resulted in a modified view of the case. This has been especially marked in that part of Industrial History which deals with the keeping of cattle, sheep and pigs during early times, and in the changes introduced into agriculture by the new methods brought in during the seventeenth and eighteenth centuries.

An error which has crept into the transcription of a document relating to this area, may here be corrected, as the point has some bearing upon matters about to be dealt with, and also illustrates how an otherwise well qualified writer may for want of local knowledge originate or perpetuate a misunderstanding. In the *Rent Roll* [1] of Sir John Towneley,

---

[1] *Chetham Society*, Vol. ciii : Vol. vi. of *Miscellanies* (p. 6).

A.D. 1535-6 we find :—" Item XIJ bests to be fothered with orts." The last word " orts " the editor translates "oats." Now a limited acquaintance with the folk-speech of the borderland concerned would have revealed the fact that "orts " are " leavings," and the word still survives amongst farmers as denoting the leavings of cattle from their fodder, which was invariably hay. The milk-cows and beasts which are being fed up for beef, as well as those not in the best of health and with weakened appetites, are generally treated to the best of the hay-crop in order to tempt them to eat to the full, so that the best and quickest results may be obtained. Like their human masters these pampered beasts often develop rather partial tastes and sort out and leave what does not appeal to their refined palates. These " orts " are collected by the stock-man and given to those other animals which are rather marking time, being younger stock and lying off adults, which it is not so important to coax to feed to the utmost. The difference is considerable, and materially alters our conception of this part of the stock-keeper's practice during these early years.

AUTUMNAL SLAUGHTER OF LIVE STOCK. The usual statement, or at least the impression gained from reading the ordinary descriptions of agricultural life, is that at the decline of the year, owing to the scarcity of winter-food and the consequent difficulty of keeping all the animals with a moderate supply during that season, such of them as were not absolutely necessary for immediate uses and the keeping up of future stock, were killed and salted to provide food for the family during the winter. On this assumption much has been written concerning the monotony and unhealthiness of the diet which our ancestors were constrained to endure, and the hardships imposed upon those of the cattle, which were privileged to stand between the difficulties of their human masters and their own race extinction. One writer,[1] whose work has passed through several editions, gravely informs us that " during the winter they (the cattle) were half-starved." This is in general agreement with the implication of others ;

[1] H. T. Warner, *Landmarks in English Industrial History*, Ed. 6, (p.286).

87

but the assumption finds little support in the facts relating to the northern hill-districts, whether we look at present day practice or at such evidence concerning the past as is available. In accounting for the winter deterioration of condition in the stocks, no account has been taken of the unhygienic conditions under which they were stalled.

A false conception of this kind is largely based upon a failure to realise the natural conditions of existence of the animals in question. Even when entirely subject to natural conditions, that is before they were domesticated, these animals like all the rest which are still with us, were able to withstand successfully the winter hardships and survive in vigour and plenty. Any highly organised animal subject for long ages to an annual " half-starving " for several months must long ago have met with extinction. Yet so far was this from being the fact with the ox tribe, that their natural qualities quite early in man's experience led to their selection for devotion to his special service. Immediately a knowledge of the art of curing and storing hay became general, and this we shall see was centuries before the time these writers are speaking of, its possessor both furthered his own interests and repaid some of his debt to his humble and obedient servant by largely correcting such natural deficiency as existed in the winter-food supply.

Another natural condition of existence for dairy cattle, which these writers have imperfectly realised, is that at all times both past and present the natural food for cattle is grass, and that the great stand-by and principal element in winter artificial feeding has been and must be hay, that is, the dried and stored meadow-grass of the previous summer. Once the practicability of utilising a portion of the summer grass-crop for feeding cattle during the ensuing winter had been grasped, it was but a small step to the setting apart of sufficient land for the purpose of hay-growing to yield enough for the end in view. So too, throughout the period from the beginning of which much documentary evidence is available, there is abundant testimony that in all parts of England the growing, curing and storing of hay was well known and extensively practised. To this point we shall return later on (Chapter vi).

THE NEW METHODS OF FEEDING CATTLE INTRODUCED INTO ENGLISH AGRICULTURE DURING THE SEVENTEENTH AND EIGHTEENTH CENTURIES. These have been represented as constituting quite a revolution in the possibilities of the winter feeding of live stock. Such a pronouncement is very disproportionate, if the case be looked at from the point of view of those elevated regions in the north where agriculture does not now, and probably never has partaken much of an arable character. As the matter has a close bearing upon the question of the winter feeding of cattle in general, the northern practice so far as it can be ascertained may here be described. The most that can be claimed for these newly adopted methods is that they did somewhat enhance the possibilities in variety and magnitude of crops both for human and animal consumption to be obtained from the land, and mildly stimulated milk production (with some doubt as to its quality), the laying on of flesh, and possibly a little earlier maturing of the animal. In the non-arable districts the system has never had more than a very limited application. Although it would be foolish to assert that no changes have taken place, it is safe to say that in all essentials the feeding of live stock in the upland dairy-farming districts which prevails to-day, is the same as that which has been known for six hundred years. Anything but the grass grown upon the land where the cattle are kept, forms but a very small proportion of the whole food consumed. The general practice of using the land mainly for growing grass both now and in the past, is confirmed by the old custom in these districts of measuring land by the " day-work," that is, the area which when used for mowing grass intended for hay, could be mown by a man of average capacity in that kind of work, in a day.

In very few cases has the use of root-crops as a food been adopted, and in fewer still are they home grown. Only for special reasons, such as the accessible town's demand for milk, butter, or beef, are the the corn miller's offal, maize-meal, linseed or cotton-seed cake resorted to beyond a very limited extent, and the greater portion of this practice has come into vogue within the the latter half of the last century. In relation to the winter feeding of stock it should be borne in mind that the last-named supplementary kind of food is used in summer almost as much as in winter. Some only adopt the practice rather sparingly even now, and it cannot be too often emphasised that such food is not an essential for keeping the stock in a fairly vigorous and thriving condition. This system of more artificial feeding has been given a great stimulus by the modern town-demand for milk, butter and cheese, and by the greatly increased importation of grain, cotton, etc., which has augmented the quantity of these foods available and reduced it's cost. In this connection there are some recent developments in the neighbourhood of northern manufacturing towns, both social and industrial, which have accentuated the use of artificial feeding stuffs. During the last century especially in its latter half a considerable reduction of dairy-lands has taken place ; firstly by desertion of out-lying lands which the restrictive effect upon imports produced by wars and corn laws had forced into an unnatural occupation ; secondly by taking up much of the richest land to provide for the growth of towns, for buildings, pleasure grounds and other purposes. The demands upon the remaining dairy-lands have been proportionately increased, stimulating a greater demand for produce which has been partially met by the forcing methods of artificial feeding and conditions for stock life. This method of enhancing produce is greatly more in vogue than attempts to stimulate the fertility of the soil, which would appear in many districts to be somewhat neglected. In the direction just indicated great changes have already taken place, many farms which fifty years ago were considered altogether too far out for taking their milk into the towns, now do so regularly. The additional work involved precludes the occupant from giving the attention to the land itself, which he was formerly wont to do.

Under the old system the milk was converted into butter or cheese, the skim-milk and whey being used for rearing young cattle, feeding pigs, or sold to neighbouring cottagers.   During a recent visit to the Ribble Valley the writer learned that a large area, which a few years ago devoted itself mainly to cheese and butter making, now sends most of its milk away into the large centres of population.   Even a limited acquaintance with the present day practices of farm-life in these regions, confined as it is to dairy produce and sheep, would convince anyone that the book-difficulties of winter food for stock before the days of turnips, clover, lucerne, etc., have been greatly exaggerated.   The stock here, reared as we have seen very largely upon the very old-time produce of the land, will bear comparison with those of any other part of England, provided that a very moderate allowance be made for hilly ground and exposed climate. We must also bear in mind that there is room for doubt whether the variety of cattle kept during recent centuries is indigenous to these rough and exposed hills.   The care, shelter bestowed, and improved herbage brought about by centuries of cultivation in response to the demands of an increasing industrial population, must have had an artificial-ising effect.   The shorthorn, which now obtains largely, could hardly have survived the more natural conditions of life, which prevailed in early times.   As stated above turnips are seldon used, clover other than a little red and white which grows wild and with little special effort to encourage it, is never cultivated and seldom used except for horses, and the present witer who has lived on such a farm for many years and been closely associated therewith for over fifty years, does not even know what lucerne is.

Facts which strongly confirm the conclusions herein set forth are furnished by the somewhat scanty documentary evidence which has managed to survive the trials of centuries. The *Extent* [1] or *Survey* of the graveship of Sowerby, within the North-west Riding of Yorkshire and the Manor of Wake-field, made in the year 1309, gives some account of five vac-

[1] The Extent (or Survey) of the Graveships of Rastrick, Hipper-holme and Sowerby, 1309. Copied and translated by J. Lister, M.A.

caries which existed in these high, exposed and lean hill regions. The graveship of Sowerby touches the ridge of the Pennines. Its lowest point is about 350 feet above sea-level, and the highest parts occasionally reach as much as 1500 feet. The valleys are very narrow, and consequently large portions of their sides are crags and scars. The soil on the moorlands is peaty and the rest clay and sand. The main portions of that which was under cultivation at the time we are speaking of would be at altitudes ranging from 500 to 1300 feet. The particulars are not in all respects so full and definite as we could have wished. But it would seem that taking the five vaccaries together 109 acres of meadow-land produced each year sufficient hay for the winter food of 3 bulls, 125 cows and 70 calves, an average of nearly two animals to the acre. These animals, it must be noted, were in each case taken elsewhere for summer pasture. Assuming then the acre to be approximately the same as the present statute acre—there is some reason to think that it was greater—this is a higher feeding capacity than most of the land in the locality bears to-day. The disparity may be explained by the following facts ; (1) that more than a third of the animals were calves, and (2) that milk production would not be the pressing necessity that it is to-day. Hence most of the stock would pick up a considerable share of their food out of doors by winter-grazing the meadow and common land ; just as to-day most of the non-milkers are regularly turned out to pasture, except during the more severe weather and when the ground is covered with snow. The fact that such vaccaries existed, and the larger and more numerous ones on the other side of the Pennines, to be alluded to elsewhere, implies that the winter-keep did not present itself to their owners as a very serious problem. There were at the same date 87 tenants and holders of land, most if not all of whom presumably kept cattle, if only for their own family use. There are, however, no specific allusions to meadow-land other than those above. The Wakefield Manor Court Rolls, however, prove that hay was commonly cut and stored at an earlier date than 1309. There are also references to corn-crops in the lower slopes of the area but of what kind of grain is not stated.

CORN GROWING AND ARABLE CULTIVATION. Apart from what has just been stated, there is no evidence that arable cultivation was ever extensively carried out in these parts. No doubt in very early times, when each little group of people tried to be, or were of necessity, as far as possible a self-contained economic unit—and the circumstances which led to the first settlements in these inhospitable regions tended to make the local people more than usually exclusive—precarious crops of oats and barley would probably be raised. From the *History of the Stansfield Family* (p. 112), we learn that in the year 1358, " the King gave licence to Ralph de Stansfield, that he may buy 600 quarters of corn, and 20 casks of salt herrings in Ireland, and load them in ships, and bring them to England for his convenience." There is in this extract no clue as to the destination of these goods ; but it is clear that England had begun to import corn, and the most likely place for it to come to was some part where that commodity was not easy to produce. Perhaps we may also infer that the districts in England where conditions were favourable for corn growing would send out their surplus produce into those areas where the conditions were less favourable. It is likely that salt herrings would be intended for some distance inland. At that time and for some centuries later, the Stansfields of Stansfield were the principal family in that part of upper Calderdale, some of its members occupying responsible offices in both of the adjoining Manors of Wakefield and Clitheroe. Is it unreasonable to think that at least a portion of this Irish cargo found its way to the family and its tenants living in the Stansfield and neighbouring bleak regions ?

Twenty-one years later we find in the *Poll Tax Returns* the name " Willelmus de Stansfield, Merchaunt." He and another in this remote hill country make up a quarter of the whole of that rank, who were there at that time in the wide parish of Halifax. On the 28th of May in the same year Ralph was granted permission to bring twenty casks of wine to England, " as well for the use of Henry, Duke of Lancaster, as for his own convenience." These two transactions afford a glimpse of the connections and activities, which the Norman favourites who had at last been able to establish themselves in these remote highlands, maintained amongst their associates and other parts of the outside world. What was the exact relationship between William of the *Poll Tax Returns* and Ralph of twenty years earlier is not quite clear. The pedigree published in the work already cited shows a Ralph, uncle of William, and another his grandfather. The importer of wine, herrings and corn, might have been either of these. Which ever it was there can be little doubt that the Stansfields of Stansfield were interested in distantly flung trading transactions during the middle of the fourteenth century ; and in these we may have some indication of the lines upon which the " Merchaunts " of the later date directed their energies. An argument based upon such evidence as is available to us would not be conclusive, but the facts are very suggestive.

In the *Wills* relating to the parish of Halifax, some of which take us back to the early years of the fifteenth century, there are occasional allusions to ploughs, harrows, or corn ; but more frequent are mentions of cattle, sheep, hay, etc. ; more frequently still do we find bequests of looms and other tools used in cloth-making, furniture, personal clothing and belongings. The evidence to be found in *Manor Court Rolls* points in the same direction. These two may be culled from a scanty choice, namely ; sometime between the years 1297 and 1286 " Alan, son of Richard Talvas, was imprisoned for taking from William del Hirst six sheaves of oats against his will, alleging that William owed him the same for preserving his corn in the night from the beasts of the woods." And at a Court held at Halifax on May 10th, 1313, under the head of " Sourby," there is this :—" Elyse, son of Ivo, 3d. for wrongfully withholding half a quarter of oats from Matilda the Webster." The wandering capacities of all kinds of live stock are potent forces towards bringing their owners into Court, so that no close analogy can be drawn between cases relating to them as compared with growing crops : but throughout the forty-two years *Court Rolls* which are accessible, cattle and pigs are a perennial source of trouble and contention ; sheep, hay, pasture and horses, only less so.

Probably when the lower slopes and valley bottoms began to be occupied, the more fertile and sheltered places would be utilised for corn growing, thus giving a greater aggregate yield, which might, however, be balanced by increasing population. After the introduction of the potato into England until the middle of the nineteenth century much of the local supply was home grown. Corn growing was at its maximum during the last quarter of the eighteenth and the first of the nineteenth century, as a result of the wars and the Corn Laws with an increasing population. Even then little wheat was attempted, a fact sufficiently attested by all the people who survived into the happier times after the middle of the century. Their universal testimony was that in former times the general mass of the people never saw flour, except when a few pounds were given out to hand-loom weavers for the purpose of sizing a warp. Oatmeal porridge and cake were the staple diet of the people.

OATS THE STAPLE DIET OF THE NORTHERN PEOPLE—GRINDING. Some light upon corn production and its preliminary treatment in the processes of conversion into food might be expected to be derived from the surviving corn-mills and their records or the apparatus which may have been used for the purpose of reducing the grain to a consumable powder. The two questions are closely involved in each other, and for that reason are here treated together. Such evidence as there is, is rather meagre and more often of a negative character. Allusions to corn, either directly or indirectly, are of frequent occurrence, but the cases of specific identification are rare. When, however, we do come across definite particulars, oats almost invariably are mentioned. During the period when the Napoleonic blockade and the Corn Laws made home grown food imperative, and corn growing was most prevalent throughout the Pennines, oats were the most prevalent crop, intended mainly for human food and for the final stages of fattening animals for beef and bacon. Whether the corn were home grown or not, the provision made for the pulverising would be the same. The presumption is strong that such as came from outside would be brought in before grinding. The packing and carriage in that state would be easiest and safest, least liable to damage by weather or temptation to illicit disposal. The provision for pulverising the grain, so far as it is known, may help us to some extent in determining the kind of grain so treated. Oats differ from other food grains in that they need to be subjected to a high temperature for thorough drying before they can be pulverised. Accordingly, where-ever that was done a kiln had to be provided. Many of the old corn-mills had in their deeds such a kiln specified, *e.g.*,[1] " A water corn milne, called Stansfield Milne, in my occu-pation, and a kilne called Stansfield kilne." There is a similar clause in the deeds of Gauxholme Corn Mill situated in Todmorden and Walsden.

It has already been noted that manorial tenants were under an obligation to grind their corn at the Lord's mill, paying mulcture at a fixed rate. There is little doubt that for centuries this was a profitable business for the miller, and burdensome to the tenants by whom the obligation was frequently evaded. It may be conceived that as holdings became sub-divided and some of them more distant as the result of increasing population, the corn produced from each individual holding might become so small that the enforcement of the duty might cease to be worth while, or distance from the mill might render fulfilment an irksome task ; or again the demands upon a convenient mill might become so great that its share of the contract could only be fulfilled, if at all, with great difficulty. Then for these and other reasons, com-pounding might proceed so far that little inducement remained to retain the mill in effective working order. There is no doubt, that, probably for a variety of reasons, the once existing rights and dues ultimately became obsolete ; and in many cases the owning and working of the mill became an affair of private enterprise, grinding such grain as was voluntarily brought thereto, or the owner on his own responsibility might bring and grind the corn to supply an expected market. In Watson's *History of Halifax* is given a list of

[1] *History of the Stansfield Family* (p. 341).

seventeen water-driven corn mills as existing in the parish
of Halifax in the year 1758. Some of these were undoubtedly
the old manorial mills, or at least the survivals of them.
Whether any of them still exercised the old mulcture rights
over their neighbours is doubtful. Their very uneven
distribution points strongly against any presumption of at
least several of them ever having enjoyed manorial privileges. Two only in the extensive Ryburn Valley, and
Stansfield Mill for the extensive township of that name
would be poor provision indeed. On the other hand,
Mayroyd, Foster's Mill, Hangingroyd Mill and Hudson
Mill seem to supply a redundancy in one locality, as do
two in Soyland, or Cragg Valley respectively, if we assume
that they were confined to local requirements. It is
at the same time worthy of note that in the year 1691 the
owner of Warley Corn Mill secured a ruling in the Duchy
Court of Lancaster, enforcing upon all the inhabitants of the
township the duty of grinding their household corn at the said
mill.

Something has already been said about the possibility
of a manorial mill ceasing to be a paying corncern. Possibly
something of this sort may have happened in the case of that
part of the old township of Sowerby which ultimately became
the separate township of Erringden. What was the origin
and former rank of Woodmill Old Corn Mill is not known ;
but it is one of those given in Watson's list ; and although
actually situated within Stansfield it is close to Sowerby
Ramble and within a stone's throw of Erringden. When
in the year 1449 Erringden Park was dispaled and the land
sold to several owners, it was expressly provided that they
need not do suit at the Lord's mill, unless he built a new mill
on the river Calder, or the water of Erringden. There is
just the possibility that one of the mills Woodmill, Hoohole,
or Cragg, may have originated about this time, either at the
instance of the Lord (which in the light of what has just been
said is improbable), or of the new owners themselves, or by
an individual effort designed to meet the anticipated requirements of the respective localities on both sides of the water.

97

In each case the waters from which they derived their power divided townships which had no mill accommodation within two or three miles, and were situated in a hill-country where roads were difficult. All the three mills just named stood at different points on the margin of Erringden, a territory practically consisting of one high precipitous hill. In any locality consisting of deep, narrow valleys intersecting mountainous land, the provision of manorial mills convenient for all the tenants, who were theoretically subject to the Lord of the Manor, would be an object always difficult of attainment and seldom completely accomplished. In the parish of Halifax, which was chosen for illustration above, inequality of distribution was very apparent. With the outlying tenants insistence upon suit to the mill must have been almost impossible of strict enforcement.

At Rastrick " Tourn " [1] on July 20th, 1286, there were many cases convicted for not doing service at the Lord's mill, and for having hand-mills. Fines of 6d. were imposed, and the hand-mills were to be laid aside. In such cases the remission or composition of service were probably amongst the first steps taken to slacken the full manorial powers. It is therefore not surprising to find material evidence of domestic grinding stones still in existence. Querns, sometimes entire, but more frequently only the upper or lower stone, are to be found in many places on the country side. At Turret Royd, Rattonstall, there is a number of parts of querns, brought there, as stated by the late owner, from Lower Rattonstall Farm, where the manorial headquarters formerly were. These were likely enough what had been seized from law-breaking tenants, although in the case of this small sub-manor—apparently cut off from Stansfield—very few tenants would be more than a mile from the manorial mill now known as Hudson Mill. At Higher House in Erringden and at Todmorden Hall there are good examples of the lower stones of very large querns. The museums of Manchester, Rochdale and Halifax each possess several examples obtained from various places within, or near to, the Pennine area. They

[1] *Yorkshire Archaeological Society, Record Series*, Vol. ii.

are of various types, some of them being very primitive. Others appear not to have been much used ; they may possibly date from the time when the mill to which suit was due, ceased to fulfil its duties satisfactorily ; or they may be even so late as the period of maximum corn growing in the latter part of the eighteenth and beginning of the nineteenth century.

There is also existing evidence which seems to point to the conclusion that in some of the more remote places, at any rate in the later dates of manorial jurisdiction, the Lords recognised the necessity of allowing their tenants to grind their corn at home, and made more provision for the drying of oats at a convenient centre, from which the nearest water corn mill was situated miles away. An old native of the district related that at Widdop, which is situated in the higher reaches of the Hebden Valley between Heptonstall and Wadsworth, and in the neighbourhood of Walshaw, which is far up on the Wadsworth side, kilns were provided by the landowner, who was also Lord of the Manor, to which tenants brought their corn to be dried. When this was done they took the grain home to grind. In the immediate vicinity of the kiln was a small piece of land—a sort of common land— on which the beasts which had carried their grain, might graze during the time of waiting for the grain to pass through the kiln. There is reason to believe that in some cases where the word " kiln " enters into a place-name, it may have been derived from this source.

Before concluding this part of our subject a very brief reference may be made to other vegetable food crops and food-stuffs known during the period of our earliest records. Some particulars will be given at a later stage of this book relating to wheat (pp. 123-4-6, 161) ; but such information as is available with regard to that cereal points to its having been grown in the more eastward part of the area, where it passes into the more open and lower lying land of central Yorkshire, where richer soils and less rainfall are found. There are a few place-names which might have been derived from the particular locality, or a portion of it, having at one time being devoted to that crop. Wheatley for instance, near the town of Halifax, may be a case in point. This surmise in confirmed by the fact that the local pronunciation of the first syllable is identical with that given to the grain, namely, *whee-at*. The place is ten miles eastward of the Pennine Range, so that some of the more favourable physical conditions just mentioned are beginning to prevail. Not so, however, with Wet Ing in Wadsworth, which some shallow purists misinterpreting the local folk-speech have written *Wheat Ing*. At this place the area of land which could ever have been put under the plough is very limited indeed, and both soil and climate are decidedly adverse to success with a wheat crop. Moreover the the folk-name for the place is *Weet*, whilst wheat invariably takes the form *whee-at* as given above.

We may also reasonably infer that some garden-crops were raised ; but unfortunately we are absolutely in the dark as to the specific kinds of produce. At a Court at Halifax [1] on May 23rd. 1275, under the head of " Soureby," in regard to a sale and demise of land there is mention of " a garden and a stubbing." Again a court was held at Wakefield [2] on May 26th, 8, Ed. II. when Roger son of Amabell of " Sourby " was fined 6s. 8d. " for putting several beasts to graze in the Earl's garden." This case suggests some confusion of the sense in which the word " garden " is used, as compared with the modern meaning : but the " garden " may perhaps have included what would now be called an orchard, in which case grass would very likely be found under and between the fruit-trees. We know too that bees were cared for, honey probably being of some value though we find no specific mention of it. At a Court held at Halifax [3] on Sunday, October 18th, 1313, we find " value of a swarm of bees from an oak in Luddenden, 10d." About December 10th, 1308, in a case of burglary, ten pounds of wax are mentioned ; in another on May 23rd, 1275, flour.

[1] *Yorkshire Archaeological Society, Record Series*, Vol. i.
[2] and [3] *Yorkshire Archaeological Society, Record Series*, Vol. i.

butter and cheese are named. Amery de Stodeley was fined
3d. for escape of cattle and gathering nuts : this last indicates
their use for food and their prevalence resulting from the
then greater quantity of copse and woodland.

EXTENT AND MOTIVE OF AUTUMNAL SLAUGHTERING
OF CATTLE. Reverting more directly to the subject of the
autumnal slaughtering of cattle, it may be observed that the
killing off, so far as it took place at all, could not have applied
to more than a small fraction of the whole live stock, assuming
that the number thereof were maintained at some uniform
relation to those of the human beings they were intended
to serve. Any other assumption must necessarily imply an
enormous consumption of flesh meat by the people. Whether
the beasts of burden were oxen or horses, winter is the part
of the year when the severest demand would be made upon
them for farm or domestic services, and so this part of the
stock could not be reduced. The dairy requirements would
not be much if any less than during summer, and in winter
the natural production per head of stock decreases, which
would imply the need to keep up numbers. Such of the
breeding stock as were coming to " noit " would be unproductive for several weeks or months previously, during
which time they would need moderately generous feeding,
if their offspring and the future production of milk for dairy
purposes were not to be handicapped. Seeing that it takes
two years for a beast to come to maturity, in order to keep
up the level of numbers at least twice as many calves and
stirks would need to be kept going as there were adults killed,
or to make up for those which succumbed to disease or accident during the year. It may be mentioned incidentally
as an illustration of how far the artificialising of stock-keeping
has gone, that whatever was the practice in earlier times,
it is certain that for considerably over a century in the northern
uplands, even from birth, calves have never been allowed to
run with their mothers : they are always fed by hand and only
receive a portion of the mother's milk.

On most of the smaller farms, which were almost certainly the most numerous, the regular slaughtering of one

full grown cow or ox per annum would, in the course of a few years, seriously deplete the numbers which the farm could support, unless indeed the resources of the land for feeding the animals had been deliberately strained to the utmost safe limit in order to make provision for the family's food supply.   In this case the contingency had been deliberately planned, and the motive of evading an annually recurring difficulty in feeding the animals had no operating effect. The relative numbers of large and small occupiers of land may be illustrated by the district flanking the Yorkshire Calder on its twenty miles upper course.   In the graveship [1] of Sowerby, the most exposed and rugged of all, eighty-seven tenants are named in the 1309 *Extent*.   Of these forty-seven are given as holding less than an ox-gang (fifteen to twenty acres), while most of them held considerably less.   Of the remainder—the greater tenants—there is every probability that in most, if not all, cases the lands were sub-let in small amounts.   An examination of the Hipperholme and Rastrick lists shows an even greater preponderance of the small men. It may also be worthy of note that the conclusions which have hitherto held the field with respect to winter-feeding have been based upon evidence drawn exclusively from those localities where climate, soil and the configuration of the land all favour the arable style of cultivation, where the use of such crops for the winter-feeding of cattle has now obtained so long, that it has acquired the force of an old and unquestioned custom.   In the absence of acquaintance with any other system of feeding nothing else has been conceived possible.

It may be admitted that the conditions of old-time rural life did undoubtedly require that at the fall of the year provision should be made for a substantial contribution towards the ensuing twelve months need of animal food for the family.   Salting and drying were the only methods then available to ward off putrefaction during the ensuing months through which it had to be stored.   Very few farm-house kitchens are to be found on these north-central hill-slopes to-day, where flitches of bacon and hams do not hang from the beams during most of the year.   In spite of official regulations about pig-styes in relation to dwellinghouses, registered slaughter-houses, and meat inspection, little more than a century ago many cottagers were in the same happy position, and supplied relatives, neighbours and friends with a portion, which in the aggregate amounted to at least one half of the total production. The " pig-butcher," who formerly had a very busy time of it during the three months beginning with the latter part of October, is now an extinct individual. His sadly waned duties are now shared between the ordinary butcher and the owner of the pig himself or a trustworthy friend, when strict secrecy is necessary to evade the official licensed slaughter house and inspection. But it is important to bear in mind that the motive involved in the practice of autumn killing even when most in vogue was not so much the difficulty presented by the feeding of the animals during the winter months as economy and convenience. Certainly any difficulties in regard to winter feeding, which showed themselves, would apply to the pig, and not to the cattle, around which all the tales of agony have been woven. With pigs fed in the open, acorns, beech-mast and other natural foods, would be at their minimum in late winter and with stye-fed pigs, which would be mainly in the hands of cottagers without land, the obtaining and storage of the necessary grain would present a difficulty.

The potent factors in the case were briefly the following. During spring and summer the cattle spend their whole lives in the open-air, which in itself is a stimulant to vigour of life and the healthy functioning of the organs. The abundance of fresh food together with more genial weather conditions, is naturally more inviting, healthy and generally conducive to growth and the laying on of flesh. When the summer is advanced until the hay harvest is in progress, the herbage of the pastures has lost something of its freshness and succulence so that at this time it is interesting to see how, if they have the opportunity of getting near it, the cattle will eagerly devour the new hay. At this time they have a real and legitimate treat in store for the near future. In a few weeks the meadows from which the hay has been taken, will have a rich crop of

after-grass, known over a wide area as " fog," which is peculiarly succulent, nourishing and inviting to the cattle.   So
much is this the case, that it is not uncommon to limit the free
range of the animals over the meadows, that they may not
overfeed themselves.   The pigs also will profit most at this
season from the abundance and freshness of acorns and other
fruits with which the waysides, hedgerows, woods and stubbles
are strewn.   In addition there is the natural tendency of
animals to lay on a store of flesh in preparation for the scarcity
of food—which as we have already seen undoubtedly prevails
in their natural habitat—and for the rigours of winter.   The
time is the one of the whole year when it is easiest and cheapest to fatten beasts.   The young, particularly of swine, are
most easily reared in the mild weather of spring and summer,
and those not intended for breeding from attain their maximum qualities for human food during the late autumn or.
early winter of their first year.   Their greater fecundity
also points to the greater liklihood of these beasts to become
the victims of the annual sacrifice.   With all kinds of flesh,
curing by salting—the only method available to our ancestors—would be most easily and surely effected during the colder
weather of late autumn and winter, the danger of putrefaction
being at that period reduced to a minimum.   Moreover the
human demand for flesh is greatest during winter.

        Thus it may be seen that there were other reasons
for slaughtering animals and salting their flesh at this season
of the year, than the simple difficulty of keeping them alive
until the time when they might be wanted for food.   The mere
convenience of a supply which could be drawn upon at any
moment, is a factor not to be lightly weighed.   Nor were
the people so completely tied to salt meat as has been gratuitously assumed.   At pp. 200 is an allusion to " butchers " in the market at Manchester during the fourteenth
century, which is suggestive.   Surely the specialising upon
that work implies a more or less regular demand for the flesh
of the animals they killed.   Even if, as might be inferred
from the association of " butchers " and " tanners " in the
quotation, the former were primarily engaged in serving the

latter, the beasts for that purpose could be slain at any time of the year, as they need not for that purpose carry any considerable amount of flesh : but such as it was we may safely infer was not thrown away, but would be made to contribute an appreciable amount to the available food supply.   Just in proportion as the surrounding population was numerous or not, would that meat be consumed fresh, or a portion of it salted.   It was only where the people who were able to procure, or were allowed to consume, flesh meat, were so few that they could not dispose of a whole carcase while it was fresh, that any considerable quantity needed to be salted.

When nearly everybody had their pig or fowls, where many had a cow or two and some a few sheep, which the widespread common lands would render comparatively easy to feed, where the means of communication were difficult and the relations between customer and seller imperfectly developed owing to these causes in addition to the lack of currency, the possibility of disposing of the carcase of an ox in such small quantities as could be immediately consumed would be very small except near the few large towns.   The hot weather would enhance the difficulties during the summer time.   Even well within the last century it was customary in districts which in the modern sense were not more than semi-rural, for people attending the service at church to learn when someone in the neighbourhood was intending to kill a beast during the ensuing week.   No one could hope to make a living by devoting himself exclusively to the supply of fresh meat where possible customers were far apart, and everybody had a cured supply in his own home.   Moreover, at times throughout the year there would be the animal which happening an accident, or showing signs of fatal illness, was slain in order that its flesh might retain a soundness which it was imagined would not attach to it, if much physic had been imbibed, or a wholly natural death had ensued.   When such a misfortune did occur, special efforts were made to dispose of the carcase, and everybody for a distance around was morally bound to take a share at a customary price.   In thinly populated districts the quantity taken by most purchasers

105

would be more than could be consumed while the meat was sound, and so a portion was put to salt. But this was quite a different matter from the over-rated annual function. This is by no means a mere fancy. Well within the memory of persons still living the custom survived in full vigour in many, if not all, rural and semi-rural localities. It was the stock-keeper's system of insurance against losses of this kind.

Nor was the animal that succumbed to a strictly natural death allowed to impose itself as a total loss upon its owner. The only reason that weighed against the free use of such meat for human consumption, was the fact of its not having been bled ; for the more fastidious people were possessed of a deep-seated but wholly sentimental fear of consuming blood of any kind, and held that the food from which it had not been let out was thereby tainted. The extent to which the caracases of both these classes of the animal-victims of man's economical aims or of nature's ruthless operations, were formerly used for human food would greatly surprise many a scholarly author of works relating to the social and industrial life of the past, no less than the ordinary health official, or the mass of those upon whose behalf he acts. Herein lies one fact which partly explains the rising prices of flesh meats, which had been coming on for some years before the great war arose with its dislocation of values. Here and there were men who, ostensibly pig-butchers or cattle-leeches, did a roaring trade as " slink butchers," receiving dead cows at the " slaughterhouse " after darkness had come on, skinning, dressing and preparing them for some distant market, to which they were dispatched before sunrise. Living in some quiet retreat, their operations could be carried on with little publicity, to which unlighted and quiet streets and roads lent a measure of secrecy.

In addition to the supplies of unsalted meat just mentioned, which were quite independant of seasons, there was another which should not be ignored. In former times the area of land in proportion to population was several times greater than it is at present. Woods were far wider and streams unsullied. It can scarcely be questioned that these yielded much greater number of beast, fowl and fish towards the domestic food supply than we are accustomed to experience in these days. A greater intimacy with natural country life was a part of the social heritage which persisted well into the last century, though in its latter part the food resources just referred to were rapidly waning. " Old men's tales," though in some measure inspired by fond memories of youth's gay frolics and an exaggerated sense of regret for the departed glories of the past, do nevertheless indicate that the modern poacher is largely a survival of an age-long and once more general passion, directed to satisfying the hunger for food through the instinct for sport. But this habit, unfortunately, the more general and strictly enforced game laws of recent times has converted into a criminal taint.

In the large upland area outside of the purview of the academic historian the very nature of the country made the contribution of the wild creatures to this end of a more appreciable quantity, and the preserved game—even where anything of the sort was attempted—more subject to illicit depredations. Facts which are on record make it clear that even the denizens of hunting grounds enjoying the privilege of royal protection were by no means free from the attentions of unauthorised persons. At a Court [1] held at Wakefield on October 18th, 1274, " Jordan de Schakeltonstal, Nelle de Wynter, John Luvekyn and William son of Elkoc de Schakeltonstal, accused of taking a stag, remain under the surety of Sir Richard de Thornhill until the next Court." There are some half a score of similar cases from a very limited area dealt with in the published records of the Wakefield Court, which only cover a period of thirty-five years. That large number of cases was drawn from the comparatively small area of the graveship of Sowerby situated in the extreme upper end of the Calder Valley. There are others less definitely worded in the records, which may be of the same kind.

[1] *Yorkshire Archaeological and Topographical Society's Record Series.* Vol. **xxix.**

Such cases as came within the range of the official eye were undoubtedly but a small proportion of the actual practices effected : the topography of the district, to say nothing of popular sympathy with the offenders, lent itself to the making of detection and conviction difficult. All classes outside of the official were engaged in the work, from the knight or churchman to the humblest individual. One case is particularly interesting, as it would seem to suggest that strict and severe laws were not in themselves sufficient. On the contrary, in order to reduce illicit practices it was found advisable to buy off possible offenders by means of bribes to influential individuals. At a Court held at Wakefield on March 25th, 1297, " Thomas de Coppeley, indicted for many misdeeds in his bailiwick, whilst he was the Earl's Master Forester in Sowerbyshire, upon the verdict of the following (Jury) . . . . who say on their oath . . . . he committed no offence . . . . *except that he killed a hart (bissa) and sent it to the Vicar of Rochdale, on behalf of the Earl, with a view to his drawing the malefactors of that neighbourhood away from the Earl's chase, so that they should not enter to do wrong there ; and he took nothing in return for the hart ; and the said Thomas avowed the gift before the Earl who pardoned him.*" Ten years later, the same or a succeeding Vicar was fined £20 for trespassing in the Earl's free chase of Sowerbyshire.

Such considerations as these lead us to the conclusion that the alleged necessity of living almost exclusively on salt meat during the mediæval winter has been overdrawn. There is every reason to believe that the salt meat consumed in summer was as large a proportion of the whole as in winter, just as the common habit of eating bacon is to-day. That in fact is a survival of the old habit of laying in a stock of meat for the year at the period when it could be cheapest and most conveniently done. A custom born of necessity, leading to an acquired taste, often continues as a habit, long after the conceiving force has ceased to act. The difficulties of disposing of a newly killed carcase would be greater in summer than in winter because of the high temperature and lessened demand. Everything points to the conclusion that the real motive behind autumn killed meat was laying up of the necessary supplies of the ensuing year ; and that that was the most economical and convenient way in which constant needs could be met and sound meat ensured at all times.

THE MEANING AND EXTENT OF DOVE-KEEPING. The great number of doves kept in some manors has been alleged as confirmation of the conventional theory. Surely if this were the only relief from monotony of diet, it could only have been such to a very trifling degree, unless the number of birds kept was truly stupendous. It would surely need several hundred of them to equal in weight a single ox. In the mountainous area, which it is the object of the present work to bring into the view of the historical student, there is very little evidence indeed of the keeping of any large numbers of doves, and any that were kept, were more likely to be provision for sport—shooting and pigeon racing and possibly as messengers. Certainly in only very few of the numerous seventeenth century buildings which still survive does there appear to have been any provision made for the shelter of these birds, and in no case can it have been intended for more than a score or two at the most : even in the few cases where the provision exists the sporting instinct has always been most strongly developed as far as the family history can be traced. There is still surviving near Bingley a large dovecote ; but the situation is where the mountainous character begins to decline into the lower, more open and fertile lands which have for centuries been endowed with the presence of the dominant upper class. The comparative smallness and intermixing of estates which have always prevailed in these upland areas, suggest a prolific source of quarrels, had anyone owned a large number of pigeons to batten upon the crops of his neighbours.

The very limited amount of corn-growing which has been customary in these upland parts after we get beyond the earliest times, confirms the presumption that at no period could any considerable number of birds have subsisted upon the free warren they are supposed to have enjoyed over neighbouring acres. If freshly killed pigeons were the only source of variety in food the people of these parts would seem to have been constrained to jog along through an unending course of monotony, and certainly they would appear to have survived the ordeal without serious adverse effects. The absence of any mention of these birds in available contemporary records, though only negative testimony, is nevertheless confirmatory of their not being abundant, and that the privileges said to be attached thereto was not of much value. Viewed in the light of such considerations as these just given, the alleged motive for the existence of the dove-cote savours of an attempt (probably unconscious) to put a generous construction upon what must, where it existed, have been a harsh and selfish privilege, maintained in the interests of a dominant and leisured class. Its existence in anything like its assumed feudal glory (?) seems to have been reserved for the pleasant places of the earth, where the original adventurer had won a complete success, and he and his descendants had been able to impose completely and maintain a thorough domination, so that the fortunate few were able to secure their own will, and chose to abide in ease and luxury. Weighing all the circumstances, the conviction cannot be escaped that the real underlying motive of the custom was rather the lordly passion for " sport," relieved of the arduous toil involved in the pursuit of the wild animal under the laborious conditions of its native habitat.

THE BREEDING AND REARING OF SHEEP. Almost from the beginning of available records sheep have browsed upon and wandered over our northern mountain slopes. They do not enter conspicuously into the *Manor Court Rolls*, so far as they have yet been published. But the extract from the Wakefield Court Rolls given on page 52, shows that there were sufficient of them in the old parish of Halifax to attract the attention of the Vicarial eye. Incidentally one wonders whether there is in this a manifestation of the increasing powers of the Norman masters, and through them of the ecclesiastical authorities over their refractory hill-country subjects. The infrequency of the allusion to sheep then in the available records would seem to need some explanation. Their wandering propensities are more marked than those of either cattle, swine or horses, all of which figure often in the *Court Roll Records* as " escapes," or in other capacities. Possibly they were subject to a different law, or they were not considered as harmful to the forest. Or again, shall we infer that their wanderings were held in check by a system of universal hobbling, a practice of tying the legs which considerably hampered extensive peregrinations, which was very common in later times amongst keepers whose lands, and consequently flocks, were limited in extent? Although documentary evidence is comparatively so scanty, it is generally assumed by local writers that sheep were commonly kept in mediæval times. In attempts to explain the presence of " Merchants " in the *Poll Tax Returns* for 1379, it has generally been assumed that they were probably dealers in wool, hides and cattle. Some evidence has already been given (p. 93 sup.) that in one case at least other things were dealt in. Probably there were few if any of what we might call great flock-masters ; but a large proportion of the population kept a few, some possibly not more than one or two.

In the information which we have relating to the Manorial Vaccaries of the Graveship of Sowerby, and in North-east Lancashire no mention is made of sheep. Possibly this may be due to the fact, that owing to the wandering habits of the animals and their living most of their time out-of-doors, being left as they are both winter and summer in the charge of servants, they were less likely to be well taken care of, and consequently less profitable than cattle, although as we shall see shortly, one of the lord's cow-herds had a small flock of sheep himself. We have already seen that the holdings of land were small. and that each had to provide for other more urgent needs of the family and its dependants in cases where there were any. But that sheep were kept is certain, though their appearances in the *Court Rolls* are few indeed. There are a few, however, which are significant.   In the year 1314, the lord's former stock-keeper is convicted of having fed eleven sheep on the lord's hay during the winter in the Vaccary of Saltonstall.   Allusion is made to a stray sheep belonging to the Lady of Rishworth at a Court held in 1316, and a theft of four sheep in the same locality, although belonging to a different owner.   At a Wakefield Court probably held in the year 1286, one Warley man was fined 6d. for allowing twelve sheep to escape, and another man the same amount for four sheep.   From the *Poll Tax Returns* (1379) we learn from their names of only two shepherds in the wide parish of Halifax.   One lived at Warley and the other at Midgely : but this may only imply the fewness of large owners.

Fowls seem to have shared with sheep a comparative immunity from official attention.   Yet we may safely assume that they were generally kept.   They would be easy to acquire by all classes on account of their low cost ; they could be kept with little trouble, and their produce, whether of eggs or their carcases, was a convenient form of fresh meat, the quality of which could always be regulated according to immediate requirements.   At a " Tourn " held at Halifax on March 12th, 1316, John Soughil and nine others were reported as forestallers of hens, pullets, eggs and other poultry, The fact of their being a marketable commodity which, like other things of every-day use, were deemed needful of regulation by the market authorities, implies that they were common.

It would be interesting to know more of the breeds of sheep, which were kept during past centuries in these northern highlands and the southern lowlands respectively.   Certainly the known and traditional practices relating to those of the former area differ widely from the information given to us of the methods said to have prevailed in the latter.   Professor Thorold Rogers [1] says, " Our forefathers advised that sheep should be kept under cover from November to April, and should not be allowed to go on the ground between August

[1] *Six Centuries of Work and Wages*, 1884 (p. 81).

and November till the sun had well purified the ground. They were fed under cover on coarse hay, wheat and oat straw, or, failing these, on pea and vetch haulm." At page 443 he further says, " Because there was no forage for them out of doors." This statement has been accepted and repeated by De Gibbins [1]. Toynbee [2] also says, " There were no turnips or artificial grasses, and consequently no sheep-farming on a large scale," thus implying that these things were a necessary adjunct to successful sheep-rearing. As a matter of fact they are seldom used even now in the northern hill country. The observations used with respect to the feeding of cattle apply equally well here. How sheep could be " the mainstay of English agriculture " [3], and how the great reputation of England as a wool-producing country for the looms of Flanders, was established and maintained, is difficult to understand, if we acccpt as a fact the statement that turnips and artificial grasses were a necessity for success-ful sheep-rearing.

Such a view is certainly quite inconsistent with all known experiences of the northern hill country, where the hardships of winter are undoubtedly greater than the southern, eastern and western districts from which last all evidence has hitherto been drawn. One is driven to wonder whether the increased weight of wool borne by modern sheep has also raised their power of resistence to severe weather : but a great deal of this heavier fleece is due to the greater size of the animals, and usually artificiality does not add to natural endurance. In these highland regions the flocks do undoubtedly spend most of their lives, and pick up most of their food out-of-doors during the winter months ; and the statement relating to " August to November" would simply raise a derisive laugh if read out to any practical northern shepherd. The only exception in respect to winter keep to what has been stated above, is that during times of extreme severity and when there is much snow on the ground, the

---

[1] *Industrial of England*, 1890 (pp. 4-6).
[2] *Lectures on the Industrial Revolution*, Edition 4 (p. 40).
[3] Thorold Roger, *Work and Wages* (p. 78).

flocks are given some, but not often complete shelter ; and are fed with hay (not rough), and sometimes grain or roots. The latter more particularly obtain when the sheep are being fed for the butcher—which academic writers tell us was quite a secondary matter with the mediæval sheep-master—and the ewes which are coming on to the lambing time. During very wet weather it is considered advisable, as a precaution against disease, to supplement the out-door natural food with dry hay : this practice acquires additional point from the fact that the rainfall of the Pennines is greater and more persistent than obtains in most of the more classical areas.

As the lambing season approaches, which is somewhat later in the north than the south, many sheep-masters house their ewes at night and improve their food. A closer watch is kept over the flocks, and their range of liberty over the moors is restricted during the winter, in order that they can more easily be brought to safety in the case of sudden and severe storms appearing likely : but no general system of keeping them under cover during the winter is known. The reports that appear in the newspapers from time to time, when a snow-storm descends upon the fells of north Lancashire, Yorkshire, Westmoreland and Cumberland, prove that as a rule the flocks are scattered over the mountainside. It is quite true that little food will be found during the winter on arable land : but the presence of sheep in any quantity in itself implies a large portion of permanent pasture. And here even during winter, unless the previous growing season has been an exceptionally bad one, the animals are able to find much suitable food. During the warmer half of the year by far the greater portion of the flocks spend the whole of their time on the unbroken moorlands. During winter the pastures and meadows are utilised so far as their smaller area will allow. A limited amount of grazing by sheep is thought to improve the herbage.

CHAPTER VI.

ON MEADOW LAND—ITS COMMON PREVALENCE AND VALUE DURING MEDIÆVAL TIMES.

IN the last Chapter when dealing with the question of winter food for cattle, it was intimated that further attention would be given to the value of meadow land and its use in former times for growing hay. This is a point which would seem to be of some importance in the light of the conclusions which have been arrived at by those historians who have hitherto given attention to the keeping of live stock through the winter. Closely associated with the production of hay as the principal winter food for cattle, and a supplementary one for sheep, is that of the meadow land upon which it is grown. The evidence to be found in some northern documents and present day practices relating to this important aspect of rural economy, would seem to point to a conclusion differing considerably from that which appears to have been drawn from an interpretation of facts, as they have been found in the south and lower lands generally. The recognised authorities seem to imply two contradictory conclusions :—(a) that hay alone is a very unsatisfactory food for live stock, and that the art of growing, curing and storing it for future use was little known or practised during mediæval times ; and (b) yet in spite of its imperfections for the purpose hay was in great demand, and consequently such land as could be rendered available for such a crop, was limited in amount and commanded a very high price. And yet the various writers frequently mention hay, meadow, and mowing—the latter term of course applies to grain crops as well as hay—but seem to think that either the stock did not get much of it, or benefitted little from its consumption. Obviously the benefits claimed on behalf

115

of the seventeenth century newly introduced feeding stuffs have not been sufficiently examined ; on the contrary exaggerated claims of enthusiasts have dominated the minds of inquirers to the extent of playing upon the very general obsession, that in early times and even down to a comparatively recent period Englishmen have been hopelessly dull and devoid of the commonest of common sense. The obsession has taken the form, not only of an undue appreciation of the great virtues inherent in root-crops and the artificial grasses, but also of a failure to appreciate rightly the real qualities of an old-fashioned, extensively used, natural product, possessed of a large measure of fitness for the purpose to which animal instinct and human intelligence had both recognised and applied it.

The idea that hay alone, or at least without root-crops and artificial grasses as introduced into this country during the seventeenth and eighteenth centuries, was a very unsatisfactory food for cattle has already been dealt with (Chapter v.). The other side of the question, namely, that before the introduction of these newer methods of feeding, winter food for cattle was very scarce, and that meadow land commanded a very high price, will now be examined. The subject divides itself into two branches :—(a) The prevalence of the custom of making and storing hay, and (b) the rents actually paid for meadow land in the cases where existing records separated this kind of grass-land from the general, and the comparison of the one with the other. Under (a) it may be said that existing documents relating to manorial life in the pre-Norman period contain numerous references to hay and meadow land [1], and certainly it is clear that the getting and storing of hay was a well known practice as early as the thirteenth and fourteenth centuries. Allusion has already been made (Chapter v.) to the five vaccaries which Earl Warrene had in the graveship of Sowerby, where the cattle were kept in winter at specified places, and were sent elsewhere to graze during the summer. Indeed in relation to

[1] V. Andrews' *Old English Manor* gives several allusions to " hay " and " meadows." *e.g.* (pp. 107, 116, 203, 280, etc.).

three of these vaccaries it is expressly stated that there is
" one grange for putting hay in." [1]   In the Wakefield *Manor
Court Rolls*, which begin in the year 1274, there are numerous
references to land taken with a grange, also to disputes about
mowing adjudicated upon in the Courts.   For instance,
at a Court held on October 23rd, 1297,[2] we find, " Holne——
Robert de Mereford sues Peter de Rodewode for trespass
. . . . Plaintiff says that the defendant had agreed with
him to mow his meadow for a week at 3d. a day :   Gilbert
de Alstanley sues John de Holne for carrying away his hay
and corn."   An old custom of which prevails in upper Calderdale of giving the area of land in units of the " Day-work "—
that is the area which an average mower could get over in
a day, and which was equal to two-thirds of a statute acre—
shows that Robert de Mereford was possessed of at least four
acres of meadow, which in an average year, according to
modern crops, would produce hay sufficient to feed through
the winter three or four milch cows, and young stock enough
to keep up the number by replacing old ones killed or dying
naturally or by accident.

There can hardly be a doubt that at the period here
spoken of, nearly all the occupiers of land on both sides of
the Pennines did keep cattle, if only for their domestic use,
and that they would prepare for the winter feeding of their
stock by storing hay during the summer.   But the numerous
fines imposed upon owners for allowing their cattle to stray
beyond their proper limits places the fact beyond all question.
One typical example will serve.[3]   At a Court held at Halifax
on December 6th, 1308, we find :—" Sourby—John Culpon,
10d., John del Rodiker, 8d., John sone of the Hermite, 6d.,
Elise de Haderschelf, 4d., John son of Hugh de Langley, 3d.,
Thomas son of John de Midgley, 1d., William del Croft of
Mancanholes, 3d., Richard de Wollenerwalle, 3d., Adam de
Kirkschagh, 4d. . . . . for escapes."   Six at least of these

---

[1] Extent (or Survey) of the Graveships of Rastrick, etc., 1309 (pp.
31-2).   Halifax Antiquarian Society.   [2] *Wakefield Manor Court
Rolls*, Yorkshire Archæological Society and Topographical, Record
Series,   [3] Id., Vol. ii.

can be identified as coming from a very narrow area, less than half a dozen miles separating the most distant from each other. They were all in sight of one or more of the lord's winter vaccaries and some quite near thereto : indeed it is perfectly inconceivable, that they and most of their neighbours would fail to note and copy the hay-making with which they were familiar. From intimate personal acquaintance it can be affirmed that the land used by the lord as meadow was quite ordinary elevated land, several hundred feet above the river level, which had no special qualities for the purpose as compard with much of the land held by others in the neighbourhood. It can scarcely be conceived that even in the earlier periods of a settled pastoral life the production and storing of hay would not be known.

It may be useful at this point to explain exactly what is here meant by *meadow land*. Except in the case of the Port Meadows at Oxford, to be referred to hereafter, meadow land is that portion of a holding which is especially set apart for growing that grass which is intended to be converted into hay ; that is, dried and stored for the purpose of feeding the live stock during the winter months, when the grass scarcely grows at all and the weather is too severe for the animals to be exposed to it generally during the night and often in the day-time. As the drying has to be done by the sun, the crop has to be grown quickly so that it may be at maturity both in quantity and quality, and ready for cutting by midsummer. In the hill country altitude makes some difference as to the actual date of " hay-time ' : but the period from the middle of June to the middle of August generally covers the time of its duration. In order to secure these ends the meadows must be conveniently situated for receiving the manure made when the live stock is fastened up in winter, and easiest for working and carting the hay. A very general misconception, which still persists in some quarters, of what meadow land is and has been, and the power and extent of utilising natural grass for hay, is to be found in the *Quarterly Review*, an extract from which is given in the *Yorkshire Weekly Post* of October 27th, 1917. In the article on " The

Place Names of England " the writer G. B. Grundy says :—
" The meads or hayland was always near a stream since, in
the days before grass-seed, the water meadow was the only
land on which hay grows." Such a sweeping and ill-in-
formed statement bears very little relation to the facts already
given and still to be adduced in this chapter.

Compared with any arable crop the cultivation of
grass or hay is very simple. Except land laid down to permanent pasture, it is the easiest of all crops, and can be done
on nearly any land, provided there be a few inches of soil.
Generally speaking all vegetable and corn crops require
a richer soil and often a more genial climate. The only
sources of anxiety in connection with the hay-crop are, too
much drought in spring which interferes with the growth,
and much rain at the cutting and drying season which mars the
value of the hay. For meadow, the surface of the land
must be fairly smooth and free from exposed stones ; for as
the grass is cut very low.projecting stones would damage the
scythe. On unwarped land the stones require to be removed ;
on warped land the silt would gradually bury them. But
if any one deposit of silt were too great, even an inch would
be sufficient to bury the roots of the grass so deeply as to
retard the growth of the crop for that season. After the first
laying down, this crop requires neither that the land should
be ploughed, rolled, harrowed, nor sown ; and the original
sowing is generally done by nature. Given this initial
preparation, it will remain permanently as highly productive
in grass if manured moderately and if in periods of drought
of a few weeks duration in the growing season it be occasionally watered, as any conditions can make it. This watering
is a very general but not extensively practised treatment of
sloping meadows. Any available small water-supply is
conducted through small temporary gutters to different parts
of a meadow, as convenience and opportunity dictate. It
obviously has its limits as to the parts which can be so treated.
Such is the only labour or expense required to be incurred,
until the crop is ready for cutting. The example given by

the late Professor Thorold Rogers [1] is low-lying flat land warped by the adjoining river. But constant water, if it verges upon swampiness in the land, will seriously mar the quality of the herbage, killing off the more tender succulent plants and encouraging rank, coarse and unpalatable grasses. It will, moreover, be a decided detriment to successful hay-making. For these reasons even steeply sloping meadow land is often artificially drained. Nor can the most perfect warping be as successful in stimulating growth as farm-yard manure. The so called " natural meadow " cannot, without a large proportion of the above-mentioned treatment and attention rank high in quantity or quality of produce.

If evidence were entirely wanting, which it certainly is not, that a knowledge of the benefits to all growing crops of farm-yard manure did not exist in these early times, the presumption is strong, that if in no other way, the value and convenience of its periodical removal from the precincts of home would soon force itself upon the minds of those responsible for the care of the cattle. When the beasts were housed or confined to any kind of shelter, the accumu-lation of droppings would be so great as soon to become both a serious inconvenience and a great nuisance. Even if only shifted for convenience, some easily accessible corner of the adjoining land would be fixed upon for the reception of the troublesome material. When this had been done, even the most backward and unobservant individuals would not be long ere they noticed a greater fertility in the immediate neighbourhood where such matter came to be.

Returning for a moment to the comparison between land suitable for meadow and pasture, and the ease and sim-plicity of their cultivation, it should be pointed out that the former must of necessity be somewhat better than the latter. Almost any land upon which the cattle can be allowed to roam with safety to themselves, may be utilised for pasture ; but such as is very ugly or of rough surface can only be made suitable for meadow at some cost in labour and manure.

[1] *Work and Wages* (p. 73).

Much light is thrown on this aspect of mediæval rural economy by some surviving particulars relating to the Lancashire slopes of the Pennines. The valuable possessions of Henry de Lacy, Earl of Lincoln, included the present counties of Lancashire and Cheshire. Of these detailed accounts were periodically rendered at the Lord's Courts, some extracts from which may now conveniently be given. The higher altitudes of the Lancashire area were largely used for cattle rearing, the lord himself having at least thirty-one vaccaries, in which were kept over two thousand six hundred head of cattle. The following is a fair sample of these annual accounts :—[1] p. 136 " Rosyndale. John, son of Odousa in place of Adam de Wordhille renders his acompotus of 37 cows and 1 bull of the remainder, and 6 of addition and 6 received from the Instaurator : total 49 cows and 1 bull. Of which two in murrain, hides and flesh 2s. 10d., 2 delivered to ye Geldhird, and 2 to the Instaurator : 43 cows and 1 bull remain. Also 6 oxen of additions, delivered to G. the parker. Also 9 yearlings of the remainder ; of which one strangled by wolf, hide and flesh 16d. : 4 steers and 4 heifers remain ; also 15 calves of the remainder ; of which 3 in murrain, hides and flesh 9d. ; and 1 in the tithe ; 9 yearlings remain (6 males). Also 15 calves of the year and 5 from the Instaurator, total 20 ; of which 3 in murrain, hides 1d. ; 17 calves remain. Total of the cattle remaining in this vaccary ; 48 cows, 1 bull, 4 steers, 4 heifers, 11 yearlings (6 males) and 17 calves."

There was also at least one horse-breeding station, as the following shows :—[2]

" Ichtenhille.

	s.	d.
Hides of 9 mares, 2 foals of the third year and 7 foals of the second year	4	9

[1] Two " Compoti " of the Lancashire and Cheshire Manors of Henry de Lacy, Earl of Lincoln, xxiv. and xxxiii. Edward I. Chetham Society, MDCCCLXXXIV. Vol. cxii.
[2] Two " Compoti " of the Lancashire and Cheshire Manors, XXIV and XXXIII, Edward I. (pp. 127-8).

s. d.

Expenses ..   ..

Two men keeping foals in the stable for ten weeks   7 6"

" Ichtenhille Grange.

Compotus of produce of the grange of the fruits of
autumn, 1295 ..   ..

Horses, remainder 52 mares of which 9 died of
murrain, their hides accounted for above,
one delivered to William de Stopham by the
Earl's letters. And 42 mares remain   ..

     Two year olds. Remainder 29 foals in the same year
of which two in murrain, hides accounted for above. And
27 foals in the third year remain, of which 14 are males.

     Foals. Remainder 22 foals, of which 7 in murrain,
hides accounted for above, and one in tithe. And 14 foals
in the second year remain, of which 6 are males. Foals of
the year 22, of which one in murrain, hide of no value. And
21 remain."

     Nor were the returns from these vaccaries the only
interests, which the Lord of Clitheroe held in North-east
Lancashire. As we shall see he had much land let out to
tenants, as well as extensive and varied activities in other
directions. A few particulars may be quoted [1] as indications
of their nature and extent :—

" Akerington.	£	s.	d.
Rent of 52 acres, 1 rood of land let	1	11	9
A plot called Pesecroft	0	7	0
The Hall, Kitchen and Grange let	0	4	0
3 Vaccaries there let, 1st September	5	3	1¾
Rent of Mill deducting tithe	1	16	8
5 acres of waste land lately let	0	2	6
Fines for entering upon lands 17s. 4d. ; fees 1s. ; impounding cattle 6s. 6d.	1	4	0
Brushwood and Ore sold to a forge there for 27 weeks	1	14	0
Herbage for Brocholehurst	0	6	8"

[1] Ibid (pp. 155, 171, 119).

	£	s.	d.
" Trochdene [1]			
. . . . cattle agisted	0	12	6
Hay sold	0	3	7"
" Cliderhowe.			
Received from Gilbert Instaurator as in compotus	77	18	4
Produce of 27 Vaccaries let out	81	0	0''
" Halton.			
Rent of 1 Saltwork in Northwic (given in both the			
compoti)	1	0	0
Produce of 10 cows let, rent deducted ..	1	10	0
Old hay sold	0	14	0"
" Congleton.			
4 acres of meadow of the demesnes let ..	0	10	6
Hay of the same meadow from last year sold ..	0	17	0"
" Congleton (2nd compotus).			
The grass and fruit of the garden and the dove			
cote, both let	0	6	6"
" Standen.			
Mowing 48 acres of meadow	0	14	0
7qr. of wheat, 3qr. 5 bus. of barley, and 167½qr.			
of oats threshed and winnowed	0	13	4½"

The two following extracts may also be given for the insight they afford us of North-east Lancashire industrial life in the thirteenth and fourteenth centuries. Whatever may be said of the difference between then and now, it cannot be denied, if we combine what has already been given with what is to come, that, much variety of interest was displayed as well as energy and enterprise in getting full advantage of all that could be obtained in material prosperity. We quote from the same prolific source :—[2]

" Akerington Grange.

Robert de Ryelye rendered his compotus of the produce of the grange of the fruits of autumn 1295.   Oats,

[1] Ibid. (pp. 155, 171, 119).   [2] Ibid. (p. 142).

Produce 53 quarters 3 bushels, from which he counts 16 quarters for seed, 1 quarter provender for work-horses and oxen, and 37 quarters 3 bushels sold as above. Work-horses one mare and one foal of last year and a foal born. Oxen, 12 oxen of last year. Dairy: 156 cheeses with 16 made after Michaelmas. From which he counts 16 for the tithe and 140 weighing 82 stone sold as above. Butter: 27½ stone, clear of tithe, all sold as above."

" Grange of Standen.

The same render their accounts of the grange for the harvest of 1295, before the same as above. Wheat: 5 bushels produce and 1 quarter 5 bushels produce of the grange; total 2 quarters 1 bushel. Of which 1 quarter 5 bushels for seed and 5 bushels sold. Oats: produce of the grange 121 quarters 6½ bushels: of which 51 quarters for seed and 70 quarters 6½ bushels sold. Oxen: 17 oxen of the remainder, 17 oxen remain."

It is quite the usual thing for writers on economic, social and industrial history, to group Lancashire with some other northern counties, whilst political and constitutional students ignore them altogether, and dilate upon their poverty and backwardness until the era of the Industrial Revolution. Similarly in the valuations given by those writers when comparing the wealth of the different counties too little notice has been taken of the comparatively large areas of high barren moorland and unfertile crag and scar. How the assumed sudden transformation then consummated could have been effected, when we bear in mind the accepted notions of evolution, the Englishman's conservatism and assumed northern slowness in particular, seems never to have occurred to the authors of the current theory relating to pastoral and general industry. Yet here we have one corner of the (assumed) most benighted county of all, for the time and the western world's development, comparatively rich in much that then constituted the world's wealth. Possibly the above named estimate of progress and poverty in the north may be but a reflection of the centuries-long attitude of mind towards that part of England which, to the " cultured " and official classes has been looked upon as a wild and lawless territory, without the ordinary amenities of a civilised life. The recorded valuations, upon which all judgments have been based seem to have been founded not so much upon existing facts as upon such partially imposed taxation and imperfect trade returns as the feeble agents of an imperfectly developed national government could exact from a jealous and elusive people.

Remoteness and difficulty of access, both physical and moral, placed these regions largely outside of the purview of travellers and chroniclers. Imperfect knowledge tends to interpret little known facts as non-existent, and things not understood as of little moment. Age-long customary views and judgments, based upon the chronicles and documents, which have been drawn upon by the investigators into the history of a limited conventional England, have been accepted by moderns from the guardians of our historical consciences as having an unqualified application to the whole of the island. Some of the sources of information, e.g., the Merchant and Craft Guilds and legislative enactments— have scarcely been viewed with a sufficent grasp of their reflecting class interests and activities. The greatly differing sources of materials relating to the unconventional outlands have hardly been touched at all, with the result that a defective and misleading picture has held the ground. That the North-east Lancashireman of the thirteenth century were quite familiar with the practice of laying by a store of winter-food for their live stock, and successful in its use, is quite clear. In the Ichtenhille accounts cited above, we also find the following :—

p. 128. " Mowing 60½ acres of meadow .. 17 7¾
Making and stacking the hay.. .. .. 12 7"

Also in the later " compotus " of September 30th, 1305, we find such entries as the following :—[1]

[1] Two " *Compoti*," etc. Chetham Society, Vol. cxii. (p. 169).

	£	s.	d.
" Akerington.			
Mowing 80 acres 1 rood of meadow	1	6	9
Spreading grass, gathering hay, carrying and stacking within and without the grange ..	1	9	7"

and this :—

	£	s.	d.
" Mowing and gathering 20 waggon loads of hay within le Rodes	0	6	8
Carrying and spreading dung	0	0	10"

In the six Accrington vaccaries 200 acres of meadow are mown besides the 20 waggon-loads referred to immediately above.

It is not necessary to say much in amplification of these details of Lancashire and Cheshire mediæval life.   They are interesting as showing that the great Earl, in endeavouring to develope his estates displayed enterprise and a progressive spirit.   Besides welcoming tenants who would work the estate in their own individual interests, he also made of it on his own part a large and varied trading concern.   The form and matter of the accounts show us that something was known of the practices and customs prevailing in the greater outside world.   But there are also some interesting differences from what we have been accustomed to regard as the prevailing methods and habits in other parts of England.   It is quite clear that cattle could be kept on a large scale, and hay got and stored for their winter food, so that there was no necessity for killing off in autumn all that were not absolutely essential for breeding from.   There is no indication of any other feeding stuffs being available besides those mentioned in the accounts of the Accrington Grange for the year 1295, where two per cent. of the oats produced are recorded as having been consumed by " work-horses and oxen."   The corn grown does not appear to have been used for that purpose.   Oats were the only kind of grain which appears to have been raised in any quantity, the rest was quite insignificant, and suggests that, contrary to the opinion of Thorold Rogers, in these parts at any rate, wheat was certainly not in common use for human food.   The relatively large quantitites of oats were disposed of as seed, provender for work-horses and oxen, and the major portion sold. The large proportion of each crop reserved for seed suggests that cereals did not yield a very abundant harvest. Neither does the price suggest a very high quality.

The prices given for mowing grass work out at 3½d. and 4d. per acre, and 3d. a day or 4½d. per acre eight years earlier as mentioned in the Wakefield *Court Rolls*, as compared with Rogers's 5d. The same authority records 3d., 2d., 1d., per quarter respectively, as the prices for threshing the three kinds of grain, wheat, barley and oats, and for winnowing. Under the head of Congleton there is an entry above for thrashing, which consisting mainly of oats, includes a small quantity of wheat and barley. Making allowance for these higher kinds, the price for the two operations works out at about ¾d. per quarter as compared with 1¼d. given by Rogers. " Produce for ten cows let " works out at 3s. each as against 5s. to 6s., although we are not quite sure that the comparison is an equal one. Lancashire butter and cheese appear to have been equally cheap ; for whilst we are told elsewhere the prices were ¾d. and ½d. per pound respectively, those produced in the Accrington Dairy taken together only yielded rather less than ⅜d. In the few cases cited above of land let, where measurements are given the rates agree closely with the succeeding prices. One works out at 6d. per acre, another just over 7¼d. The Congleton demesne meadow lets at the rate of 2s. 7½d. per acre. It is also interesting to note that the previous year's crop of hay, sold during the year following its gathering and presumably consumed on the ground, as the meadows had not been let the previous year and so the crop had remained over—which may or may not include the whole of the crop— sells at the rate of 4s. 3d. per acre. This affords an interesting comparison with Roger's Oxford example given on p. 131.

There are some other items contained in the foregoing extracts which are worth a passing notice. The farming out of a " saltwork in Northwic " is in direct contradiction

to Thorold Roger's statement [1] that "the English did not use them before the beginning of the eighteenth century; I am quite certain." In connection with this point the following extracts from Leland [2] may be of some interest. "Northwich is a grate Market Toune but foule, and by the Salters' Howses be great Stakkes of small clovyn Woods to sethe the Salt Water, that thei make white salt of. The Salt Water pitts is hard by the Brinke of the Dane River."
Again :—" Ther be II Salt Springges at Middlewich . . . . . and one at Nantwich, the wich yieldeth more salt water than the other III. Wherfore ther be at Nantwich a III hunderith Salters. The pittes be so set aboute with Cannales that the Salt Water is facily derived to every Mannes Howse. And at Nantwich very many Cannales go over Wyver River for the Commodity of deriving the Water to Salter's Troughs. They sethe the Salt Water in Furnesses of Lede, and lade out the Salt, some in cakes of Wiker, thorough the wich the Water voydeth, and the Salt remaynith. Ther be also a ii or iii but very little salt springs at Dertwiche."

At Congleton was a dovecote let with " The grass and fruit of the garden at 6s. 8d. for the year." We have no idea of the size of either the garden or the dovecote, but the price given does not appear to strongly confirm the high value usually associated withe privilege of the manorial dovecote.

The reference to " Brushwood and Ore sold to a forge there " is one of several contained in these records, which prove that both iron and lead were worked in East Lancashire in the thirteenth century, and also indicate the wide variety of the De Lacy interests. There are also numerous entries, such as —" carrying and spreading dung," " two men keeping foals in the stable for ten weeks," mowing, haymaking, as well as some of the produce sold : these are evidence that the regular staff was not always equal to the work of the farm, and that apparently if customary labour existed at all, it was not in sufficient amount to meet the requirements of these estates, but that there were people in

[1] *Work and Wages* (p. 96). [2] *Itinery*, Vol. v. (p. 87).

the neighbourhood willing to sell their labour, and buy of the lord's surplus produce. Then there is John son of Odousa of Rossendale, who accounts for one of the cattle as having been " strangled by the wolf." This phrase occurs in relation to one or more beasts in nearly everyone of these vaccaries. There is also in one case an entry of wages paid to a man for minding the cattle against the attention of wolves. Herein are facts which indicate that this apparently prosperous community was face to face with difficulties from which nowadays we are happily free.

We come now more definitely to the values of different kinds of agricultural land, and particularly meadow land, as evidenced by the rents actually paid, and shown by the available records. It may first of all be noted that meadow land would at all times command a value, when isolated from the rest, somewhat above the average. This arises from the fact that it is necessarily a superior quality of land, if we take into account all those features which make it suitable for its purpose, namely, soil, situation and convenience for manuring and winning the crop, nature of surface, etc. These conditions may be partly natural, but frequently are in the main artificially imposed. Much of the existing hay-land has thus been made. Nature has been greatly improved upon ; but most of the improving methods are purely mechanical, and well within the capacity of our early English ancestors. But once the conditions are secured, little besides periodical manuring is required to make the improvement permanent. Moreover, most of the lower prices for general land related to natural unimproved land. Meadow may be said to be invariably land which has been improved. Professor Thorold Rogers [1] gives 6d. an acre as the usual thirteenth century rent for land for the whole of the districts with which he was acquainted, namely, the south, east and west of England. As this price is very nearly equal to that which has been found to obtain in the northern parts of England now under investigation, no comment is here necessary. But when

[1] *Work and Wages* (pp. 40, 41, 52, 58, etc.).

he comes to treat of the special case of meadow land, the figures
he gives, strike one as quite irrational : he says :—[1] " Natural
meadow.   About Oxford it is constantly let at 7s. 8s. or 9s.
an acre ; aftermath . . . . being let at 2s. 6d."

Any criticism of so high an authority must be undertaken with great hesitation ; but in this particular instance
it would seem that the learned Professor had not given to the
facts his usual penetrating insight and judgment.   These
figures give an annual rent which is from nineteen to twenty
times those which he quotes for arable land, which by the
nature of things cannot be the poorest of all.   The price is as
great as most northern upland dairy-lands pay to-day, certainly more if allowance be made for houses, buildings and
other owner's improvements, which are let together with the
land.   Of course there will be a difference in the natural
possibilities of the soil.   The low-lying warped land by the
river at Oxford will have an advantage over the bleak uplands
of the north, even if the soils were identical.   Oxford, however, will have a superior soil.   Both these advantages of
climate and soil are clearly evident from the two annual
crops mentioned by the Professor, which are apparently
usual as the year comes round.   But the difference between
the two districts in this respect is not so great as the facts
given would by themselves seem to imply.   In seasons very
little above the average, second crops are frequently gathered
from the northern meadows ; this would be still commoner
if the morning dews were less heavy, and the rainfall less
persistent during the latter part of August and the whole of
the month of September.   The difficulties of quickly drying
a second crop militate against the practice of making it into
hay being more frequent.   For this reason much is eaten
off the ground which with a week or two's longer growth
would make a good second crop of hay.   The yeild of the first
hay-crop in the northern hill country is little, if any, less
than that of the lower lying lands elsewhere.   There is even
an advantage for the former over those localities, where there

[1] Idem (p. 73).

is much arable land to swallow up a large proportion of the manure.

An interesting point arises here as to how far the extension of arable cultivation resulting from the introduction and growing of the new feeding stuffs led to the neglect of meadow lands, and the consequent deterioration thereof being allowed to ensue. This might arise partly from a reserving of an undue share of farm-yard manure for the ploughed land, and partly from the excessive estimate in which root-crops and artificial grasses appear to have been held as food for the live stock. Sufficient information is not available for a definite and general judgment : but the grass-crops seen on the meadow lands in some parts of North-east Yorkshire and the West of England, where arable cultivation is much more common than in the Pennine uplands, would lead to the conclusion that in those parts with their better soils and climates the hay-crops barely come up both in quantity and quality to the average of the northern high-lands.

The enormously high rents quoted above for a class of land which would be substituted with comparative ease, and also far above the values which obtained elsewhere, in itself would suggest grave doubts to the mind of the practical farmer of grass-lands. There is, however, another damaging feature which tells against the alleged contention. The terms in which the statement of rent is given, suggest that in this case the learned Professor misunderstood his facts. Separate quotations for first and second crops almost certainly imply two individuals, who, as the case is stated to us, must have both been tenants of the same ground at the same time. For though each might come in at the appointed season for his own crop, the use of the ground for grazing, etc., at other times, certainly there would be a period between the gathering of the second crop and the oncoming winter and the necessary work upon it, manuring, irrigating and other processes, all of which would need to be done during the other seasons, open out possibilities of friction and misunderstanding which would be hardly endurable. A very likely explanation of the whole case is, that the figures 7s. 8s. and 9s. an acre for the first crop and 2s. 6d. for the aftermath, are the prices at which the first and second crops respectively were sold, the grass or hay being bought by the acre, and not rent at all.

On that assumption the holder of the land, who was was also its occupier and worked it to raise a crop or crops for sale, undertook all the work and expense incident to culti-vation, while the purchaser would have nothing to do but simply walk in at the proper time and secure his crop. Quite possibly, although by no means certainly, the cutting of the grass and making it into hay might be done ready to his hand. Most of this explanation must certainly apply to the after-math, as the man who was to have that crop, could not enter the land until the first crop of hay had been cleared off, while his occupation would be limited to the short period between that harvest and the preparation of the land for the next year's crop. The much lower price paid for the second crop would be explained by its smaller quantity, inferior keeping quality, and lower nutritive value owing to the absence of seeds, in all of which qualities the first crop would be relatively high. It is quite likely that buying hay regularly would be a practice which would commend itself in a place like Oxford, where everybody had unstinted rights of pasture on a large common like the Port Meadows [1]. An enterprising use of these rights by people who had little or no other land would increase the demand for hay for winter fodder.

In order to prevent misunderstanding, it is needful to say a few words more respecting the owner's responsibility with regard to the raising of these two crops. In the case under consideration, if no manuring were done to the land, the renewing of the fertility of the soil would depend entirely upon occasional flooding for the sake of the silt brought down by the river during late autumn, winter

[1] N.B.—The word *meadows*, which I believe is the local term applied to the land in question, is in this case used in a different sense from that which it bears in all other parts of this Chapter. Elsewhere it is always used as applying to grass land intended for hay. Port Meadows are used for pasture exclusively.

and early spring, and the short interval between the two crops. This method, however, if exclusively relied upon, would almost certainly result in a fairly rapid deterioration of the soil, and be less effective for the purpose in view than a dressing of farm-yard manure. But the latter would involve outlay in buying the manure, its carriage and spreading upon the land. In any case, for flooding, sluices would require to be kept in order, and regulated at suitable times. For more uniform and regular irrigation gutters to conduct the water on to different parts of the land would need to be cut, fences to be maintained, or watchfulness to guard against trespass and damage to the growing crop and other minor matters. So the sum given per acre for the crop, which the Professor would seem to have confused with rent, would include quite a number of other items :—wages for labour and attendance, cost of materials, interest upon and redemption of capital, etc.

We may now direct our attention, for the purpose of comparison with other received deductions and confirmation of the theory just enunciated, to the rents paid for land in different parts of England during bygone centuries, so far as access to records has been possible. The figures presented will show some amount of variation, as we might expect for convenience of situation, quality of land and other causes. But in only one case we have come across and that an extreme one, does the value given amount to one quarter of that put forward by Rogers for the " natural meadows " of Oxford. The same authority[1] gives the rent of arable land at 6d. per acre, in one case stating that figure to be the maximum. On the eastern slope of the Pennines, in the graveship of Sowerby[2] and other places within the Manor of Wakefield,[3] the rents enumerated run generally from 4d. to 6d. per acre, the former being for *oldroyd* land and, the latter for new land. Grinding at the lord's mill, and aids when he married a daughter or

[1] *Work and Wages*, (pp. 40, 41, 52, 58, 73, etc.).
[2] Extent (or Survey) as refrreed to several times above (pp. 30-43).
[3] *Wakefield Manor Court Rolls*, Yorkshire Archæological and Topographical Society's Record Series.

his son was knighted, are the only dues imposed. In the neighbouring graveships of Rastrick and Hipperholme, whose mean altitude is a little less, the slopes not so abrupt, and the soil presumably slightly richer, the rents paid in money are upon the whole slightly less ; but the tenants have to render several other dues and services besides those to which the people of Sowerby are subject.

The only definite allusions to "meadow" found in this *Survey* relate to the vaccaries in Sowerby. In three of these there appears to be none but meadow land, which it is stated produce hay sufficient for the winter keep of the given number of beasts, which are sent elsewhere to pasture during the summer. In each it is stated for what sum the place could be let to farm, if the lord chose so to do ; so that we have a means of learning what was a lessor's estimate of the rent value of meadow in this region. The total area of these meadows is 84 acres, and the estimate of rent is 106s. 8d., or an average of nearly 1s. 3½d. per acre. The highest is 1s. 8d., and the lowest is 10¾d., per acre. The two most highly rented places each include also " an ox-shed and one grange for putting hay in." (It is still a universal practice in these parts to house hay in barns, strongly built stone structures. Weather conditions make some such protection necessary). To render the comparison, say with the Oxford case, a fair one, we should have to make some slight allowance for these buildings, which might not be so massive as their modern representatives, and thus somewhat reduce the quoted rent of the local examples. In addition it should be noted that the rent mentioned is for the full use of the land, not merely for a crop which, as we have seen in the Oxford case, was probably produced ready to hand.

Crossing over to the western slope of the Pennine Range and looking around us, we find ample confirmation of the view we have formed as a result of our search on the morning side ; namely, that meadow land for yielding hay to furnish winter food for cattle was quite common ; that by virtue of some superiority, either naturally inherent in the contour of the ground and soil, artificially imposed, or both, such land naturally commanded a higher rent than was paid for any other, whether it be arable, pasture, or general. But we find that that enhanced price was nothing like the exaggerated height to which the imaginations of academic inquirers have been wont to soar. The figures found on the eastern side are so uniform, and agree so nearly with Thorold Roger's particulars of the rents paid in other localities for arable and general land, that it has not been thought necessary to give much detail. On the western side, however, we find greater variety of prices, arising largely from the greater area under our purview, and the consequent fact of more choice of quality and convenience. We are not now so entirely confined to bleak hills with abrupt slopes intersected by ravine-like recesses ; but find a large proportion of gently undulating lowland, watered by numerous streams, thicker deposits of soil consisting largely of occasionally replenished river silt, and fine glacial drift, often richly impregnated with lime. As our enquiry specially relates to the rent value of meadow land, it is of interest to us that that is more frequently specified than hitherto, although still only occasionally.

It will be convenient first to pick out those particulars relating to lands most nearly identical in physical qualities with those in the upper portion of the Yorkshire Calder Valley, with which we are already somewhat familiar. We may begin with :[1]

" Colne, 151 acres of land in Demean devised to
    divers tenants   ..   ..ix l iij s viijd "
" Worston, 30 acres of land in Demean   ..   xv s
5 acres of meadow   ..   ..   v s
48 acres of Heirable Land   ..   ..   ..   xvj s "
" Standen. 80 acres of Land in Demean   ..   xxvj s viii d
36 acres of Meadow   ..   ..   xxiiij s "
" Penhulton. William Querderey of holes (holds)
    30 acres of waste land paying yearly   ..   xxs "
" Great Marsden. 335 acre of Land in the hands
    of divers tenants at Will   ..   ..   .. cxj s viijd "

[1] De Lacy Inquisition of February 16th, 1311, Chetham Society, Vol. LXXIV.

"Padiham.   John de Whiteacker 44 acres   ..   xxv s "
" Briercliffe 166 acres and ½ of Land ..   ..   l v s vjd "
" Habergham Eves.   248 acres and ¼ of Land
     yearly for the same ..   ..   ..   iiij l. ij s x d. "
" Cliviger. 80 acres . . . . yearly   xxvj s. viijd." [1]

All the above are on the slopes of Pendle Hill, the
Pennine Range itself, or the higher grounds in the neighbourhood of the two, and open to the full blast of the prevailing
south-west winds and the accompanying persistent rainfall.
The soil is mostly of the sparse and clay variety.   The rent
of the Colne land which presumably is general in uses, is
very high, just over 1s. 2½d. per acre and nearly equal to the
average of the Sowerby Meadows, while it is 40 per cent.
higher than the lowest of them.   The rest vary from 4d. to
8d. per acre, the former figure being the more general, while
the latter singularly enough applies to the one item of " Waste
Land."   Two other items of undefined " Land " are given
for this locality which work out at the very common rate of
4d. per acre.

On page 11 of the De Lacy Inquisition, immediately
following an entry relating to this place, is a number of mis-
cellaneous items referring to various places, some of them
many miles distant.   Then comes this, " profits of Hay
sold there for each cart load carried off jd . . . . One
year with another vj s. viij."   The amount of hay sold off
would thus seem to have been about 80 cart loads per annum.
It probably applies to various holdings, being compensation
to the lord for injury done to the land when deprived of the
manure which would accrue from home consumption of the
hay.   Such a custom is universal to-day.   On the Yorkshire side of the border one-sixth of the value of the hay sold
off is claimed by the landlord.   The two items of " meadow "
given above work out at 8d. and 1s. respectively, a proportion
to the price of other land in the immediate locality only slightly
lower than we found to hold on the opposite side of the great

[1] De Lacy Inquisition of February 16th, 1311, Chetham Society,
Vol. LXXIV.

divide.   Personal knowledge of the two districts warrants
the statement that neither could be warped land.

We may now pass down to the next lower grounds,
land, the physical characters of which are somwehat easier and
richer than those just dealt with, and approximating more
closely to those to which inquirers have hitherto devoted chief
if not sole attention.   Clitheroe and the Ribble Valley will
be more familiar to the general reader at least in name, as a
richer and more fertile district than that in which we have up
to now been more particularly interested.   The following
are fairly typical examples, namely :—[1]

"Clyderhowe.   4½ acres of Meadow worth yearly   iij s.
There are 20 acres and 3 roods of Demean Lands
    which Adam Russell holds by grant . . . .
    for life   ..   ..   xx s. iij d. "
"Brunely.   John de Whiteacker for 8 acres of
    Land   ..   ..   iiij s. "
"Dennon.   In Dennon he holds 107 acres of
    Heirable Land . . . . . 60 acres pay yearly   xl s.
And 75 acres . . . .   xix s.
. . . . 10 acres of Meadow . . . .   xx s. "
We are still not far from the familiar figures : 6d. to 1s. the
acre still holds the field for land which, judging by the
terms in which it is described, is available for general purposes.
" Meadow " actually stands about midway between others.

Of the Dennon (Downham) items it should be pointed
out that the two sets of figures 60 and 75 do not square with
the total given of 107 acres.   Reverse the digits of the latter
constituent reading 57 for 75 and they are much nearer and
would give the exact rate of 4d. an acre which is so common.
Probably there is here a misprint.   The " meadow " yields the
unusually high rate of 2s. per acre, which is not, however, so
surprising when we reflect that the district as a whole is a
rich one, and that the rest of the holding pays on the scale
which, though frequent, is a low one.   Passing still further

[1] De Lacy Inquisition of February 16th, 1311, Chetham Society,
Vol. LXXIV.

down the river basin about twenty miles beyond our previous examples, we select one from the low lying rich lands near the mouth of the Ribble, namely—" Penwortham.[1]   24 acres of Meadow Demean 1xxij s." This rate of 3s. per acre is the highest that has presented itself in the course of these inquiries ; but it is less than a third of the total of the lowest and only a little more than a fourth of the highest in amount of the Oxford examples quoted by Professor Thorold Rogers.

In all the cases given in the two valuations, the one relating to a large area in Yorkshire, the other to a still larger one in Lancashire, by far the great majority supply no direct information—beyond the occasional mention of " meadow," which is presumably for hay—as to the quality of the land, and none as to the purposes for which it is used ; simply so much " Land " is named.   The presumption is, that in most of these instances, the land is used for various purposes such as pasture, meadow and arable.   It is also reasonable to assume that the land used for growing hay would be a large proportion of the whole.   Most holders, if not all, would have rights of common pasture, although such is seldom mentioned : but in some cases the commons still survive, and in others they are known to have been enclosed within a century or two of the present time ; so that on this assumption a greater quantity of winter food would be needed than the actual measurement of land given as held by each person would suggest.   As has already been stated, over a considerable portion of the area climate and soil are neither of them very favourable for arable cultivation.   It has already been shown (pp. 118-120), that certain surface features are essential, if land is to be used for the production of hay.   In very hilly districts such as the higher altitudes of Lancashire and areas above described, it is only the best of the land which has these qualities.   It is scattered in numerous small patches amongst others which are comparatively rough and sterile, while some degenerate into valueless crag and bog.   Thus we may see that a relatively high percentage of each individual rent may be ascribed to the hay-growing land, and the high values recorded for

[1] Ibidem.

" meadow " land are more apparent than real, since in each case it will be a piece of the best land carved out of an inferior larger area.   In very hilly districts such as the Pennine expanse, the proportion of land which cannot be utilised fo any purpose, or is nearly worthless, is higher than in low-lying flat lands.

In the valuations from which the preceding particulars are drawn, that for the Yorkshire side gives a number, and the one for the Lancashire side a majority of the holdings in *Oxgangs* and *Carucates*.   When dealing with the higher grounds the first term is used.   On the east side where the size of the oxgang is variable, the rent is from 3s. 4d. to 6s. per oxgang.   On the western side the rent-value is generally 3s. per oxgang and sometimes less, though one in Burnley gets as high a rate as 7s.   Generally too on the Lancashire side each oxgang bears an annual charge of iiij d " for works neglected to be done."   This would seem to indicate services once rendered, but now compounded.   With very few exceptions, no other services or dues are mentioned.   On the De Lacy side, " One pair of Greyhound collars," " One pair of Spurs," " One Pound of Pepper " and " One Pound of Cuminseed," each occurring but once are the only ones recorded, and in each case the money due is less than the ordinary, by the value of the goods.

It is interesting to note that on both sides of this upland region, the part of England which it has been fashionable to regard as being slow in enterprise and generally backward in social and economic development, was in the early part of the fourteenth century less subject to feudal dues and services than those further south, and presumably nearer the current of " progressive " thought and intercourse.   As stated on pp. 69-71 the Wakefield tenants as far down as Halifax were subject to very few impositions.   Even the really onerous one to which they subscribed—the Lord's mill— was easier than the rest ; they gave " mulcture [1] of the 20th

[1] Extent (or Survey) of Graveships of Sowerby, etc., 1309, Halifax Antiquarian Society, Record Series, Vol. ii. (pp. 28, 43).

vessel," whereas others gave " one vessel in sixteen." Likewise the De Lacy tenants, as far down as Clitheroe, appear to have been little troubled in this respect. Nothing beyond what is mentioned in the previous paragraph is found in the records which appear to be available. The special dues of those whose holdings are given in oxgangs with about four others have already been noted. The rest, who constitute the great majority of this group of tenants, are but rarely subject to any mention, the natural inference being that no dues beyond the money payments were recognised. In the Sowerby graveship it is specifically stated that tenants do not recognise any other land dues than the few mentioned in the Survey. Distance from centres where personal service and tribute in goods to the Lord could be conveniently rendered, does not seem to explain this freedom ; for there were the five vaccaries of Earl Warrene on the one side of the Pennine boundary, and the Clitheroe Headquarters of the Earl of Lincoln on the other side, respectively only a few miles from the most distant tenants. Probably the explanation will have to be found in the nature of the country and the temperament of the inhabitants. The more remote parts and extreme recesses would in the early times be difficult of access by official forces seeking to enforce unpopular demands. It is likely also that the inhabitants were composed largely, if not entirely, of refugees from the lower districts who had refused to acknowledge the authority of the successive conquerors. Consequently upon men of this hardy and independant spirit, located in, and familiar with all the intricacies of territory which enemies could only penetrate with difficulty, if at all, uncongenial tasks and obligations could not be imposed. Feudal disciplne would come late, always be indifferently enforced, and only brought about gradually and by bargaining between two parties of uncommon equality in position.

In the neighbourhood of Clitheroe we begin to find a number of days service at the Lord's periodical Courts imposed as a condition of tenancy. Here we also come upon the richer soil of a limestone district. The easier lying land of the more open country also presents itself.   Still further down, as we approach the west and south-west, alluvial flats not necessarily all at the present level of the river, constitute a large proportion of the land.   The superiority shows itself, not so much in enhanced money rents, though that is evident, as in more frequent and greater variety of personal services and payments in kind.   A more docile race of men, less possibilities of successful resistence, and a richer, consequently a more adhesive soil, constrained them to cling on in spite of more harassing terms.   The personal services and dues in kind do, however, somewhat ease the money rents, if we allow for the better quality of the land.   But even the most extreme terms do not come up in amount and variety to those with which hitherto published inquiries have made us familiar.

By this incursion into the thirteenth and fourteenth century records of two large areas which appear to have lain outside the domain of previous enquirers, some new light has been shed upon the pastoral pursuits of the English people during the middle ages.   The contention that the making and storing of hay and its successful use as a winter food for cattle, has been practised and served its intended purpose more than has generally been thought to be the case, has been confirmed. The exaggerated estimates of the value of meadow-land, with the suggestion that hay was a difficult and scarce commodity have on the contrary been rather refuted than confirmed,   From near the middle of Yorkshire to the major portion of Lancashire and Cheshire, the act of making hay was evidently universally practised, while the land for it was nearly everywhere available, although the ground concerned is, and always has been, much of it the least likely for any cultivated crop.   Indeed, the cattle-breeding stations of Saltonstall, Hathershelf, Rawtonstall, Cromptonstall and Ferneyside—on the Yorkshire side—and on a much greater scale, those of Accrington, Rossendale and Pendle Forest districts in Lancashire strongly support the view that this was the most profitable use that could be made of the land in these remote uplands.   Their long continuance is strong proof that the undertakings were successful.   Hence is driven into

141

oblivion the academic notion that the keeping of cattle in fair condition through the mediæval winter was a particularly difficult business in the absence of root-crops and artificial grasses.

Moreoever, the killing-off at autumn of any surplus stock even if carried to the extent of absolutely glutting human consumption—and the records bear no trace of anything of the kind—would have but an insignificant effect upon the numerous herds. Another thing seems to be suggested by the De Lacy and De Warrene records. It would appear that many of the vaccaries along with live stock were let out to farm, and that this corner of England generally assumed to be little removed from its primitive inertia, had anticipated by a century and more the Stock and Land lease system, by which impoverished land-holders in the more *progressive* parts of the country sought to solve their economic difficulties when, after the Great Plague, labour was for once successful in asserting its claims to a larger share of the means of life.

CHAPTER VII.

EARLY TRADE AND MANUFACTURING INDUSTRY IN THE CENTRAL UPLANDS OF THE NORTH.

POLITICAL AND SOCIAL RELATIONS OF THE PEOPLE COMPARED WITH THOSE OF OTHER PARTS OF ENGLAND.

THE Social life of this country, of which industry forms a principal part, has in the past had its history written almost exclusively from the point of view and the materials supplied by the older cities and towns. These places together with the typical rural Manor of the same lowland areas, have also supplied the only types known to writers upon the subject of English life. Naturally these aggregations of humanity are all situated in those parts of the island, which in its early period as a trading community were easiest of access to the continent, and in close touch with land rich and easy to primitive methods of agriculture, and became earlier and more completely subject to succeeding conquests. This greater subjection to the outside influences of the better known areas, as compared with the more remote and exclusive, has made the hitherto prevailing accounts reflect the real national character, temperament and activities of our country during those times less truly than would have been the case, had a wider outlook been taken. A genial climate would also be a determining factor in deciding the localities of those settlements both from the point of view of personal comfort and a convenient trading centre. The successive bands of conquerors who contrived to establish themselves in these islands, as is always the motive of such adventurers, looked for fertile lands and pleasant surroundings ; thus they unconsciously brought themselves and their activities

143

into prominence during the later times. The warlike methods by which they established themselves, were of the kind which has invariably impressed the whole incident and its results upon both their own and the surrounding peoples. It afforded to a considerable extent the very pith and marrow of the materials which have appealed to scribes, and out of which all written history has for centuries been largely made. These conditions were only to be found in the southern part of the country, and in the broad belt of comparatively flat lands lying between the lower slopes of the central highlands and the sea on the east and west, and to some extent along the larger river valleys.

Even the descendants of those tribes of settlers, who in their early career seem to have eschewed towns and town life, having further renounced the life of adventure and settled down as farmers, eventually recognised the benefits to be derived from mutual trading and could not resist the gregarious instinct which leads to town life. The repugnance felt to living in dense aggregates seems to have survived longest in some upland areas such as those bordering upon the Pennine ridge. It appears to have largely escaped the notice of historical inquirers, that outside of those favoured regions previously referred to, were others which though somewhat more sparsely populated, were not the desolate regions devoid of population, social movements and industrial arts, which they have been assumed to be. On the contrary, at any rate so far back as Neolithic times, they were certainly visited by, and were very probably the abodes of men. Here topographical features, if nothing else, were in those early times decidedly against the growth of towns : but probably during Saxon times, and certainly during the early Norman occupation, no great areas, except the most exposed and barren hill-tops, were without people scattered along the countryside. There is even some reason to believe that at least at some periods of the past these bleak moorlands may have had more use made of them than is the case at the present day.

It is quite possible that voluntary choice may have had little part in determining the original settlement of the people who selected such rugged and ungenial surroundings for their home, and the causes which determined the original settlement also influenced their descendants for centuries afterwards. Elbowed out by mere growth of numbers, or more likely driven forth from their earlier homes by ruthless conquerors, they may have found here a harder physical lot, but sweetened by the sense of personal independance, preferable to continual struggle for doubtful possession or abject submission in more fertile and less exposed situations.   Some compensation for deficient produce was to be found in greater area, if less rich land.   At all events the strategic advantages of a hilly country, the difficulties of access and transit, and the very barrenness of the land discouraged adventurers and gave to the settlers in their new home a safety from the attacks of oppressors or tyrants.   In the eyes of both these latter such land would be worth little, its conquest exceedingly difficult, and therefore to be left alone so long as the occupiers abstained from aggressive acts.   On the steep hill-sides, and in the treacherous recesses of the valleys, a small body in possession would have a decided advantage against any invader. The early people must have perforce had to put up with a monotonous and coarse mode of life.   Sheep rearing was possible, and probably was largely indulged in, partly for food, perhaps mainly for wool for clothing, which would be a specially stern necessity in these parts.

Such a tract of country as the great area flanking both sides of the Pennine Range of hills lay open to them. Besides being unsuitable to the growth of mediæval towns or offering temptations to early adventurers, it presents but a poor stage for the display of feudal state-craft and ambitious politicians to disport themselves upon at a time when national organisation and political institutions were alike imperfectly developed ;   and least so amongst a scattered population, with whom communications were at best difficult to establish and maintain.   The political activities and constitutional developments being the aspects from which the history of the past has been studied, and the only ones (until quite recent times) worth the attention of scholars, perhaps naturally, the regions which could afford little material for the construction of the dramatic element, or the satisfaction of the appetite for political intrigue or official vanity, have come to be looked upon as outside of the pale of the historian. The habit has become fixed, of looking elsewhere for the history, the social life and customs of the English people.

What May be Expected to Result from a Wider Outlook.

There is, however, much reason to believe that such a view is a very incomplete one. In so far as the past life of the whole people comes to be embodied in an account of the development of modern English life, these hitherto neglected regions will come into more prominence. It is perhaps on the side of Industrial and Economic History that this restricted outlook on the part of historical writers has resulted in the greatest misconception. The conclusions arrived at have not in the main been wrong from the point of view from which the problem has been approached and the limited range of facts upon which they have been based ; but rather, narrow and incomplete, from the leaving out of sight of a large area occupied by a strong and virile people. A district and people have been neglected in which, from the conditions in which they were placed, customs and habits have prevailed, which if known, would have modified the conclusions adopted. Some of these customs that relate to pastoral industry have already been noted. Others affecting more strictly manufacturing industry will receive attention in the succeeding pages. It is not intended at present to pursue that theme, the fact is merely noted. For both these purposes in the enquiries with which we have hitherto been acquainted the records of Craft Guilds, Livery Companies, legislative enactments, Government ordinances and such other documentary relics as relate to the customary historical areas, have been freely drawn upon for the building up of the story of Social and Industrial Life ; but this is nearly all. In those parts of the country where the absence of records relating to trade organisations which controlled the operations, or made united representations to the Government of the time, the usual sources of information were not found, it has been assumed that no trade or industry worth mentioning existed. True, the records and comments thereon do in some measure recognise country enterprise, but only in so far as these entered into direct competition or relation with the town monopoly, confined to a comparatively small area around the towns, which the organisations strove to limit in their operations or to render ineffective as rivals. These are some of the reasons why Industrial History occupies a principal place in this work, partly because some operations at least of the area sought to be brought more into view have during the greater part of their occupation by mankind been pre-eminently industrial in their interests and activities ; partly because that phase of the nation's past life has of recent years begun to occupy its right place in historical, economic and social studies. All social and political reformers now recognise that the claims of those concerned in industry must for many years occupy a large share of their attention. Most of all is this so, because that phase of the mountain life herein dealt with appears in many respects to have been different in its course of development from that depicted for the rest of the country, while its maufacturing industry has been more considerable in extent than has been generally realised.

When we come to investigate such evidence as exists regarding these mediæval and historical outlands, we find that there is reason to believe that maufacturing industry and trade were by no means so late in establishing themselves throughout a great part of these obscure and unknown regions as has been generally supposed. Nowhere concentrated or organised so as to force itself upon popular or official attention, as was the case at such places as London, Norwich, Exeter and York, but scattered over the length and breadth of the countryside generally, it might very easily aggregate a total greater than that of the official centres. In some parts at least, almost every family early came to be engaged more or less in some industry for which the locality found a call. Moreover, in this connection it is generally overlooked that there was a great preponderance of rural over town population ;

consequently there was available in the aggregate a relatively great mass of this scattered array of workers. This comparatively great volume of trade, although largely ignored, could not fail, even it if were done unconsciously, to affect the fortunes of the recognised operations. Even most of the towns had but a population which we in these days regard as that of moderately sized villages, and their habits sympathies, and modes of life would be emphatically rural. In this light a moderate estimate would put the proportion of the population to that of the towns as not less than ten to one. Rogers gives it in the fourteenth century as 12.34 to 1. This is a point of some importance, because though in any given unit of rural area the produce might be small, the much wider area of the whole might easily produce a quantity exceeding that of the towns.

This consideration suggests that besides home consumption and a modicum which found its way into the towns, there was also some quantity of these manufactured goods which found their way into markets as yet not clearly recognised. It is a singular fact that in all the allusions to trade contained in the personal and other local documents from which the materials for this northern history have been drawn there are scant references if any to the reputed headquarters of the cloth trade. Yet it is abundantly clear that these *entrepreneurs* fared far and wide, and had frequent dealings with distant places. In the light of the imperfectly developed national administration and the crudely enforced feudal system, it can hardly be contended that the government was able to keep anything like a strict eye upon the operations of traders who would from the very nature of the case have the active sympathy and support of the whole countryside in evading and defeating the representatives of a government whose principal objects were interference with the free enterprise of the traders, and its own enrichment at their expense. Professor Thorold Rogers forcibly says, " there neither did nor could exist any adequate police for the collection of other than small dues at the principal ports. In all likelihood the imports and exports at the numberless smaller ports were necessarily neglected." In addition to this, in case official attentions were at all harassing, or traders' and shippers' convenience suggested, every creek or strip of accessible beach, which could not in the humblest sense be designated ports, would be utilised for clearing off cargo.

RURAL INDUSTRIES OTHER THAN AGRICULTURE.

It has been usual to assume that in the times preceding those at which England definitely took a place in the world as a principal trading nation and for a long time afterwards, those people living outside of the towns and the immediate circle of town influences were engaged almost wholly upon agricultural pursuits. But if this were so, the obvious question at once suggests itself, what became of the produce, seeing that even with agriculture in its mediæval stage of development each worker therein must have produced several times his own requirements, and the much smaller town population could not have taken the surplus. That some corn and cattle were exported we may readily admit, although we have already seen (sup. p. 93), that as early as the fourteenth century there were imports : but such evidence as we possess does not lead us to think that the exports were a very large proportion of the whole produce of which the then rural population would have been capable. Again the sheep farming which produced the wool for the home looms, and, we may allow, a considerable amount for the continental weavers, could not employ a very large proportion of the rural population ; for that branch of agriculture is admittedly the one requiring the least amount of labour. Such considerations as these lead us to the conclusion, that many of even a sparse population of the country in these bygone centuries must have had some other means of earning a livelihood than by digging, delving and following sheep and cattle. Rogers [1] who had specially studied the district, was of opinion that " Even in Norfolk, which was their special home in the thirteenth century, they (the manufactures of textile fabrics)

[1] *Work and Wages* (p. 47).

were carried on in villages where agriculture must have been a principal employment."

That the rural cloth production was a matter of some concern to those who, having experienced the privileges which Guild organisation brought them, considered themselves to be the rightful monopolists of the trade's profits and advantages, is evident from the records of many of the town organisations. Attempts were often made to regulate or altogether prohibit this unlicensed production, either by supervising the operations in a certain area around the town, or prohibiting the sale of goods in the privileged town save in bulk, and that to the freemen of the town. The lesson had apparently not yet been learned that enterprise, baulked in any direction often displays a facility for venting itself in another. At the same time, there would be a limit to the extent to which restrictive ordinances could operate. The more scattered and remote areas could be but little influenced thereby, partly as the result of distance from the centre of authority, partly as a result of sparseness of operations over any given area. To have supervised these enormous areas effectively, especially where there was active antipathy to the motive prompting it, must have demanded an energy which would dissipate the resources of even the largest towns, and the strongest organisations.

Professor Unwin's [1] opinion upon this question of rural cloth-making may be appropriately introduced at this point. He says :—" There was a considerable trade in cloth long before the industry was organised on a handicraft basis. . . . . . Down to the fourteenth century this surplus produce of the home-worker was still very probably the trader's main source of supply. Three or four centuries later the country districts had become once more the chief seat of the woollen industry, owing to the spread of the domestic system . . . . . From the middle of the twelfth century onwards the towns, many of which had acquired their first importance as cloth markets, began to be centres of the industry. Gradually

[1] Organisation of Industry (p. 27.)

the processes of the manufacture were specialised, and as each was appropriated by a special body of trained workers, there grew up side by side the several handicrafts of the weaver, the fuller, the burereller, the shearman or finisher, and the dyer."

When the industries of the country had passed definitely beyond the family system, and specialisation had become generally recognised to have a place in the industrial organisation, those places where fertility of soil, facility of transit, or other advantages conduced to favour agriculture, might be expected to devote their energies mainly to the production of food-stuffs, wool and such pastoral pursuits. But even here, a supplementary industry which could be carried on independently of the weather and so be made to fill in the natural slack seasons ; or by those who did not care for, or through physical infirmity could not follow the more exposed occupations of agriculture, would commend itself ; especially as it could be carried on at home, and at their own convenience, making a welcome addition to the family income. Moreover, the economic base of the community would thereby be broadened, or shall we say the primitive breadth retained : for this new order would conform more to the pattern of the old domestic system, it being generally recognised that the narrowed basis of modern rural economic life is the greatest evil which centralisation and production on a large scale have imposed upon the countryside by drawing away the home industries which they at one time practised. This we may regard as the one extreme, where conditions operated most favourably for providing a market for the goods produced in the towns, in return for which the towns would directly or indirectly take food-stuffs, wool, skins, etc., from the rural areas. But there was also another extreme consisting in those districts where conditions of climate and soil severely limited the quantity and variety of necessaries and comforts which could be produced.

SPECIAL NEEDS OF ISOLATED AND UNKNOWN UPLANDS :—

Such a district is the extensive area of narrow valleys, barren rugged slopes, and bare uplands flanking the higher ranges of the Pennine Hills and other mountainous regions. Until well on into the Middle Ages, the sheltered bottoms of the confined valleys, where more fertile soils and a kinder climate could have been found, were shunned as dangerous tangled swamps, almost impossible to cultivate with the primitive methods and tools then is use.   The people lived on the upper slopes and only gradually pushed their way down into the more sheltered and fertile lands bordering the stream, as necessity, increasing confidence, and improved tools and methods made it desirable and possible to deal with the difficulties there facing them.   There is conclusive evidence that these inhospitable regions, that is the grounds high above the stream levels, were occupied by men long before the time at which conventional Industrial History begins, and have been so continuously up to the present time.   The present day population of the uppermost regions is probably less than it has been for several centuries ; certainly it is below that of the 15th, 16th, 17th and 18th, and most of the 19th centuries.   Such means as we have of estimating the numbers occupying these parts in early times—say, *The Poll Tax Returns* of 1379—lead us to the conclusion that, taking the population of England and Wales at two-and-a-half millions, the recognised inhabitants were about one-seventh of the present proportion to that of the whole country, judging by the townships of the upper portions of the Yorkshire Calder Valley.   We are not, however, without reasons for thinking that the actual population was somewhat larger.

Apparently in less elusive and better known parts of the country, and at a somewhat later date, it was possible for discontented labourers to escape from the clutches of the law.   Commenting upon the position of the labourers and their attitude towards official attempts to keep down wages after the Great Plague, Professor Thorold Rogers [1] says :— " Many to avoid punishment or restraint, fled into the forests where they were occasionally captured."   In the *Poll Tax Returns* for the township of South Ourum 23 names are given. These are the particulars usually relied upon for basing an

[1] *Work and Wages* (p. 228).

estimate of the population of the period. By the accident of a dispute between two land-holders in the locality, during the years immediately preceding, some names are revealed to us of men very probably living there at the time.[1]   In the Assize Action six names are given which do not appear in the *Poll Tax Returns,* either because though holding land in the township they did not reside there ; or possibly they were too poor to pay their 4d. or otherwise managed to escape the tax-collectors.   We cannot of course, definitely infer from this that the recorded population of Southowram in 1379 can be increased by 25 per cent, if we want to get at the true numbers.   But it does show us that in the one township out of the twenty constituting the parish, into whose unofficial life we can get a glimpse, and that township the least favourably situated for concealment, there is a great probability of some having escaped the imposition of the tax-gatherer, and that the real numbers were proportionately greater than the official figures suggest.   Nor are we precluded from suspecting that many others may have escaped the tax.   Allusion has been elsewhere made (Chapters ii and iv) to the difficulties of approach for others than natives to the recesses of the great hill-slopes, and to the jealous distrust of outsiders which the previous experiences of the inhabitants have fostered.   There are still surviving in the Upper Calder Valley and other places traditions of outlaws and of some of the natural and artificial shelters in which they took refuge, and the protection given them by the less adventurous natives.

A recently published series of articles by a much respected journalist who spent his younger days in the immediate neighbourhood referred to, contains a description of one of these reputed refuges and its associated occupants. Its site is the crest of a hill 1300 feet or more in height and backed by a stretch of wild moorland miles in extent, overlooking the old town (now degraded to the rank of a small village) of Mankinholes, which is probably near the oldest human settlement for many miles around.

[1] J. Lister, M.A. and J. H. Ogden, Halifax Antiquarian Society, Vol. i. (p. 26).

" Jackson's Rock [1] was one of the old stony subjects. Up to 184— it had maintained its existence for ages . . . . . . then the covetous eyes of the stone-getters fell upon Jackosn's Rock . . . . .For Jackson's Rock had a tradition, which was something, though not important to us, and it had a cave, which was both romance and fact . . . . . The legend was that the rock apartments had been inhabited by a hermit . . . His chimney proved, by showing that fire had acted upon it, that he had some comfort. . . . . . .The piece of evidence that Jackson had lived was that above the rock-house was the ash-midden . . . . . of coal ashes and broken crockery . . . . The pot scars were not of red clay with the dark or treacly glaze, but of grey with a creamy coloured surface with ornamental lines and small patterns. Some pieces collected from the spot, we kept after Jackson's Rock had been hewn to bits and cast away. It was said by some estimators ' there was stone enough there to build a city as big as Manchester,' an estimate I could not accept. The midden has been claimed by some grave-robbers and barrow-diggers as the leavings of early history. Hard to believe that ; harder to prove."

It may, however, reasonably be held that in any case, when the population of any considerable given area had to be sustained mainly, if not entirely, by native grown food it would be impossible for a soil such as exists in the locality under review, to maintain a population equal to that of those richer soils obtainable in those parts of the rest of England, which have attracted the chief attention of industrial and economic writers. Indeed a principal part of the case here sought to be made out is that the paucity of natural resources made it imperative that the upland natives who had settled in these hill fastnesses, being in excess of the normal natural resources to be found there, must provide themselves with means of obtaining supplies from elsewhere. Those means must of course take the form of some sort of locally created wealth, which could directly or indirectly be exchanged for the surplus food of other localities.

[1] *By the Fire,* by A. B. B. *Todmorden District News,* February 25th, 1916.

Most of the area, with which we are concerned, taking it in its wider sense as including the elevated ground in the middle of northern England, contains or borders upon that portion of the country for which no *Domesday Survey* exists, nor apparently ever has done. Whether any sufficient reason for this omission has ever been given or not, is not the point at present ; but it is very probable that the character of the country combined with the jealous exclusiveness of the people, the unusual nature of which has already been dealt with, supplies much evidence towards that end, that it was beyond the power of the Norman to quell. Hence the people escaped his domination by retreating into these fastnesses, where his emissaries for long afterwards could not, or dared not attempt to enter. At pp. 67-68 something has already been said upon this point in relation to Heptonstall. This implies that these people were partly or entirely outside of the pale of Norman control for a considerable period under the earlier reigns of that dynasty. The inability of both King and Lord to whom the lands were granted to enforce their authority, is suggestive of a good deal in the earlier history of some of the remote regions. Take for an illustration our now familiar upper part of the Yorkshire Calder Valley. Its two extreme arms push upwards and into, and on the west side of the stream embrace some of the Lancashire territory of the Earls of Lincoln. The early *Manor Court Rolls* for this area are defective ; and some other records hereafter to be cited, which though copious are but for a limited period and relating to matters which probably applied only to the specific districts, for the neighbouring parts over the hill within the watersheds of the Irwell and the Lancashire Calder, are absolutely silent about that portion of the De Lacy territory which is within the eastern side of the water parting. We are not justified in assuming from this absence of records that there was no population. Instances are given elsewhere (pp. 158) of men from " Todmorden " and " Walsden " during this period of obscurity, who took land in the adjoining and farther east Sowerby. This Hundersfield part of Lancashire will be referred to again. Its situation and character, together with its obscurity in the records, suggest that here we may have a detached portion of that greater north and western area, where Norman law and administration for a long time ran a very feeble and halting course. These very acts of migration just alluded to may imply either that the individuals were unable to find in their old haunts suitable land for a home, a surmise which suggests sufficient population there to take up most of the land considered worth having, or a disposition to regard submission to the Norman authority as including some advantages over continued resistance. It is not an unreasonable presumption that in many of these extreme recesses of Norman England there was living a larger population than official records were able to take into cognisance. All these were outside of the range of lawful authority, refusing to acknowledge the dominion sought to be imposed upon them, while both King and Lord were powerless to make them submit. They resented interference, and from the strategical advantages of their chosen homes were able to enforce their own independence : they were refugees from an alien, meddlesome tyrant, who in their judgment only sought their acquaintance for his own benefit. Their ancestors were of a stock which had always declined supervision or dictation. Nay, some of them may have been refugees from the Conqueror's terrible harrying of Yorkshire.

This self-imposed isolation does not necessarily imply that they sought to evade what they conceived to be the obligations of society, or to get an easy living by subsisting upon the plunder of others who might have submitted, and thus secured a modicum of the richer products of the more fertile lands now held by less scrupulous adventurers. They simply wanted to be left alone, to manage their own affairs in their own way, to secure to themselves the fruits of their own toil and the produce of their own land. Had these people been less inclined to rely upon their own efforts in pushing their interests regardless of outside influences, had they been more assertive in seeking for themselves a privileged position like their rivals in the east, south and extreme western towns, they might have made more " history," and figured more conspicuoulsy in available records, thus providing for themselves a more prominent place in historical narrative. The English excluded parts would have had more justice done to them. We may safely conclude that the border people of the outlands were not sharply divided from those of their neighbours who had submitted to a more or less nominal jurisdiction of the greater, and elsewhere supreme, ruling and administrative authority. The temperament, sympathies and habits of both would be largely identical, while from the point of view of the authorities the one would be a shade better than the other. Those parts of this debatable land to which the earlier records apply, are such as were to early ideas in the main preferable for residence, being safer against surprise, easier to work, if anything more fertile and of such military quality as the advancing power could safely creep up to, as opportunity offered. Here the more rational and less stubborn would realise some advantages in moderate payments for occupancy coupled with a measure of protection. To this end official colour could be given, provided that its powers were exercised discreetly, without too much interference with the prejudices of their subjects, and too great a strain upon the popular opinion of the neighbours of the latter across the border-line.

In such a difficult territory as the one here described, escape from the purview of an outside official class, which was viewed by all with jealousy as an interfering and self-seeking body, would be comparatively easy. There are some considerable areas, e.g. the old township of Hundersfield, a large part of which though within the watershed of the Yorkshire Calder is in Lancashire, as already referred to (p. 155), and extends from Cliviger to Rochdale, embracing two of the Pennine Passes which connect the counties of Lancaster and York, and covering a distance of a dozen miles in one direction, where there is almost a complete blank in such records as exist for neighbouring areas. Yet we cannot consider it as uninhabited, because in some parts of it the remains of the late Stone Age men are more plentiful than in some other localities of which more documentary evidence is at hand, and occasionally in later times we find men coming from these dark regions and taking land in those parts where the light of records does exist, although it may flicker somewhat feebly. Thus at the *Wakefield Manor Court*[1] of June 11th, 1298, " Michael, son of Richard de Todmereden gives 2s. to take half of all the land at le Helm, left unoccupied on the Earl's hands by Jordan Peule, for ever." So too in the *Court* at Halifax of November 1307,[2] we find :—" Roger de Walsdene and Alice his wife give 6d. to take two acres of land in Sourby fron Richard son of . . . . . . " Both Todmorden and Walsden, though apparently within the Earl of Lincoln's Lancashire domains, join up to the Earl of Warrene's Manor of Wakefield and its graveship of Sowerby on their western edge. The two uppermost arms of the Yorkshire Calder separate the two territories and also drain them. Other entries in the *Wakefield Court Rolls* would appear to locate " le Helm " within the old township of Sowerby, which was formerly larger than it is now, including as it did the later township of Erringden, and at some points came within a mile of the hamlet of Todmorden, and for a distance joins up to that of Walsden. Besides several conveyances of land during the thirteenth century, Colonel Fishwicke[3] mentions the fact that " The names of Stephen de Todmarsden and Elias his brother appear as witness to a grant of land in Whitworth."

[1] and [2] Yorkshire Archæological and Topographical Society's Record Series.
[3] *History of the Parish of Rochdale* (p. 107).

CHAPTER VIII.

THE POSSIBILITIES OF THE NORTHERN UPLANDS FOR AGRICULTURE.

THE writers on general Industrial History have familiarised us with a system of agriculture in early times in which each local community worked collectively upon an area large enough to supply their united wants. Such a system of arable cultivation could have but a limited application in the parts of the country we are now considering. Typical of what prevails throughout the Pennine regions, Mankinholes, Heptonstall, Eastwood and other small areas such as Shore and the part now known as Cross Stone in Stansfield, Sowerby Town and Wadsworth, places which figure in the earliest records, all now present fairly smooth stretches of land on their higher slopes, although limited in extent for the most part. Besides these little groups—the towns of their day—there were quite a number of individual homesteads nestling in sheltered nooks or attractive holdings on the slopes, so limited in extent that anything approaching in size to the academic arable field was impossible. The neighbourhood of the seat of the earliest representative of the Norman Earl Warrene in the higher portion of the Calder Valley, in later times known as Stansfield Hall, gives little indication of the possibility of arable cultivation on the large scale, so rugged and irregular is the land, immediately it rises out of the swampy valley bottom. On the Langfield side, where it joins the original Sowerby, there is Stoodley. Here the lie of the land does show conditions approaching the possibility of communal cultivation on a small scale : but the number of cows and calves of which we have evidence as kept there by individual owners as early as the year 1277,

159

precludes the probability of the giving over of anything more than a very small area to arable purposes. There is also a great probability that a considerable number of sheep may have been added to these grazing animals.

The takings of land at various points in the graveships of Hipperholme, Rastrick and Sowerby, as recorded in the earlier *Manor Courts*, and the numbers of cattle of which their owners were possessed, or were responsible for, suggest the extensive prevalence of individual land-holding. The omission of references to common land other than unimproved waste is also suggestive. The sizes of these holdings are such that they are within the capacity of being worked by a single family, so that the inference must be drawn that if there existed many landless men, or very small holders such as would have to rely for support mainly upon communal lands or assistance given to large holders, the population of these parts must have been much greater than has been generally believed to have been the case. Of these individual holders were those, such as Richard del Pendant—mentioned in the *Court Rolls* of 1274 and several times subsequently—who appear to have had holdings some miles apart, but each consisting of only a few acres. As regards others, such as Hanne del Schaghe and Hugh del Hagwe (1298), and John del Hassenhirst (1313), we have no indication of their possession of more than their places of residence. Their homes—the first and last in Stansfield and the two others in Langfield—were at least in the instances of Ashenhurst and Pendant inconveniently situated for sharing in the work and oversight of any possible arable common land.

The evidence is conclusive that all were originally thickly wooded, and judging from the steepness of the slopes and some un-reclaimed portions still remaining, which are both capped and ribbed with rocks, were strewn with blocks of grit-stone. To have found an area large enough to be rendered available and of sufficient magnitude to employ an ox-team, must often have been difficult and when found, must have involved the expenditure upon it of an enormous amount of labour to fit it for the plough. The stony character which there is abundant evidence for believing that this land possessed, places it quite outside the possibilities of the arable cultivation which we ordinarily associate with primitive agriculture. Throughout very large portions of these hilly districts cultivation on a large scale was impossible either individually or collectively. The irregular surface, broken by cloughs and large stretches of scout and scar, all told against that. Of the five vaccaries already referred to, the largest had but 30 acres of meadow, and the inference is that this was the maximun amount which could be broken up and laid down for the growing of grass at any one place, for the cattle were taken elsewhere to pasture during the summer. We do not know that these thirty acres were all in one piece. At that time (1309) less than one-eighth of the individual holdings within the whole graveship of Sowerby equalled this one in size, and most of those which exceeded it, were probably sub-let in parts. The scanty references to corn crops to be found in the *Court Rolls* or elsewhere are in terms which imply individual cultivation and ownership.

We have also to bear in mind that the climate of these exposed hills, as well as the soil—soft, spongy peat on the flat tops, and sand or clay, all very stony, on all the slopes amenable to any sort of cultivation—rendered corn crops, especially wheat, as well as vegetables and fruit, highly precarious. As the lower grounds and more open country are approached, *e.g.* at Hipperholme and Rastrick in the lower portion of the Parish of Halifax, the condition for these purposes improves somewhat ; and the available records confirm the natural inference that in those parts more corn was grown. Sheep could be pastured in fairly large numbers almost everywhere ; though it certainly seems singular that an animal possessed of such a roaming instinct as compared with say, bovine cattle, should figure so little in the *Court Rolls* for wandering out of their owner's lands. There could hardly have been any large proprietors ; but likely enough most people had a few running on the commons and cropping the grass of the small farms which were nearly if not quite

161

universal.   Mr. Lister [1] has cited some figures from the accounts of the Priory of Lewes, which enable us to form an estimate of the numbers of these animals kept in the old Parish of Halifax in the year 1367.   It appears that the tithe of wool amounted to three sacks, so that the total of the clip for that year would be about 30 sacks.   Taking the sack at 26 stones, as given by Thorold Rogers,[2] and 14 lbs. to the stone we get 30 x 26 x 14=10,920 lbs.   Thorold Rogers gives the average weight of a fleece at that period as 1 lb. 7¾ oz. We may take it at 1½ lbs. which gives us :— $\frac{10920}{1\cdot5}$ =7280 fleeces, also the number of animals from which they were taken.

The number of tithe lambs—252—gives us another method of calculation, namely, the number of adult animals necessary to produce a yearly supply of 10 x 252 young. There are some difficulties in settling upon a correct multiple of the number of tithe lambs, as well as the adult animals from which the fleeces above were taken, in order to get at the number of animals themselves.   At a *Manor Court* held at Halifax on July 7th, 1277, complaint was made that the Vicar had imposed upon the parish a tithe of one in six, instead of one in seven as previously.   On the other hand, as already stated, although sheep-keeping was common, in most cases the number of these animals kept was very small, in not a few instances probably less than the six or seven upon which, from what has just been said we may infer that the levy could be made, even supposing that all came within the meshes of the clerical tithe net.   Hence there is a great probability that the total flock was greater than could be used for the profit of the parson.   We have no data to enable us to compare the prolificness of ewes, and the proportion of survivals to births five and a half centuries ago with what obtains at present.   Practical sheep-masters in the district say that now each lamb surviving to the autumn may be fairly taken as representing one ewe.   On that basis we should

[1] *Yorkshire Coiners and Old Halifax* by H. Ling Roth and J. Lister (pp. 134-5).   [2] N.B.—An age-long local custom, which prevailed until the great war gave 16lbs. to the stone.

have :—Number of breeding ewes 2520 ; these would necessitate the keeping of rams at least 80 ; to keep up the breeding stock there would be of year-olds, one-half of the number of ewes 1260 ; total 3860. Add to this one-fourth for losses by disease, accidents, etc. 965 ; grand total of adult sheep 4825. By this means we get a total about one-third less than that previously attained. Some at least of the difference may be made up by the inferior fertility of the breed kept, care, etc., in attendance at the lambing season of older times as compared with the modern. If we take the mean of the two results we shall have $7280 + \frac{4825}{2} = 6052\frac{1}{2}$.

That is no inconsiderable number for a small portion of a district, which has been assumed to be of little moment in the general affairs of the nation. The number is three and one-third times that of the human population, estimated upon the numbers in the *Poll Tax Returns* of twelve years later, allowing three children under sixteen years of age for each married couple, a mendicant for each township and seven clerics for the whole parish. Possibly this extra-ordinary result may suggest a revision of some of the less certain data. Roger's average weight of a fleece certainly looks small ; and if the northern sheep exceeded it, the numbers of the animals would be proportionately reduced. Or, was the real human population much larger than the estimate based upon the local *Poll Tax Returns* ?

SOCIAL AND ECONOMIC POSITION OF PEOPLE TENDING TO AN EARLY GROWTH OF WOOLLEN AND OTHER MANUFACTURING INDUSTRIES.

The rational presumption to be drawn from what we have already seen would seem to be that the life of the people occupying the regions previously described, would be rather a comfortless and monotonous one. Their food and clothing would be coarse, their comforts meagre, their supply of higher quality corn, vegetables and fruit-crops uncertain. Very probably the earliest acquaintance with the outside world would open to them the possibilites of more certain supplies and better qualities of fish, corn, and it may be fruit and vegetables. Certainly in the thirteenth century, and probably much earlier, many of them—say, those of the upper Calderdale—had regular communication with Wakefield twenty-one miles distant, and still more with Halifax and Rastrick. Besides a market for wool and cattle at the two first named places, the possibilities of disposing of cloth would soon become apparent. All the circumstances of their life, through the many generations that they and their ancestors had occupied these hill-slopes and valley recesses, must have tended to cultivate a power of adaptation and facility for turning to account all the possibilities that presented themselves. What more natural than that, already acquainted with the art from the fact of their having been accustomed to supply their own needs in clothing, immediately a market presented itself, they would lay themselves out to make the best of it, and so add to their slender resources ? The wool they produced, could be converted into cloth before selling, instead of disposing of it in the raw state, and thus contribute to that end. The lean fare which we have considered before must have been inseparable from the lives of these folks, we may readily conceive would stimulate a desire to improve their economic resources, an end which there was now some hope of reaching.

The eight merchants named in the *Poll Tax Returns* for Halifax in the year 1379 may quite probably have been engaged largely in buying cloth from their neighbours and selling it in the fairs and markets elsewhere. The freedom from political and military disturbances which the natural conditions of such localities favoured and the whole history of the country confirmed, gave a security and quiet, which are powerful factors in stimulating industrial enterprise, and conferring upon it permanence and success. The climate too would tend to the same result. The rainfall, not so much the amount as its persistence and comparative frequency, the frequent and sometimes long continued snowfalls, and the general rigours of an elevated and exposed region, would encourage the adoption of occupations which could be carried on under cover.   Thus we may reasonably infer that this combination of favourable conditions, namely, some acquired skill, the raw material at hand, a felt need for better means of living, and a known market, the hill-folk would very early apply their spare time to the tasks of spinning, weaving and finishing woollen cloth.   The very distance from the market would act as an additional impetus to the putting of the greatest value into the goods to be conveyed there and thus tend to the production of the highest quality.   As early as the year 1301 Richard Scissor is witness to a deed by which Thomas Clerk, of Wadsworth, conveys a piece of land to John Culpon, probably a neighbour living in the adjoining township of Sowerby.   It may be inferred that his presence in such company and the name by which he was distinguished, imply that by his business he had established himself as a man of substance and standing.

One other piece of evidence seems to point to the presumption of an early devotion to at least some sort of trade in the upper Valley of the Yorkshire Calder.   In the *Extent or Survey of the graveship of Sowerby*, we find that as early as 1309, with the exception of suit at the lord's mill and two rather remote aids, the whole of the rents were paid in money. It has already been pointed out (pp. 69-71) that this was scarcely likely to be entirely due to difficulties in rendering payment either in personal service or goods.   Laxity of manorial discipline and the difficulty of enforcing unpopular terms may have had something to do with it   But in any case the fact implied sufficient trade to enable money for those times to be fairly plentiful in these parts.   This date (1309) is an early one for the complete commutation of payment in goods and personal services, and affords a further confirmation of the presumption that trade was the medium which enabled any inconvenient dues to have been commuted, if any ever existed.

The available records are scanty and indirect ; but so far as they go at all, they point in the direction of strong confirmation of the above presumption.   Hitherto, not a shred of evidence has been found indicating the existence within these extensive regions of an organisation for the furtherance of class interests or trade regulations. Until the later centuries when the guilds elsewhere were becoming corrupt and declining, and the woollen trade was admittedly becoming established as the principal centre in the West Riding, and other textiles in Lancashire, no traces are found of united action in the way of representations or appeals to Parliament and the governing authorities. This absence of organisation and therefore of records of their doings, together with non-appearance in government and other official documents, is probably largely responsible for the industrial development of these parts of the country having been so completely overlooked. What has been written has been based almost entirely upon the surviving records of trade guilds and government departments. Where no such bodies existed, records of course could not be compiled, and therefore the modern inquirer found nothing. Perhaps he is not quite without excuse in coming to the conclusion that nothing therefore had been done. Those towns and cities which have been credited with being the homes of particular industries, had populations sufficiently dense and in close touch to render association and organisation not only possible but quite natural. In all rural districts the reverse of this must have always held, real and effective combination must have been severely handicapped, if not quite impossible. The folks were too scattered and their time was too fully occupied, for the close association necessary for combined action in large bodies. Although there is no evidence that the little communities of the counties were ever in active opposition or rivalry with one another, yet there is much to show that a spirit of jealous exclusiveness was always rampant, and that individual energy was the one essential quality which made for success. Combined with this was an alert inquisitiveness into the doings and affairs of their neighbours, and no qualms about copying anything which promised advantage.

Perfect freedom of enterprise would seem to have been the keynote of all social and industrial activities. At the same time, until the eager capitalistic ambition began to manifest itself in the seventeenth century, few were solely dependant upon the cloth or other industry with which they had associated their fortunes.   Nearly all combined some branch, or the whole operation of cloth-making, with dairy farming and the production of their own domestic supplies besides some wool as the raw material of their industry. Even the very poorest of all, those who were unable to provide themselves with either raw materials or tools, spread their energies amongst the varied tasks of the more fortunate ones. Until quite recent times the custom of cultivating a garden patch attached to nearly every cottage, survived ; and all were so familiar with the simple farming operations, that the alternation between textile industry and pastoral occupations, or *vice versa*, was quite easy and of daily occurrence.   The patches of grass land, some of them once under spade culti- vation, reclaimed from the most stony and barren scars in sheltered situations, which are a marked feature of some of the remote recesses of these districts, testify both to a once intense land hunger and to general familiarity with pastoral work.   The smallness of most of the farms, frequently less than ten acres, demonstrates conclusively the impossibility of supporting a family upon them and presumtively the existence of some supplementary industry.   But few were entirely dependent upon the capitalist, fewer still upon one species of industry.   Before the great changes of the Indus- trial Revolution, changes which in their suddenness violated some of the social instincts which centuries of custom had crystallised, to which only the strongest, physically, mentally and morally could easily adapt themselves, the considerations just submitted helped to protect the workman and saved the face of the poor from being hopelessly ground.

The history of the Poor Law, with the low rate of pauperism in these parts, the rareness of charitable institutions for the relief of poverty—and such few as do exist date mainly from a time subsequent to the beginning of the great up- heaval—the proud independence and sturdy thrift of the hillside native, are the products and evidence of a social and economic status which has prevailed through the centuries. The opportunities which the textile trade offorded for people of both sexes and all ages to work and contribute to the maintenance of themselves and their family, has done something to develope this character.   Every farm-house, every cottage was a hive of industry.   At a later date, Defoe in his *Northern Tour* noted this universal energy in the Halifax district devoted even then to cloth-making.   His oft quoted observations depicted a feature common to many a locality on both sides of the Pennines, and were probably suggested by his discovery of facts so different from generally accepted assumptions.   This widespread interest and facility in a complex industry implies a long course of development. There are earlier manifestations too, which point the same moral.

ADDENDUM—(CHAPTER VIII.).

It may be that the statement made on pp. 166, and alluded to or assumed elsewhere, to the effect that there is in these highland areas no evidence of the existence of trade guilds, will bear some slight modification.   But such fragments of evidence as will now be given bears no relation to the textile and iron industries which form the main theme of the manufactures dealt with in this work.   On a few of the principal buildings of earlier dates are to be found a few mason's marks, testifying to the fact that there penetrated into these parts craftsmen who had some direct or indirect connection with that guild which still survives vigorously, although now bereft of that influence over the craft which originally called it into existence.   By far the principal example of these buildings to be here referred to is Halifax Parish Church (12th to 15th century).   Here may be seen no less than thirty-five patterns of these individuals' identification marks.   The high-class character of the building and the authority responsible for at least its management—the southern

Priory of Lewes—do but confirm the inference suggested by the large number of marks, that the work was executed by a body of men almost certainly imported, but quite certainly trained by and under the authority of an effective organisation.

Other buildings distinguished from the much greater number by the possession of mason's marks, have them, however, of very few patterns, seldom more than three. Of these mention may be made of Hurstwood Hall, near Burnley (1579), Lower Ashes in Stansfield (1612), Higher Underbank, Stansfield (1611), and a few others. These buildings although undoubtedly good as examples of domestic architecture, cannot be compared either in magnitude or style with the church first mentioned. Neither do other ecclesiastical buildings improve upon the paucity of guild craftsmen's presence shown by the domestic buildings. Almost, if not all of these buildings both domestic and ecclesiastical, date from the time when the power and influence of the guilds or the trades they represented had begun to wane, or even ceased to exist.

With the exception of the Halifax Parish Church, which for reasons already stated, and the additional one that its situation is nearer to the more orthodox territory than the rest of the buildings mentioned, the slender evidence afforded by the very few masons' marks can hardly justify the conclusion that there existed in these remote regions an organisation that can be at all compared with those we know to have held sway elsewhere. In one case at least—Underbank—the marks are crudely executed. The few instances there are being most likely a spreading and survival of an influence which came from outside and continued long after the originating cause had ceased to have operative force. It was common until quite recently (in fact it may be so still) for stone masons to mark their tools by special figures acquired from their ancestors, the origin of which they had no knowledge, but which they accepted as an obligatory custom.

CHAPTER IX.

DOCUMENTARY EVIDENCE OF EARLY TEXTILE AND OTHER TRADES IN THE WEST RIDING OF YORKSHIRE.

EARLY MANUFACTURES IN THE WEST RIDING OF YORKSHIRE.

IN an analysis of the 1379 *Poll Tax Returns*, Canon Isaac Taylor [1] gives some interesting particulars relating to the West Riding of Yorkshire. A considerable portion, at least one-half, of the area under consideration rightly belongs to the low-lying, comparatively fertile portions of England, which it is the object of this work to show has had undue prominence given to it in historical writings. It includes the more southern parts of the county, and on the east stretches to within a few miles of the gates of York itself. The ancient towns of Pontefract and Wakefield are the only two within the area, which Canon Taylor mentions. " At Pontefract there is a Lyster who employs two men and two maids, another who employs two men ; and there is a Webster who employs two men. At Wakefield there is also a Lyster who employs two men . . . . . . There are also twelve Textors and four Sheremans." Thus there is clear evidence that clothmaking had passed beyond the family stage and also that specialisation together with an employer-class had definitely set in, most markedly in the towns. At the same time we may expect that in the more remote districts, owing partly to distance from the specialists and partly to the necessity arising from the poorness of the land, the system of more generally combined tasks would operate to a later date, where the work was devoted to supplying family requirements and

[1] *Notes and Queries*, December 17th, 1898.

Clothier's House (pp. 186-190).   *Photo. by H. Hardaker.*

possibly to some intended for the market. Within the Riding " The Taylors number 407, of whom 104 are called by the Latin name of Cissor, or more correctly Scissor . . . . . . There are 83 Drapers, 24 Mercers . . . . . 75 Merchants . . . . . Two Coverlet Weavers . . . . . . The Chapmen (25), and the Pedder (Pedlar) travelled with goods." Further, " The manufacture of leather seems to have been important, showing that leather jerkins and breeches were commonly worn. We have 19 Skynners, 40 Barkers, 6 Saddlers, 3 Cordwainers, 167 Souters (Shoemakers) and 8 Glovers."

Confining our attention to a more restricted area, Mr. Lister [1] has shown that in the old parish of Halifax the cloth industry was early established on an extensive scale. Mr. S. C. Moore [2] has also dealt with the same question for the area of Sowerby graveship, which is within the parish. There are reasons for believing that similar results would be eatablished for other localities on both sides of the Pennine Range, if the necessary investigations were undertaken. The parish named is an extensive one, embracing the valley of the upper Calder and its tributaries. It touches the very ridge of the Pennine Hills for several miles and stretches eastward for $16\frac{1}{2}$ miles. The exterme north and south range is $14\frac{1}{2}$ miles, and it has an area of 82,539 acres, being the third largest in the kingdom. It is at least large enough to be taken as a fair sample of our greater whole, the lofty grounds of the north. Rising in places to over 1500 feet, much of it is near to or above the 1000 feet altitude. Most of its lower slopes form the steep sides of narrow valleys with barren scars and rugged scouts visible everywhere.

Some of the documentary evidence in support of our main contention may now be adduced. For much of this we are indebted to the article by Mr. Lister on Halifax trade and the growth of the town, included in Mr. Ling Roth's book

[1] *Yorkshire Coiners and Old Halifax* by H. Ling Roth and John Lister (pp. 143-151). [2] *Evolution of Industry in Sowerby Division*, paper read by S. C. Moore at the Sowerby Conference of Youth in 1913.

The Yorkshire Coiners and Old Halifax. " As early as 1297,
a fulling mill was in existence near the North Bridge, Halifax,
showing that at that time sufficient cloth was made in the
town and adjoining districts to find work for at least one mill.
It is also evidence that there was some division of labour,
and probably production for an outside market.   This mill
and its owners are frequently mentioned in later *Court Rolls*,
and its trade was sufficient to establish its owners as of some
importance to the affairs of the locality.   The Wakefield
Court Rolls begin with the year 1274 ; in some of the earlier
volumes allusions are made to John the Weaver of Warley,
Adam the Tailor, William the Mercer, Thomas the Mercer
of Warley, Ivo the Webster, and John the Webster of Hipperholme, which occur in the rolls of the time of Edward II.
As early as May 7th, 1297, at a Court at Wakefield, under the
township of Sandale, William le Chapman and Geoffrey le
Folur are mentioned.   At Halifax, four days afterwards we
find appearing at court in various capacities, Richard the
Tailor, Robert son of William the Tanner and John le Baggere.
A year later Robert the Tanner makes his appearance from
Sowerby.   In the year 1296 Richard Lormier of Stansfield
is cited.   On February 2nd, 1275, at Wakefield from the
township of Sourby, William the Fuller makes himself a
pledge for a neighbour.   On January 6th, 1308, there are
from the same township William the Mercer and Bate the
Lister.   On July 12th, 1307, John the Skinner appears and
Geoffrey the " Colier's " wife.   Coming from Sourby where
no coal exists, we are quite safe in taking the word *collier* in
its original meaning of the maker of charcoal.   Some of this
was likely enough used for iron-working, as will be seen later.
But most of all it was in universal demand for wool-combing
operations.   In the days of Edward I. the name of Thomas
Textor appears in a charter relating to land in Hipperholme ...
our clothiers of the seventeenth century . . . . . also allege, in
some legal proceedings . . . . . . that " their mystery " had been
practised in the parish, " time whereof the memory of man
was not to the contrary," *i.e.* at least as early as the coronation
of King Richard I.   From the Halifax *Court Roll* of 1414,

we learn that a tenter croft was surrendered in the Hall Moot.

A Comparison Between an Academic Centre and the Parish of Halifax.

Some help to the solution of the problem before us might be obtained if we could get anything like a complete list of the occupations of, say one of the northern districts, and another situated within the area which has been looked upon as the mediæval textile district.   As none is available, perhaps some indication of the relative prevalence in the two localities of the trade—although at best an imperfect one— may perhaps be obtained from other existing material.   In the fourteenth century a considerable proportion of the identification-terms of individuals other than Christian names, were derived from occupations.   In a smaller number definite statements as to occupations are given in the documents to which access may be had.   The large number of names derived from places of residence, parentage, personal characteristics and the like, give no indication whatever of occupation.   It is also to be borne in mind that the uses of all these sources of nomenclature is quite arbitrary, and therefore the proportion of any one of them at any time and place as compared with another may give no exact indication of the real state of affairs.   There is, however, one of these sources which tends in a specific direction, and is of some importance in the comparison about to be made.   This is the use of the name of a person's place of residence or origin, for the purpose of identifying him.   The nomenclature of the period under review was always directed to the end of certain individual identity, just as is the case to-day when, however, we have fixed surnames to help us.   But in a town where the number of persons or families residing at a definitely named place, such as Townend, Eastwood, Horsfall, Hill, Clough, etc., this method of naming does not give a very distinctive result.   Indeed, it can only be applied to a small proportion of the people who may live at some such circum-scribed spot ; so that there would be a tendency to adopt other means of identification.   It is a reasonable inference, where the people are scattered over a wide area, that residential nomenclature will prove more useful, and therefore will embrace a larger proportion of the whole.   These consider-ations suggest the inference that in the comparison given below, the town area would have a larger proportion of trade names than the rural one.

Coming now to the comparison itself, Thorold Rogers [1] gives us some information about Colchester, which town is situated, if not actually within yet near to, the academic early textile district, and is for the year 1305.   With this will be contrasted the very large parish of Halifax with its scattered population ;   the time will be three-quarters of a century later.   Those two dates are the nearest at which the necessary information is available for the respective places.   The Professor's estimate of the population of the first named place in the year 1305 is two thousand ;   for the latter the editors of the *Poll Tax Returns* [2] (1379) give 1826.

As stated elsewhere (pp. 152-153) the population of Halifax parish at the time named may have really been some-what larger, although that, if a fact, would not necessarily affect the comparison, as the assumed omissions would include various classes.   Nor would the fact of Colchester's population at the later date, which in Roger's opinion was over 4000, in-validate the comparison, unless there were reason for thinking that the ratios of occupations had been materially altered by the rise in population.   The comparison follows :— (Occupational names in Halifax do not include such as Harper Crowder and the like.)

Occupations.	Colchester.	Halifax.
Total Designated	166	87
Weavers	8	6
Scissors or Tailors	4	9
Fullers or Walkers	6	9
Listers or Dyers	3	4

[1] *Work and Wages*, 19188 (p. 121).   [2] Halifax Antiquarian Society Record Series (p. 40).

Occupations.	Colchester.	Halifax.
Smiths	10	8
Carpenters	3	4
Milners	4	6

As suggested above, the occupation names given in Colchester is larger than in Halifax, being in fact in the proportion of nearly two to one. The difference is largely, if not wholly, accounted for by there being in Colchester 16 shoemakers and 13 tanners, while in Halifax there are but 5 (which probably included both). The southern town also has 8 butchers, 7 bakers, 6 girdlers, 5 mariners, 3 fishermen, 1 wool-comber and several others, none of which are represented in Halifax. In the first-named place there were 10 persons of " considerable substance " and in the latter—if we include eight merchants—eleven. Colchester with its population of two thousand in the year 1305 had twelve clergymen ; but in the Halifax list there were none, the list being that of the *Poll Tax Returns* 1379, from which the clergy were exempted. Included in the estimated population numbering 1826 for that year there is an allowance of seven churchmen. There are, however, in the list of names of tax-payers, an Abbot, a Priest, a Clerk and three Clerksons, the last all being married, so presumably they were not in Holy Orders. The name Abbot occurring in Halifax township, the seat of the old church of the parish, may be significant. When we come to the textile workers, weavers, tailors, fullers and dyers, the members twenty-one and twenty-eight respectively give the balance decidedly in favour of the north country ; although we might have expected to find the town craftsmen specialising more than would be possible or necessary in a very rural area. In the wider area more " milners " would be a necessity. To smiths and carpenters would fall the task of making looms, shears and other implements of industry, thus accounting for their practical equality in the two lists.

175

Evidence Afforded by Government Documents.

Mr. J. Lister [1] gives us some further valuable information about the matter in hand. " In the Record Office . . . . ulnagers accounts, *i.e.* the accounts of the officials appointed by the crown to measure and seal the cloth exposed for sale, and collect the subsidy . . . . The Royal Officer—Thomas Trygott— . . . . . . gives the towns in the West Riding that made woollen cloth and paid the subsidy . . . . . during his year of office. These towns are nine in number ; Ripon, we see heads the list with . . . . . . 889½ cloths, for which that city pays . . £16 13s. 4½d. But which is the next to follow ? Why, Halifax, which has produced 853¼ cloths . . . Wakefield is a bad third with only an output of 249 . . . . Leeds only 177, Almondbury, Pontefract and Selby are comparatively nowhere. Bradford . . . . is not even named . . . . These figures . . . represent *not* the *towns*, but the *parishes*, against which the towns are set. The total production of the West Riding in 1469 amounted to 2506 cloths (Halifax being credited with 853). The cloths made at Halifax at this time were kerseys, *i,e.*, narrow cloths, each piece about 13 yards long. In the accounts of the collector for the two years 1473-1474, Halifax has out-stripped Ripon and heads the list with a production of 1488½ pieces and a payment to the King of £24 8s. 10d., while Ripon numbers only 1386½ pieces and pays £23 2s. 3d. Bradford appears on this list in the sixth place out of the ten West Riding towns, having an account of but 178½ cloths."

The smallness of amount on the part of what are now the recognised seats of the trade may have misled inquirers who contented themsleves with looking for early evidence only to those places which are now identified with the industry, and thus warped their conclusions. The name of " Halifax Cloth " had become famous in the days of Edward IV. for we find in the inventory of the stock-in-trade of a wealthy York tailor of that date many references to it. Thus are enumerated :—9½ ells called " Halyfax Tawney " 7/- :

[1] *Old Halifax*, J. Lister (pp. 149-150).

Item 7 ells and 1qr. " Halyfax Grene," 6/- : 2½ ells " Grene Tawney," 16d. :   Item 2½ ells " remelands Halyfax " 2/- : Item 7 ells and 1qr. " Halyfax russyts," 3/8 : Item 2 ells of black " Halyfax Carsey," 20d. . . . . . Probably Sowerby or Hipperholme boasted a larger manufacture than that of Halifax . . . . . the specialities of the trade of the town in the reign of Edward IV. were not so much the weaving as the fulling and dyeing of cloths." In various quarters emphasis has been laid on the point that the cloths made in Halifax were mainly, if not entirely of the coarse kind known as " carseys." But surely at most places the main part of the production must necessarily have been of the lower grades.   This conclusion becomes obvious, if the relative numbers of the different classes of consumers be reflected upon.   It is also of some interest to note that in the year 1379 Elland had its " Shalunhare," presumably Challoner, a maker of Shalloons. It is also worthy of note that of the six kinds of cloth enumerated above in the stock of the York clothier only one is specified as a Carsey.

LOCAL WILLS AS INDICATORS OF OCCUPATIONS AND INTERESTS.

A valuable source of evidence, indirect though it be, is to be found in the *wills* of these old-time worthies.   In the absence of specific trade records, as must be the case where no trade organisations existed, and where all classes sought as far as possible to pursue their way independent of government interference, these old wills supply a field of research from which many interesting fragments may be picked up, supplementary to the otherwise scanty particulars.   The first from which we quote gives more clearly than anything else we have yet seen, an indication of the magnitude of the trade going on in these localities.   It points also to a considerable anterior period of development, before such result could have been achieved.   This was within a few years of the time (1503) when, according to Thorold Rogers the manufacturers of Norwich were " migrating southwards and westwards."   He makes no mention of northwards.   In

1518, William Hardy [1] of Heptonstall died ; and in his will he says : " I give and bequeath to Margaret my wife . . . . and my children my booth which I have at St. Bartholomew, Juxta London." This would seem to indicate that the testator was doing a considerable trade not likely to be confined to his operations in London. Moreover, we may fairly assume that at least a considerable proportion of his goods would be produced in the immediate neighbourhood of Heptonstall. The natural inference is either that he was a capitalistic employer, in which capacity he collected weavers, etc., around him, or put out weft and warp to be worked up in the homes of the weavers, or that he was merely a middleman buying up with a view to marketing from his neighbours the products of their principal or bye-industries. In any case, this elevated remote country town was little, if any, behind its more recognised competitors either in knowledge of available markets or in ability to supply existing demands.

Eighteen years later, namely in the year 1536, provision is made for the administration of the goods of " Henry Draper,[2] late of Brodbothome, chapelry of Heptonstall, Clothier, ... killed in London." This individual from the neighbouring township of Wadsworth was one of a remarkable and prosperous family which figures prominently in the district from the time of Richard II. and possibly earlier. His presence in London, a journey not to be undertaken lightly in those days, may fairly be presumed to have had some weighty business affairs associated with it. Similar allusions are to be found in others of the local wills of this early period, proving that the local connections with distant business centres were not an occasional or merely incidental one, but a general practice.

Reference has been already made to the fact that Halifax had half-a-century before a reputation in trade, as is shown by the inventory of a York tailor's stock-in-trade. William Hardy's commercial enterprise confirms and extends that

[1] *Halifax Wills* edited by E. W. Crossley.
[2] *Halifax Wills.*

reputation.   Others of a like kind are to be found.   A few years later a Sowerby man, Thomas Stansfield,[1] bequeathes his two booths in the same fair.   The foregoing surmise respecting Merchant Hardy's source of trading commodities can have some evidence adduced in its favour.   Some of the earlier histories of the parish of Halifax have had an inkling of the extensive trade carried on in the neighbourhood of Heptonstall during earlier times, as for instance [2]:—" It seems that trade was once in a good estate at Heptonstall, that they had some kind of a market there ; for we have seen a deed, dated 2 Charles I., wherein it is recited that John Sunderland, late of Horsalde, in Ayringden, purchased of Sir Arthur Ingram, of London, knight, William Ingram, doctor of laws, and Richard Goldthorpe, of London, gent : all that house and building called Hep- tonstall Cloth Hall, in Heptonstall aforesaid, by indenture dated November 9, 10 James I."   In the quotation already given from Doctor Whitaker (p. 61), the author speaks of manufactures and commerce as familiar courses into which the genius of the natives of the districts naturally bends itself.   Surely such remarks were founded upon that order of things as having been long established as an ordinary and prevailing one at the time and places with which he was familiar, namely, the two Calderdales falling off from the place of his mansion at Holme in Cliviger during the eighteenth century.

The initial bequest in the *will* of Hardy in conjunction with parallel clauses in the two next to be cited, illustrates the growing power and confidence in industrial affairs at this time and place.   He follows a custom which had been almost universal during the previous century on the part of people, who having accumulated some wealth, found it desirable to make provision for its disposal, when it ceased to be serviceable to themselves, and at the same time to make their peace with or fulfil their duties to Mother Church.   William Hardy's

---

[1] *Halifax Wills*, E. W. Crossley.   [2] Watson's *History of Halifax* (p. 232).

bequest to the representative of the Church embodies in substance the purport of all of them. " I bequeath to the Vicar of Halifax my best beast in the name of my mortuary as the custom is." The reason why the bequest generally took this form is to be found in the fact of the very common association of the people with the land and consequently with the keeping of cattle. These, therefore, were an easily available and acceptable form of the transfer of wealth. They often figure in the *wills* as bequests to relatives and friends. It has already been noted that this scattered people pursued its own industry side by side with such agriculture as would supply an important contribution to the domestic food supply, while the keeping of sheep was mainly for the wool. In their bequests they naturally followed the old established, and to all parties convenient, custom. Soon after the beginning of the sixteenth century, however, the wills begin to provide for this pious duty in a modified form. The same principle is there, but expressed less definitely in kind, the phrase being, " for my mortuary as the custom is." Evidently other things besides cattle had come to have current facility in the liquidation of ecclesiastical obligations. In the year 1520, George Hanson, also of Heptonstall, supplies us with a definite break from the traditions of the past ; thus :— " Also I gif and bewitt the Vicar of Halifax my best lowme for my mortuary." This bequest suggests that the testator was something more than a mere craftsman working his own loom and nothing more. The reference to his *best* loom implies that he was possessed of a number of looms, probably more than would be required to employ his family, as apparently he had a wife, a son and daughter. This case seems also to indicate the beginning of the practice of devoting the efforts exclusively to cloth-making and leaving the keeping of cattle to others.

The increasing wealth of documentary survivals, as we pass onwards in time, bears fruit in providing definite evidence that the weaving craft and all the preparatory and finishing operations of cloth-making were generally diffused throughout these central highlands. In the year 1524[1] a Property Tax was levied ; and it is interesting to note that in the township of Wadsworth—the lowest fringe of which is about the 350 feet contour line, but rises rapidly to 800 feet or more, and in places to considerably over 1000—adjoining Heptonstall, 28 persons paid the tax. Of these 21 did so on goods and only 7 on land, a proof that the major part of the inhabitants derived their means from some other than the primitive source. Additional point is given to this fact, when we reflect that the seven paid altogether on land the sum of 18s. 8d. whilst six paid on goods 20s. each, the total of the remaining fifteen individual contributions coming under that amount. Collateral evidence points conclusively to the manufacture of woollen cloth. This township also stands highest in the list of payments of all those in the great parish of Halifax and exceeded either Bradford or Huddersfield. The subsequent growth of these two last-named districts, which in early times enjoyed somewhat less of the quiet and seclusion favourable to industrial pursuits than the more remote uplands, has been recognised ; but the source of their prosperity has been misjudged. More favourably situated for modern trading purposes, they have succeeded in annexing that of the traditional headquarters. The very great increase of population which recent centuries have seen in these two towns, as well as Leeds, has been largely the result of immigration. It would be an interesting point to have worked out, what proportion of those immigrants, both heads of industry and employees has come originally from the older seats of the industry in the hills.

PARLIAMENT RECOGNISES THE HALIFAX DISTRICT.

The same point is further enforced, and some others to which allusion has already been made, by the preamble of an Act of Parliament passed in the reign of Queen Mary to regulate the wool trade of Halifax. The following has been quoted from Mr. S. C. Moore [2] :—" The parish of Halifax

[1] J. H. Ogden, Halifax Antiquarian Society, Vol. ii. (. 83).
[2] *Evolution of Industry in Sowerby Division*, quoted from Crabtree's *History of Halifax* (p. 303).

being planted in the great waste and moores where the fertility of the ground is not apt to bring forth any corne, nor good grasse, but in rare places and by exceeding and great industry of the inhabitants ; and the same inhabitants do live by cloth-making ; and the great part of them neither getteth corn, nor is able to keep a horse to carry wools, nor yet buy much wool at once, but hath ever used to repair to the town of Halifax, and there to buy upon the wool-driver, some a stone, some two, some three and foure according to their ability, five and six miles off [1] . . . . above five hundred households there newly increased within these forty years past." Here we have official evidence, not only of the universality of the industry throughout this very large parish at least a century earlier than has been customary to recognise its existence at all ; but also that the people who were able to monopolise the available stocks of raw material, and had little hesitation in doing so, were becoming a power and objects of public concern : for the object of the enactment seems to have been to protect the small manufacturers from the attempts of the great ones to monopolise the stock of wool. Further it seems to imply that there was a demand for more wool than was grown in the area affected.

Whilst confirming much that has been said above about the physical conditions of the locality and their influence upon the industrial occupations of the people, the document just quoted also amusingly reflects the current official and dominant classes' conception of the general conditions existing in that part of the country which was outside of their personal ken. It may be noted too that the Act was an evidence that the lesser organised power of the northern industrialists was beginning to influence the legislative and ruling authorities. It sought to exempt the area to which it refers from the operations of a general Act which had been passed some years previously, very probably upon the in-

[1] This was almost certainly the " long mile," which was about 1 1/3 of the Statute mile. V. J. J. Brigg, *Some Old West Riding Milestones.* Yorkshire Archæological Journal, Vol. XXIII.

stigation of the controlling bodies of the south, which made it difficult if not impossible for the small man to get supplies of raw material.

A PARISH REGISTER.

If it be permissable to jump forward a couple of centuries—and the facts of the northern development during the next two centuries are so strong and obvious that the prominence could be no longer ignored by purely academic inquirers—we come across another significant item pointing to the same conclusion of the universal application of northern upland skill and energy to cloth-making. In any case it will have a bearing upon the real character of the so-called migration of the industry at the period of the Industrial Revolution. Mr. Moore [1] has examined the Register of Baptisms in Heptonstall parish and finds that in the year 1749, more than a decade previous to the reputed beginning of the Revolution, which is credited with having finally brought the cloth-trade northwards, of 191 baptisms, there are 131 or nearly 69 per cent. where the father is described as a *webster*. Other entries of " Yeomen " and " clothier," indicate plainly the existence of a staple trade, in which employer and workman are clearly marked off as separate classes. These workmen were all engaged mainly in weaving ; indeed the numbers who were not entirely so employed would be very small. On the other hand, it is quite probable that a considerable proportion of the remaining 31 per cent. did weaving as a part-time or subsidiary occupation. Included in this 31 per cent. was the " clothier," which denoted employers as well as servants and assistants necessary to complete the finishing and marketing of the cloth. Consequently the numbers actually engaged in the trade would be somewhat larger than the 69 per cent. literally doing the weaving. The moral of the numbers is clear enough and cannot be strengthened by emphasis. Defoe's frequently quoted description of the town of Halifax about the same time, extends the area and varied completeness of the tasks which were undertaken.

[1] *Evolution of Industry*, as above.

Local Wills Indicate Varied and Widespread Interests.

But we have been anticipating somewhat. It is a common feature of the *wills* of the sixteenth century and onwards, to give indications of the testator's interest in the cloth trade, and that not merely a local interest. In so far as the details of wills on the Lancashire side of the border have been published, they confirm the evidence drawn from other sources, that common interests climbed upwards to the higher reaches of the watersheds and joined those of their neighbours on the eastern slope. The testators give these indications by describing themselves as "clothiers," or by bequests of tools, implements, etc., of the industry, or again by reference to persons, things and debts, the latter often spread over a wide area, e.g.,[1] "Oct. 24, 1527, A—dm. of goods of William Crabtree, late of Heptonstall, cloth-maker." Again[2]:—"Dec. 9, 1539, Robert Sutclif of Hirst (Wadsworth), to Richard and John Sutclif, my sons, all my walker sheares." "April 7,[3] 1538, Richard Sutclif, Heptonstall, Thomas Sutcliffe receive all my dettes which are owinge to me of Kendall men, the one half of it to his own use, the other half to the use of Alice my wife." [4] "Sep. 17, 1540, John Steide of Northlande, Thomas Stiede, my brother, ... to be goode to Elizabeth my wife, and Agnes my daughter, as to sell their cloth in the faires in Yorkshire." Here there is an indication that the district supplied this class of goods to others in Yorkshire which did not supply their own. Possibly they thus found their way into the hands of dealers, who collected for more distant markets.

[5] "July 12, 1551, John Michell of Stryndes (Stansfield), Thomas Hylye oweth to me iiij markes for wolle. I will that he pay and delyvyr to Alicie Michell, my doughter, towards her marriage." [6] "June 7, 1502, John Deyn of Halifax, four pairs of my cropping shears to Johanna my wife and John my bastard son . . . . . one pair of my shears to Laurence Hargreaves my servant, also one pair to John Clerke my servant, and one pair to Richard Ward, servant."

[1, 2, 3, 4, 5, 6] *Halifax Wills*, edited by E. W. Crossley.

[1] " March 24, 1529, administration of the goods of John Widdope .... Wadsworth .... clothyer was committed to John Midgely of Heptonstall, clothier." [2] " April 22, 1541, John Northende of Northorom, John my son, one pare of my best walker sheres .... Margaret my doughter, iiij stone of wooll, William Northende my son . . . meases, lands, tenements, mylnes, in Stanburie and in Sourbie." [3] " 1555, James Fletcher of Heptonstall, I give to James Flethcer my son iiij sheep, and one piece of carsey price xxv s . . . . . . iiij part of one great panne, etc." [4] " John Hilliwell of Sowerbie .... . debtes owen to me .... Richard Hogeskyne of Walles, xvj s. Item, Thomas Hill of Leeds, xxiij s. Item, Thomas Marton of Leeds, iij LL. iij s." The following is not directly concerned with the point immediately before us, but it is interesting as showing both the magnitude and wide distribution of the business relations of some of these men :—
[5] " February, 1541, John Kent of Halifax :—Gryndinge stones standing and being in Leeds, Skipton, Kigley and Heptonstall, with all the axiltrees and crooks and all other things belonging to everyone of them."

There is in the porch of the sixteenth century Church at Heptonstall, on one of the brackets supporting a rib of the stone roof, a shield on which is inscribed the form of a pair of shears. In the absence of an understanding of the former industrial position of the parish this device has given rise to some unnecessary surmising. For in the light of the long and intimate association of the locality both with sheep rearing and cloth-making, the explanation becomes very simple indeed. To the uninitiated it may be useful to say that both for the clipping of the wool from the sheep and those used formerly for the hand-dressing of cloth, the shears employed were very similar in appearance.

HOW PRIVILEGED CENTRES SOUGHT TO HAMPER FREE ENTERPRISE.

It will at least make the chronological order of this narrative more consistent, if at this point evidence be given

1, 2, 3, 4, 5 *Halifax Wills.*

of the disadvantages to which external districts were frequently if not continuously subject, at the hands of the more favourably placed regions. Besides the privileges and advantages coming from the organisation which town life made possible, and the being part of the England *par excellence* of those days as already referred to, the mere fact of being in nearer and more constant touch with London, the centre of gravity of all social, legislative and administrative affairs, has always given, as it still does, an advantage to the South in having its outlook realised, its interests furthered and its wishes fulfilled. From these sources, both in the mental attitude and the directly appreciable evidence furnished by the numerous documents, has originated the much greater attention paid to the activities of one part of the island as compared with the other. The flattered and pampered habit of mind naturally revelled in privilege and monopoly. One manifestation may be seen in an instance given by Professor Unwin, [1] who tells us that, " It is accordingly, in connection with such a grant of exclusive right to carry on a species of maufacture, which they claimed to have introduced into England, that we find the mayor and aldermen of Norwich obtaining the first legislative sanction for the new species of corporation. The trading element which had supplied the capital for the undertaking was to be represented by the mayor, six aldermen and six merchant citizens ; whilst the element of handicraft was found in " eight of the most discreet and worthy men of the mistery of worsted weavers.' By this Act of 1554, etc." Other instances of the same spirit are given elsewhere. Possibly there is here an attempt to stay or check that industral decline of the city, which Professor Thorold Rogers has told us was already proceeding. Whatever its motive, it is interesting to note that the usefulness of workmen on a body which was to be responsible for the regulation and management of an industry, was recognised nearly four centuries ago, even though they were only a minority of the whole ; while the object of the combination was to secure and maintain a monopoly, by means of which both were to gain at the expense of the rest of the community.

[1] *Organisation of Industry* (pp. 96 seqq.).

"Takkin' in Shop" (pp. 186-190).

Photo. by H. Hardaker.

The mention of worsted in the above quotation suggests a very brief reference to that branch of the woollen industry. The very nature of most of the sources from which the information relating to early northern industry has had to be drawn, makes the allusions almost necessarily general in character. Very seldom indeed do we find anything of a specific kind ; so the notices there are of the cloth trade are in indefinite terms. In the *Manor Court Rolls* there are occasional references to " coliers " living at places where no " sea coal " has ever been found. They were really the makers of charcoal, the manufacture of which of course implies a use for their product. No doubt, there were uses for charcoal, such as iron smelting, which—as will be subsequently shown—was practised in these upland regions, and for the work of smiths generally. In the lower part of the Halifax parish, where coal measures do occur, there is evidence that coal was used at an early date for iron working. In the year 1274 Richard the Naylor [1] gave 6d. for licence to dig sea coals that year for his smithy. But for smelting iron, and probably for some of the higher class iron-working charcoal must have been used, unless it be assumed that the local craftsmen were considerably in advance of what is generally understood to have been the practice in other parts of the country. The extent to which former woodlands have been diminished suggests an extensive use to which the timber was put, beyond what those uses already enumerated, namely, building, domestic fuel and iron-working, would account for, unless it were consumed most recklessly. Another use would be found for it in wool-combing, which would be necessary if worsted were made. In the *will* of John Lacey [2] of Cromwellbottom, dated April 5th, 1474, there is the item, " To Richard Fourth . . . . . . a black tunic of Worset." Of course this does not prove much, as we do not know that the material was of local manufacture ; but it does show that *worsted* was known and that in a district where there is good reason for thinking that cloth-making was a very common

---

[1] *Wakefield Manor Court Rolls.*
[2] *Halifax Wills* as above.

occupation, while the spelling of the word exactly reproduces the local pronunciation which prevails in the whole of the Upper Calder Valley to the present day.

THE NORTHERN CLOTHIERS BEGIN TO EMERGE FROM OBSCURITY.

Of the seventeenth century and the first half of the eighteenth there is no need to say much. That the North of England had an increasing trade at this period is generally admitted, though it is doubtful if its extent and variety are fully realised. To say nothing of the *wills* and other documentary evidence, which when examined reveal much, anyone who is familiar with the country knows that much substantial evidence survives to-day. Throughout the area of which Halifax parish forms the centre and the adjoining parts of Lancashire, fine specimens of the houses which these prosperous traders built in which to live and carry on their business, are to be found in great numbers. Very often we may still see the doorway of an upper room—sometimes the steps leading up to it are still there—where the master clothier had his " takkin' in shop," or the warehouse where he gave out weft and warp, and took in the finished goods. Picturesque, pleasantly situated, substantial, the buildings have stood well the assaults of the fierce elements during the intervening centuries, and are a fine testimony to the sturdy character and substantial social position of those strong men. That they were keen on their rights and in defending their interests is shown by two law-suits [1] in which they were engaged with the official *aulnager* during the first half of the seventeenth century. That they knew what they were about and managed their case well, is shown by the result ; victory rested with the clothiers. The question in dispute was as to whether they should pay 1d. or 1½d. per piece for sealing the cloth. Among the witnesses were men from all parts of the Halifax district. It is quite plain that in such affairs as these there was some sort of concerted action between the larger and more public-spirited manufacturers ; but these rare

[1] J. Lister, *Bradford Antiquary.*

instances afford the only evidence we have of any organisation amongst either masters or men, the absence of which has been referred to above.

We have a striking illustration of the magnitude and widespread operations of these enterprising men in the reign of James I.[1] " The complaint of the merchants trading to Spain . . . . Besides these were the northern and Devonshire clothiers, the makers of the new drapery and the hosiers, who, instead of being content to serve the merchants as they used to do, had made it their business to be informed of the demand of the Spanish market, so that they could supply it directly." Thus it would appear that the long-privileged classes, the slaves of self-interest, when more original and sagacious rivals had adapted themselves to new opportunities and the demands of fresh or changing markets, still thought that the newer fabrics should be reserved as a monoploy to themselves. This petition also affords evidence that as suggested above the centres usually credited with being the headquarters of the textile industries, acquired at least a part of their reputation from the flowing to them of the products of distant, unrecognised rural districts, and may have been the foreign marketing centres as much as, or more than the manufacturing places. Poor " merchants trading to Spain " ! The exclusive spirit, bred of self-importance and fostered by the narrow policy of their trade organisations and the interested regulations of the government, which was eventually to help on their undoing, had rendered them unable to see that the world had not been made for their special exploitation. From what we have already seen and shall shortly further see, we may safely conclude that the enterprising traders from the hill country had very little respect for the pleasant illusion, had taken their full share in destroying it, and undoubtedly " had made it *their* business to be informed of the demands of the Spanish market (and others) so that they could supply it themselves."

Some particulars of a very remarkable firm, bringing our inquiry up to the eve of the Industrial Revolution, may now

[1] Unwin's *Industrial Organisation.*

be given.   In the first half of the eighteenth century there existed [1] at Soyland the firm of Samuel Hill.   In order to understand fully the marvellous achievements of this prosperous undertaking, it is necessary to realise the remote and difficult nature of its situation.   The place stands at an altitude of about 1000 feet, and within three or four miles of the very ridge of the Pennines.   Far removed from all the main arteries of communication, unless the craggy road between Lancashire and Yorkshire across Blackstone Edge be considered to be such, before turnpike roads were at all general, or canals and railways had come to facilitate traffic, this busy hive of industry throve valiantly and defied the disadvantages both of an exposed climate and seventy miles distance from Hull, its nearest port of shipment.   The pattern-book shows a marvellous range of patterns, styles and colours.[2]   Considering the out-of-the-way situation, the generally assumed backward state of these parts of the country, that mechanical power had not yet been applied to the operations of the making and finishing of cloth, except perhaps fulling, the products of this moorland village strike us as nothing less than amazing.   This enterprising house had a turn-over of close upon £30,000 a year.   Nearly all of its goods were exported ;   Flanders, Portugal, Italy, Russia and Persia, all were indebted to the skill and energy of these obscure and remotely situated people.

SOME OFFICIAL RECORDS IMPERFECT : OTHERS PARTIALLY INTERPRETED.

Another thought already suggested (pp. 148-150) is renewed at this point : leave has been taken to doubt whether the official records of foreign trade represent fully the facts.

[1] H. P. Kendall, Halifax Antiquarian Society, 1916.

[2] One of the principal alleged deficiencies of early English and especially northern cloth, is in regard to the dyeing.   The following figures show that at any rate Yorkshire was largely engaged in this branch of the trade at a very early date.   " Anno 1213.   Sums accounted for by sundries woad importing, viz. :—Kent and Sussex Dover excepted £103 13s. 3d. ; Yorkshire, £9813s. 3d. ; London, £17 13s. 4½d. ; other places less.   For the above, V. Crabtree's *History of Halifax* (p. 290).

This may now be supplemented by asking, are they any more reliable than the conclusions hitherto set forth respecting the location and amount of the early English textile industry? Arnold Toynbee [1] states on authority of Macpherson's *Annals of Commerce*, that in the year 1770 the total woollen exports of England amounted to £4,000,000. Yet here we have a single firm located in one of the most dis-advantageous positions that could be found in all England, on the very extreme edge of the West Riding, a region which it has been the custom to look upon as just beginning to feel its feet in industrial life, was sending out, as its account-books show, nearly one per cent of the whole. It has already been shown that others within a few miles went far afield to dispose of their goods, and the suspicion cannot be repressed that the amount of finished woollen goods produced for foreign con-sumption was greater than has generally been thought to have been the case. Nay, it seems highly probable that some of the supposed centres of industry, such as York, Norwich and London in England, and Flanders abroad, may have acquired their reputation largely from their being the commercial centres, rather than the producers of the whole of the goods which passed through them, or were dealt in by their merchants.

[1] *Industrial Revolution*, 4th Edition (p. 46).

CHAPTER X.

THE WIDER FIELD OF UNKNOWN INDUSTRIAL
ENGLAND.

SIMILAR CONDITIONS SUGGEST SIMILAR RESULTS.

THE area mainly drawn upon for the facts and
illustrations already given, relating to the industrial
developments in the English Northern outlands,
is but a comparatively small proportion of the whole.
There is reason to believe that many others of the valleys which
drain the great central ridge both east and west, together with
their intervening elevations, would yield similar results if
the evidence were diligently investigated. Looking north-
ward, the highest reaches of the Yorkshire Calder Valley
join the watershed of the romantic Worth, one of the
tributaries of the River Aire. We enter here into Haworth
and Stanbury, a locality of literary and evangelical fame from
its associations with the Brontes, and Grimshaw its one-time
unconventional vicar. Its topographical, climatical, social
and economic conditions remind us of those we have already
noted in the heights of Calderdale, only more so. The soils
of the two districts are almost identical. The average
altitude is greater than that with which we are already familiar,
and it is even more remote from the world as conventionally
understood. In the absence of mechanical means of traffic
this isolation must have been more pronounced. The social
and industrial life of the last two or three centuries has been
reflected with a considerable degree of fidelity in the writings
of the Brontes, and Mr. Halliwell Sutcliffe has portrayed
for us much of its old-time life and activities ; but into both
of these the conventional flavour has intruded itself, as might
be expected. Through these means many who have not had
the opportunity of visiting the scenes and observing for

themselves, have learned that this moorland retreat has been the twin counterpart of the district which has hitherto occupied our special attention. Dairy farming, almost invariably on a small scale, sheep rearing, wool-combing, spinning and weaving, have engaged the time and energies of the two hill peoples whose social history and characteristics during three or more centuries supply an exact parallel. We may therefore safely infer that identical results, immediately preceded by similar developments, even though our knowledge of this be limited, point to general likeness of the origin and stages of development. Although, so far as we know, the details have not been worked out, there is a strong presumption that the evidence when brought to light will have a striking likeness in its indications to those with which the preceding pages have already to some extent acquainted us.

We could hardly expect to find everywhere exact parallels to say, the Halifax district ; but that many areas hitherto considered blanks will if diligently searched, yield if not exactly prizes, at least much towards repaying the effort made, is very probable. Some have started and grown with local variations and on different lines. At a time when transport was a greater task than now confronts us, distance from available markets was a more serious bar both to the initiation and development of industry. An intervening hill such as the ridge of the Pennines would considerably accentuate the difficulties of conveying goods by no means easily moveable in themselves. The textile trade of the Yorkshire side, having the lean-to of the continental market and even of the principal English one of the eastern and southern counties, by virtue of the Great North Road, to that extent had the advantage of position. Close association, however, and generally identical conditions, naturally engendered an upward flow from the western slope into the neighbouring border lands, as well as from that part of geographical Lancashire within the eastern watershed. We need not then be surprised to find a somewhat smaller manifestation of textile industry, when we come to the more remote western slopes. But even there we are not without early indications of that facility in industrial pursuits, which ultimately became the foundation of the world's greatest cotton manufacturing centre.

Descending the Lancashire slope we find physical conditions very like those we have left behind. A similar temperament of the peole is reflected in the saying that " in Colne everybody owns th' house they liven in." But in our present search for material we are seriously handicapped. The sources of information which have served us so well on the Yorkshire side are not paired with a western parallel. On both sides of the high border line access is possible to published lists of the tenants who held land under the respective great Lords, and of practically the same date, namely, the merging of the thirteenth into the fourteenth century. For our general purpose, however, neither of these helps us much, as they contain little information respecting the occupations of the people. The *Poll Tax Returns* of the Lancashire side do not appear to be available, or only to a limited extent ; and the *Manor Court Rolls* are far from being so complete as those which have rendered such good service to Yorkshire inquirers. Neither have the *wills* been published, any more than a mere list of names and localities relating to the testators. The documents themselves are preserved more or less completely at Chester, York and Richmond, whilst we are told that for one considerable period they have been lost or destroyed. To search those in existence would involve the expenditure of an enormous amount of time by an expert in that class of work, as well as of considerable expense. Occasional glimpses can sometimes be got in cases where they have been looked up for a special purpose, such as a family pedigree, *e.g.* " A genealogical Memorial of the Fielden family of Todmorden." But in spite of these disadvantages we are not entered upon an entirely hopeless quest, although, as has already been said, the developments upon the two sides of the dividing ridge are neither in time or character always quite parallel.

South East Lancashire.

The parish of Rochdale dips down from the Pennine axis towards the south-east Lancashire and Cheshire plain. The town which has imposed its name upon the larger unit has exercised its control from near the lower corner. It has been for at least three centuries recognised as a centre of one branch of the woollen trade, that of flannel-weaving though cotton is now probably in the ascendant. There is too a probability that even in the earlier centuries of England's manufacturing career, the activities of this locality in the manipulation of wool have been greater than its own very capable historian has quite realised. He has been largely influenced by the prevailing conception which has hitherto obsessed the historical mind, that in the absence of guild records and government ordinances instigated by the representatives of an organised body of trade adherents little was going on as compared with the districts which, situated nearer the centre of authority and by virtue of organised effort, have contrived to obtrude themselves upon the attention of the world. The earlier *Manor Court Rolls* do not appear to exist except for about ten months previous to 1556 and these are somewhat imperfect. To the late Lieutenant Colonel Fishwicke we are indebted for their publication.[1] During this brief period included between November 10th, 1335 and September 21st, 1336, there were twelve Courts held : in 167 entries, in which many details are deficient, we find allusions to four *Cissores*, a dyer and a mercer, some of which appear more than once. William le Suker, which is unintelligible as it stands, may be a mis-reading or spelling of Tuker (Fuller), or Sutor (Shoemaker), of which there are one or two others. The other cloth-workers almost imply a Fuller. The *Poll Tax Returns*[2] for 1380-1, for what is apparently the same area have also been rendered available by the same author. The impost was, however, levied upon a different principle from that already alluded to in dealing with the neighbouring parish of

---

[1] Lieut.-Col. Fishwicke, *History of the Parish of Rochdale* (pp. 289-292). [2] Id. (pp. 34-50).

Halifax, every individual being rated at one shilling. This high and uniform rate suggests that the list can hardly be accepted as anything like a complete census of persons of taxable age. To do so would imply a most unusual degree of material prosperity for a very limited and scattered population. It may reasonably be presumed to contain a high proportion of land-holders. The list consists of eight-one entries and includes one hundred and thirty-five persons, amongst which we have two " Listers " and one " Taleor." (Curiously enough, the two dyers are in " Hunresfelt," the largest township of all, the highest in altitude and the one which includes the part of the western county dipping into the Calderdale of Yorkshire. The continuous supply of pure soft water flowing off from these hills may afford an explanation of the dyers' presence here, so that these two may be virtually an addition to the West Riding list). An entry under " Castulton "—" Alic S le weker(*sic*) " may be a mis-spelling or mis-reading of either *wever, webster* or *walker*. Imperfect as these lists evidently are, they appear to point to a proportion of cloth-workers at least equal to those given for Colchester and Halifax.

A century-and-a-half later we find somewhat similar evidence to that with which the Halifax area has supplied us, though perhaps not so striking. The Lay Subsidy [1] of 1523, reached thirty-two persons in the parish, who paid on land a total of £5 19s. 8d., and nineteen who, levied at half the rate, contributed on goods £4 18s. 4d. These figures though not so disproportionate as was the case in Wadsworth, still point to a considerable degree of industrial activity. Eighteen years later [2] manufactures and trade would seem to have acquired a very decided ascendancy : for of a total sum of £17 0s. 6d., twenty-one persons paying on goods at half the rate contributed £13 0s. 6d., while only £4 came from the land-holders. One township, Spotland, did not produce a single contributor under this latter head. It would appear that by some means or other the greater portion of the land-holders

[1] Lieut.-Co. Fishwicke, *History of the Parish of Rochdale* (pp. 36-8). [2] Ibid. (p. 46).

were either exempted or otherwise managed to evade the impost. Their numbers are considerably less than those in the previous list, as well as in that of 1596 [1]. The latter seems to have entailed a much heavier demand, but the numbers paying on land or goods were equal, fourteen in each case and the amounts were £7 16s. 0d. and £7 8s. 8d. respectively. It is quite plain therefore that something other than land was contributing to the wealth of the community in quite a substantial manner. About this time the evidences of trading activity were so far asserting themselves, that Fishwicke can no longer fail to be conscious of them. He says :—[2] " We have abundant proof that the inhabitants of the parish were alive to the importance of the rapidly developing industry and that if they did not themselves manufacture, they were giving their attention to the buying and selling of the goods fabricated." The order of things here assumed is just the opposite of what had up to recent times been invariably the case, and as we have seen elsewhere was almost certainly the case here. Such extensive purely trading operations might by themselves be taken as presumptive evidence of corresponding manufactures. When viewed in conjunction with other facts the case passes beyond mere conjecture. Camden [3] describes Rochdale as " a market town of no small resort." In the thirteenth century a plot of land in Butterworth, named Flaxpughill, [4] is recorded. In 1356 [5] Richard de Wardleworth had a *fulling mill* and *lands* in Ashworth ; and in 1615 " a walker bank " is mentioned in some Wardle deeds.

Ashton-under-Lyne may be said to be at the foot of the Pennines, just as they enter upon the western plain. The inducements to manufacturing industry can hardly have been so strong here as in the more elevated and exposed regions of the east and north. Its physical features partake more of those found in the topical areas familiar to the writers of the

[1] Fishwicke's *Rochdale* (pp. 36-38).   [2] Ibid. (pp. 39-40).
[3] *Brittanica sub. Lancashire* qs quoted by Colonel Fishwicke.
[4] and [5] Three Lancashire Documents, Chetham Society, Vol. LXXIV (p. 96).

past. The comparative isolation of the place, the great range of hills behind it, and in front its long distance from the sea—and that sea on the wrong side for the world's markets—constituted a serious handicap, when all traffic was conducted under primitive conditions. Yet even here we have evidence of some industrial enterprise, though our one source of information is of the kind which is always least prolific in material for the purpose at present in view. From the *Customs Roll and Rental* of Sir Ralph Assheton ,Lord of the Manor, made in the year 1423, we learn that there were several persons engaged in cloth-making. Robert the Walker pays " for the Walk Mills 26 shillings and 6d. and at Yole a present to the value of 12d." There is also William the Walker, who, whether he works on his own account, or servant or partner with Robert we have no means of knowing. " Jack the Mercer [1] " seems to indicate that there is sufficient trade to absorb the purely commercial energies of at least one individual. The presence of four Croppers [2] suggests that enough cloth was dressed and finished to more than supply the requirements of a population represented by 126 entries in the *Rent Roll*. Thomlyn [3] the Tailor, if he were limited to the operation of making up the finished cloth into garments and were the only one so engaged, might supply the needs of his neighbours in that line, but could only consume a mere fraction of the production alluded to above.

There is also one significant item in the roll relating to corn. It is provided, that if the tenants buy corn and therefore none of the Lord's fuel be required for drying before grinding, the grinding must be done at the manorial mill, but only paid " muller of one twenty-fourth," instead of one-sixteenth, which the home grown article paid. This allowance to the extent of one-third, seems to suggest that the possibility of the home production of grain not being sufficient for the requirements, was at least not a remote contingency : yet the soil and climate of the place are not the least likely for that purpose. The inference seems to be,

[1] Chetham Society, Vol. LXXIV (p. 99). [2] Ibid. (pp. 101-10).
[3] Ibid. (p, 116).

that a considerable portion of the people had found other occupations which took up their time and energies ; else would they have grown not only a supply of corn to meet their own needs, but something to spare. The mention of " drying " seems to suggest that the corn referred to was oats, and consequently that that grain comprised at least the principal portion of the food of the people.

COTTON SETTLED IN THE HOME WHICH HAD BEEN PREPARED FOR IT.

Manchester's prominence as a commercial centre was not born of its association with cotton ; although the marvellous growth of that industry in the town itself and the surrounding districts has certainly contributed to its modern greatness. We cannot conceive of its so completely and rapidly monopolising the newer trade without a previous intimate acquaintance with the world's resources and requirements on the part of its leading men, and a long established facility in the making of textile fabrics amongst the mass of the population. These must have already been there, to make the working of the new fibre successful, and to attract the workers whose presence made the later great developments possible. Hollingworth [1] tells us " One writeth that about Anno 1520, there were three famous clothiers living in the north country, viz. Cuthbert of Kendall, Hodgkins of Halifax and Matthew Bryan, some say Byrom of Manchester. Every one of these kept a great number of servants at work, Spinners, Carders, Fullers, Dyers, Shearmen, etc., to the great admiration of all that came to behoulde them." The fact that cotton wool was imported regularly into England, beginning as early as the end of the thirteenth century, although for a time only in small quantities, indicates that there was a textile industry other than the wool and linen, which form the subject matter of those treatises on the history of trade and commerce, with which we have up to late years been familiar. The conservatism of the Craft and Trading Guilds may have prevented its use in the classical cloth-working districts, even in combination with

[1] *Mancuniensis.*

199

the customary older materials, and thus may have been responsible for some of the obscurity which has surrounded the subject. This attitude would necessitate the exclusive use of the newly introduced material in the ex-classical parts of the country ; thus the presumption is strengthened that the textile industry of those regions was in reality greater than documentary evidence can be found to support.

In mediæval times [1] Manchester had advantages as a market which were widely recognised. About the middle of the fourteenth century a dispute as to the status of the town, and the powers of the Lord of the Manor in relation to the weekly market came up for decision. As might be expected from the large number of cattle which we have seen (p. 23), were reared in the north-east of Lancashire, there must have been somewhere a conversion of the hides into leather. The men of the county, it would appear, were not content to allow these skins to pass into the outer world without their having been made the means of contributing their maximum to the economic resources within their power. Although no information as to the exact location has yet presented itself, it appears certain that a tanning industry was carried on somewhere. That may be shown conclusively from the award given at the close of the inquisition referred to above. Besides other liberties of the market, all of old standing, mention is made of " punishment [2] of butchers and tanners as to merchandise sold against the assize, the law and custom." This specific mention can only imply a well recognised trade of some magnitude.

In the *Rental* of 1473, we find [3] "Hughe Bothe, Geoffrey Newman and others the fulling mill there £2." Also [4] " a piece of land called Tenter leaker 12d." seems to allude to one of those pieces of ground on which woollen pieces were stretched on frames in the open air to dry and bleach. The *will* [5] of George Manchester, A.D. 1483, mentions the " garthyn and my newe orchard that is called the Tenter

[1] Manchester Chetham Society, Vol. III)pp, 438 seqq.). [2] Ibid (pp. 450-456). [3] Manchester Chetham Society, Vol. III (p. 504. [4] Ibid. (p, 504). [5] Ibid, (p, 506).

Bank." Apparently this was a plot of land which had previ-ously been used for that purpose, and then devoted to the requirements of a domestic dwelling. The item[1], " George Manchestre one singing house 6d," is doubtful. Mr. Harland the editor comments upon the obscurity of the original Latin, and the difficulty of a correct translation ; but judging from his allusion to *purple*, there is just a possibility that the place may have been one where dyeing was carried on.

"Camden [2] writing in 1582, says that Manchester excels the towns immediately around it in woollen manufacture '." Again,[3] " Leland reported in 1536 that Bolton market standith most by cottons and divers villiages in the moores about Bolton do make cottons '." Fishwicke's academic leanings do not prevent him from saying :—" The woollen trade had now become of considerable importance in Lancashire. Very early in the (sixteenth) century Manchester was doing a good business in the making of linen and woollen cloths ; amongst the latter was a coarse kind of woollens known as " ' coatings ' or ' cottons ' " We are told by [4]Mrs. A. S. Green, that in the year 1567, " the Lord Deputy Sydney made the last attempt to save, as he said, ' the manufacture of commodities within the country (Ireland) ' by an Act which not only forbade the export of yarn unwrought, but restrained the deputies for ever from granting any licences over sea. This effort was vain. The Queen was besieged for patents to bring Irish yarn to Manchester, where 4,000 hands were employed in weaving." Thus we get not only some indication of the extent to which linen-weaving was an occupation amongst the people in the neighbourhood of the modern cotton metropolis, but also evidence of one of the sources of their materials.

Whether the derivation of the word " cotton " as given above be one which will meet with the approval of philological experts or not, it seems certain that the term was applied to a class of fabrics which was produced in Lancashire long

[1] Ibid, (p, 504). [2]a *Echoes of Old Lancashire,* W. E. A. Axon (p. 107). [2] and [3] Quoted by Colonel Fishwicke *Rochdale* (p. 39). [4] *The Making of Ireland and its Unmaking* (p. 146).

before the newer vegetable fibre was brought in such quantity as to constitute it the principal raw material used. The vegetable fibre, the imports of which were increasing and did so very considerably during subsequent years, was up to this time used little if at all except for weft. It found its use for fabrics in which wool, flax and possibly silk, constituted the warp. Hence in judging the magnitude of the industry into which cotton entered, the fact of its being probably less than half of the whole quantity of material used, should be borne in mind. Besides, most of the cotton came in the raw state, having to be wholly prepared in the district, whereas we have seen in the case of linen yarn, much of the other material came in already prepared for weaving. By the end of the seventeenth century the imports of cotton had reached nearly two million pounds in weight. Manchester and the Lancashire around it displayed their business enterprise and facility for manipulation by making the most of the new industry and the call for its products in the world markets. Bolton marketing concentrated in Manchester ; but the old moorland centre manifested its deftness in the production of yarns by soon becoming the world's centre for the production of fine counts. There is one other reference which is suggestive of much. On February 24th, 1341, an inquisition which had been appointed [1] " to inquire into the true value of the ninths and fifteenths granted for two years to our Lord the King " makes exception of the citizens and burgesses not living by agriculture." Obviously there were craftsmen and traders sufficient in number to justify mention. On the general subject of the inquiry it is interesting to note, in the light of what has already been said (pp. 23) respecting the wealth of the northern counties before the era of the Industrial Revolution, that the inquisitors expressed grave doubts as to the sufficiency of the returns made by the locality for the benefit of " our Lord the King," and would not pass them without the direct sanction of the higher authority.

[1] Manchester Chetham Society, Vol. III. (p. 438).

Reverting to the linen industry, a piece of legislation enacted in the reign of Henry VIII may have been in a measure responsible for the flax-growing suggested by the foregoing allusions, and helped to develope the sixteenth and seventeenth centuries' Manchester trade. M. B. Synge [1] gives the following quotation from the Act :—" The King's Highness calling to his most blessed remembrance the great number of idle people daily increasing throughout this realm supposeth that one cause thereof is by the continual bringing into the same the great number of wares and merchandise made and brought out and from the parts beyond the sea into this realm, ready wrought by manual occupation ; amongst which is linen cloth of divers soils." Again, " Therefore for reformation of these things . . . . . and to avoid that most abominable sin of idleness out of the Realm, every person occupying land shall, for every sixty acres under plough, sow one quarter of an acre in flax and hemp." Probably too the quantity of Manchester goods coming into use interfered with the virtual monopoly enjoyed in some directions by the older woollen goods. In this we may have an explanation of the jealousy manifested by southern traders against the north, which amongst other things at a later time eventuated in legislation enforcing burial in wool.

NORTH-EAST LANCASHIRE.

A very brief reference to the north-eastern corner of the county must suffice to show that this industrial development in early times was not exclusively local. The mention in the De Lacy Inquisition [2] of " A plot for flax, 1d." does not go for very much : but in conjunction with the one near Rochdale already mentioned, it shows at least that flax-growing was known at widely separated parts of east Lancashire, and may indicate the beginnings of that industry, which starting with home-grown raw materials then drew upon the sister isle, as has been already mentioned (p. 201) and eventually found it necessary to utilise a new fibre and press

[1] History of *Social Life in England* (pp. 143-144).
[2] Two " *Compoti* " of Lancashire and Cheshire Manors of Earl of Lincoln, Chetham Society (p. 116).

into service two continents for its adequate supply. [1] A document dated 1415, mentions the " Flaxfeld in Pynington."
Colne, Walverden and Burnley are the parts of Lancashire nearest to the old established cloth market of Halifax, though separated therefrom by a high ridge covered with miles of bleak moorland. They were all early in the trade of making woollen cloth. The De Lacy Inquisition [2] 1311, tells us " There are at Colne and Walfreden 2 watermills and a fulling mill worth v l. vj s.viii d, and at Burnley [3] a fulling mill yearly worth v s." The earlier *compotus* is a little more explicit, for it gives " Rent of the fulling mill at Kaune, 1 Sep. £1 13s. 4½d." Also [4] *Bruneley* " Rent of the fulling mill there this year the first 6s. 8d." Again in the *Clitheroe Expenses* we find " Repairing the fulling mill of Kaune 12s. 8d. and Brunley fulling mill built anew £2 12s. 6½d." Four-and-a-half centuries later namely in 1727 in a list of occupants of rooms in Halifax Piece Hall, out of 293 are the names of twelve persons from " Colne." " Walfreden " is only two or three miles from Colne, and it is quite likely that any cloth-making that was pursued there at this time had become centralised in the hands of the Colne men for marketing purposes. The frequent references in these records to *water mills* may be taken as almost invariably alluding to the manorial corn mill. Amongst others is a mention of " Clivacher Mill," but no reference to a fulling mill. The presence of a fulling mill at *Guxham* (1316-1317) causes Professor Rogers to remark, " a proof, by the way, of these domestic industries." There is, however, in one of the lower parts of the present Cliviger, a small village always known as Walk Mill," the name of which has traditionally been regarded as coming from the fact that it saw in early times the practice of fulling carried on by the old system of literally " walking " the cloth in the stream. It is quite probable that this method of thickening the cloth

[1] Lancashire Inquisitions, Chetham Society, Vol. XCV. (p. 103).
[2] Three Lancashire Documents, Chetham Society, Vol. LXXIV, (p. 8). [3] Two " *Compoti* " Chetham Society, Vol. CXII (pp. 119, 122, 123, 126). [4] Lancashire Inquisitions, Chetham Society, Vol XCV., (p. 103).

may have been commonly practised in the numerous streams by individual cloth-makers, where no specialised fulling existed. This may quite conceivably have been the case in places which were too far from a mill, or where the weaving industry carried on side by side with farming was too scattered to justify the erection of a mill for the special branch of fulling.

CHAPTER XI.

PRIMITIVE IRONWORKS.

THE RECOGNISED POSITION IN RELATION TO EARLY IRON-WORKING.

FOR two thousand years iron has been known in England as a material for weapons, probably also for some kinds of tools and implements. Whether these earliest examples of utilising the most useful metal were of native production or not, is not quite certain. When, however, the Romans had established a footing in the country, they took advantage of the surface deposits of ore existing in those parts of the country which they brought under their sway, and utilised the abundant woods for fuel wherewith to smelt it. When the imperial legions deserted the natives, some of whom they may have cowed in spirit and degraded in general capacity, during the strife and confusion which reigned throughout the ensuing centuries, it is probable that some of the acquired arts were lost. But the extraction of iron from its native minerals was not one of these. Primitive methods of working the metal were too simple, and its usefulness, nay its absolute necessity, were too great to allow of the taking place of that event, to say nothing of the age-long practices of some parts of the island in mining and working various kinds of metals. We have little knowledge of the places where the industry was carried on in these earliest times, and in many cases of later date, save the remains of the furnaces and slag-heaps, which have been found from time to time. Most of these are in the immediate locality in which modern known ironstone bands come to the surface ; some, however, are many miles away from the sites where any available deposits occur. During mediæval times, and up to the seventeenth or eighteenth century, the furnaces and methods of working were primitive, the production being from the very nature of the case exceedingly limited in amount. We have, however, the satisfaction of feeling that in this industry at any rate, so far as the methods used are concerned, England was little, if at all, behind the rest of the world.

Sussex, the Weald of Kent and some adjoining parts have been credited with at least half of the national production before the sixteenth or seventeenth century, while the rest was distributed through the iron-bearing localities of the academic historian's England. Like the practice in other industries, the only evidence which has hitherto been able to reach the notice of inquirers, has been that gained through the records of organised workers and traders, government regulations, fiscal devices, reports and accounts of the goods regularly dealt in and bought by manorial officers and farmers at the great fairs. The production which went on in the regular and ordinary course of daily life beyond the recognised haunts of traders, travellers and officials, has been in the main ignored. The academic mind does not seem to have realised that valuable light, though often in fitful glimpses or enshrouded in mist, may be sent forth from other sources than trade records and travellers' tales. All this unseen production was probably small in any given place, and being effected outside of the official area was little noticed. Still it was so continuous and widespread in operation that in the aggregate its magnitude was relatively considerable. Like all other matters, such activities as were displayed in the back-woods bestriding the Pennine Hills have remained entirely unknown ; yet in the department now under consideration there was much activity. So far as we are able to judge from available evidence, these districts, engaged in agricultural operations of the more strictly pastoral type and more in textile and skilled industries than it has been the custom to recognise, did at least supply most if not all of their own needs in this useful metal. Herein may be seen both native exclusiveness and the practical energy which manifested itself in supplying at home whatever wants were capable of being satisfied. The southern centres of the iron industry (Sussex) being in the very heart of official and classical England, with a fertile soil, a comparatively mild climate, easy to travel and consequently eminently agreeable to the privileged classes, besides being within easy reach of that part of the Continent favoured by the ruling and official orders ; being moreover reasonably close to the seat of government and the select circle which dominated knowledge and culture, has not been suffered to have its glories obscured, or its achievements neglected. Others too, such as the north-east corner of England, being places of political and military importance, have likewise loomed large in official records and the minds of chroniclers. Those areas, however, which consituted the remote outlands and were on the official black list, have suffered from the results of cultured ignorance, highly placed indifference and haughty incapacity : consequently they have been largely ignored. The evidence which may be adduced in support of the conclusion that the art of smelting iron was widely distributed in these upland regions during former centuries is of a two-fold nature. There are the actual remains of the furnaces ; there are also some documentary references, though a positive and direct connection between the two cannot be very definitely traced. The remains here enumerated as existing about the higher reaches of the Yorkshire Calderdale are most of them known to the writer.

RELICS OF EARLY IRON WORKING IN UPPER CALDER-DALE.

Quite in the passes between the West Riding on the one hand and South-east Lancashire on the other, are to be found relics of these early Vulcans. Little more than a mile from the summit of the southerly pass, at an altitude of over one thousand feet, is Waterstalls. Here there is the site of one of these "bloomeries," as they are usually called. Judging from the quantity of ferruginous slag and scoriae still to be found, the work must have been on an extensive scale, either long continued, or in magnitude of operations. Every little mound is crowned with it, the ground around is often scattered or thickly coated with it, while all is overgrown with turf. Hundreds of yards of road and footpath seem to have been covered by the stuff at some time or other. Add to this, that the principal mound and some of the strewn soil, are close to a rapid mountain stream, which is often swollen into a torrent, whereby much must have been carried away, and we may to some extent realise the quantity which originally existed. It could not be measured by less than many hundreds of tons. A good many years ago the late Mr. John Aitkin [1] conducted some investigations relative to this old bloomery ; referring to some chemical analysis which he had made, he observes that " it is very evident from even a cursory examination of the slag from any of the old spoil-heaps, that only a comparatively small percentage of the metal was actually secured from the stone." This fact seems to indicate the most primitive skill on the part of the operators. Near the principal mound already referred to is a bed of iron pyrites ; but it is highly improbable that this material was used, even if known to the early workers to contain iron, for the purpose of the furnace or furnaces, for these reasons. (1) There are no signs of any mining operations, or other works for getting the mineral. (2) The large quantity of sulphur contained would very materially impair the quality of the iron when smelted, and thus would suggest that in that case a very inferior quality satisfied. (3) Or most improbable of all, a method of purification was known to these primitve workers, which would be highly prized by modern iron masters.

On the opposite side of the main valley, half-way up a small tributary glen, there was a little farm called " Furness " or " Furnace." By this name it had been known from time immemorial, few people suspecting the reason why. Much of the site is now covered by the Ramsden reservoir of the Rochdale Corporation Waterworks. During the early eighties of the last century the works were constructed and it was at this time that conclusive evidence of iron-working at the place during some former period was revealed. The

---

[1] Manchester Geological Society, Vol. XV. (pp. 261 seqq.).

usual kind of spoil-heap was found, and in addition several large lumps of cast iron were discovered. On a wall in the locality was also picked up a mass weighing a dozen pounds or more of highly ferruginous matter. Its precise nature has never been definitely determined ; but several people, judging from external appearances, are of opinion that it is a piece of chain-armour which had been rolled up, thrown aside and forgotten, until corrosion has converted the whole into a solid mass. Assuming this explanation to be the correct one, the object may or may not be connected with the iron-works, but its presence at that place is certainly a remarkable coincidence. It may also be noted that the site of the disused works is near two old pack-horse roads connecting Yorkshire with South-east Lancashire. The Waterstalls bloomery furthermore is not far from the ancient road between Sowerby and the same parts of Lancashire. Just as this goes to press Mr. M. Barr has shown me at a lower point in the same valley what may be the remains of another bloomery. At present the evidence is not sufficient to warrant a definite statement.

Mr. Aitkin mentioned several others in this part of Walsden, and if his assertions are well founded, there must have been half-a-dozen within a couple of miles and another not much further away. It is to be noted, however, that the present writer has searched for these furnaces without success so far, except that in one case there certainly does exist behind Birks House some slag with an oak-tree growing over it. Undoubted evidence of charcoal hearths, however, has been found and this may have misled Mr. Aitkin and his friends. Charcoal would indeed be required for working the iron, but it was also largely used in the neighbourhood by wool-combers, until some distance into the last century. A little more than a mile northwards on the same hillside as Ramsden Clough is the Dulesgate Valley. Several eye-witnesses have reported a bloomery high up above the Gorpley reservoir : but the making of the waterworks appears to have destroyed all traces of it. Not far from here is the one at Saunderclough mentioned by Mr. Kerr, who will be quoted below. Then on the south side of the main valley, high upon Langfield

Edge, where it overlooks Mankinholes, are the puny remains of Jackson's Rock. Near by are quantities of the slag, which may be in all cases more accurately described as imperfectly worked iron. An analysis of this and others will be given in due course.

Passing down the main valley about two-and-a-half miles, we find on opposite sides of it in Beaumont Clough and Rattonstall Wood respectively, two other bloomeries. Both of these are situated at the altitude of several hundred feet less than most, if not all, of the others in the district of Upper Calderdale. Rattonstall Wood occupies the steep insecure slope below the official headquarters of the ancient Manor of Rattonstall. This circumstance suggests that the iron-making at this spot may have been associated with the manorial privileges. Beaumont Clough is in sight of the manorial offices. No exhaustive examination has been made in these cases, but the slag to be found at each place puts the fact beyond a doubt. Higher up the hills above Callis Wood through which Beaumont Clough runs, is a farm called Kilnshaw. Whether this has any connection with the activities of the bloomery or not, there is no evidence to show ; but both are within Erringden, which ranked as a Royal Deer Park from the twelfth to the sixteenth centuries, and is part of the old township and forest of Sowerby. Another coincidence is that from the Halifax *wills*, several times referred to previously, we learn that as early as the first half of the sixteenth century, we have mention of a " George Fornesse " in an Erringden document. Both of these facts, the place-name and the family-name, may or may not be connected with the iron-smelting, which once took place in the locality. The point is one upon which we cannot dogmatise ; but the possibilities that arise out of the coincidence can scarcely be entirely overlooked.

Passing still further down the Calder Valley at another mile-and-a-half the Hebden Valley branches off to the north. Along here are certainly the remains of two, or more probably three, ancient furnaces ; one of them situated at a place known by the suggestive name of Smithycliffe. More detailed particulars of these bloomeries are given in a paper read by the author before the Halifax Antiquarian Society on September 7th, 1918. It should also be noticed that near most of these derelict furnaces are to be found remains of charcoal burning places. We cannot, however, infer much from this, as some have tried to do, as sources of fuel for the furnaces. The fact might be of more weight, if no other use could be assigned for the charcoal. But in this locality, where, as we have already seen, an extensive woollen cloth industry was carried on continuously from the thirteenth to the nineteenth centuries, we find an all-sufficient reason for the charcoal hearths which are to be found, not only near some of the bloomeries, but in considerable numbers all around. Each individual wool-comber's consumption of the fuel would be small in comparison with the charge required by an iron furnace : but then these consumers were much more numerous, and their operations continued over a longer period. Moreover, when we come to the documentary evidence which will be adduced later, it will be seen that there is room for doubt whether in the earlier times charcoal was used exclusively for fuel in the iron-working operations.

OTHER REMAINS OF EARLY IRON MANUFACTURE IN THE NORTHERN HILL COUNTRY.

Saddleworth is another of those high moorland districts whose situation has hidden it from the sight of the historical inquirer. There is not wanting reason to think that much of what has been said in preceding pages relating to the woollen industry of Halifax parish and other upland districts applies also to these upper recesses of the Yorkshire Colne Valley. Other associations of Saddleworth with Rochdale in Lancashire—i.e. ecclesiastical—suggest that its textile and other trading operations may have taken that direction, rather than that of the Yorkshire centres, a fact which may account for the rare mention of it in West Riding documents. But we are at present concerned with the iron trade. Mr. Ammon Wrigley [1] gives particulars of several bloomeries that occur in that district, most of which he has personally investigated. He speaks of several bloomeries at " Cudworth, South Clough and Far Owlers," and makes passing allusion to some others. The " Old bloomery Furnace, Cudworth near Castleshaw," is of special interest because it retains the low ring of rough stones which constituted the principal structural part of the furnace. This feature is very rare indeed amongst the various bloomeries known. Another interesting point which he mentions is that " the bloomery remains in Diggle have long been known to the dales-folk by the name of Cinderhills." This is a place-name which occurs elsewhere, one being about midway between the Walsden bloomeries descibed above and the next example further down the Calder Valley ; that is, at Cinderhill on the Stansfield hillside about a mile below the centre of Todmorden, and within half a mile of the home of the important Stansfield family already noticed. Nothing is known, however, of any remains having ever been found there, which may in any way be connected with the origin of the name. The place is, however, situated in the midst of one of the early seats of both the pastoral and the textile industry. There is too, one, or it may be more, Cinderhills in the neighbourhood of Halifax. In the cases known to the writer nothing further can be said as to their association with iron-smelting ; but the situations and names, taken together are somewhat suggestive.

CHEMICAL ANALYSIS OF THE " SLAGS."

In all these cases the extraction of the iron was very imperfectly done, as the following analysis will show :—

CUDWORTH.

Silica	..	..	29.70%
Alumina ..	..	..	11.90%
Iron Oxide	..	..	52.60%
Manganese Oxide		..	3.84%

[1] *Songs of a Moorland Parish,* 1912 (pp. 163-177).

Lime	..	..	..	1.98%
Magnesia	..	..	..	nil.
Phosphorus		..	..	.130%
Sulphur	..	..	..	traces.

Such is the analysis as given by Mr. Wrigley.[1] He also mentions two other analyses which gave 37 and 46 per cent. of iron respectively.

Of the slags in upper Calderdale the following analyses have been given, namely, Mr. Snoxell (Halifax) provided the following :—

Analyses of slags from bloomeries at

	Jackson s Rock	Water- stalls	Beaumont Clough	Hardcastle Crags
Silica	.. 20.70%	16%	10%	32.4%
*Phosphoric Acid	.. 1.08%			
Oxide of Manganese	.. 1.55%	2.8%	10.2%	2.00%
§Ferric Oxide ..	.. 74.25%	80.0%	78.6%	64.4%
Alumina.. ..	.. 2.42%	—	—	—
Lime	.. traces	1.2%	1.2%	1.2%

*Equals Phosphorus .47%.   §Iron 52%

Mr. T. Stenhouse, F.I.C., F.C.S., also made an analysis of a specimen from Jackson's Rock, which confirms the above.

As is the case elsewhere, the iron-stone itself is extremely rare in the immediate vicinity of the iron-works themselves ; but in the neighbourhood of the one at Cudworth a few small fragments of hæmatite ore have been found, which leads Mr. Wrigley to suggest Barrow-in-Furness as the source. In the absence of local knowledge on the present writer's own part and with all due respect to the above-named gentleman's very high qualifications to speak on this local topic, though his conclusion cannot be denied, the very great distance seems to make the suggestion almost incredible.

The complete interpretation of the analyses just submitted, and any light which they may throw upon the

[1] *Songs of a Moorland Parish* (p. 175).

problem of the sources of the ore used at the respective places, are matters more for those experts who have made a special study of the metallurgy of iron. Unfortunately Captain Aitkin does not give the full particulars of an analysis which he had made for him of the Waterstalls " slag." He does, however, give us one important item, which declares that " the iron-stone is a carbonate of iron and contains 39.2% of metallic iron." He is also surprised to find that the iron component in the slag exceeds that in the raw iron-stone from Ruddle Scout, by 1.8%. This total of 41% is somewhat less than that revealed by the foregoing analyses. It would seem, however, in the light of facts about to be given, that the surprise is rather in the opposite way to that which struck Captain Aitkin, in that, the ore having been subjected to two heatings, so little purification should have been effected. We are also told by Aitkin that the first operation, that of roasting the ore, was effected at the mouth of the Ruddle Scout mine. This simple process, and to a greater extent the heating in the rude smelting furnace, must have resulted in the driving off of much of the impurities in a gaseous form, the percentage of the iron contained in the mass all the while increasing. The primitive method of recovering the iron is generally believed to have consisted in heating the iron-stone, until it assumed a pasty character, and then beating out the iron ; or would it be more correct to say, by beating out the remaining impurities from what had by heating been converted into a mass of impure iron ? Or may it be said that what we find left behind at the bloomery sites was that portion of the partly purified mass, in which the reduction has not been satisfactorily accomplished ? In the earlier times at any rate, sufficient heat could not be generated to reduce the metal to a fluid state.

So far as a non-expert may be able to judge, there is nothing in the analyses given above, which is inconsistent with the use of a carbonaceous clay iron-stone, unless it be the rather considerable differences shown in the quantity of silica, and the greater amount of iron shown by all other than the Waterstalls sample as noted by Mr. Aitkin. Possibly in those cases we may have indications of a richer ore brought from some distance. We may reasonably expect some differences to be shown by samples of " slag " from different sites and even from the same place, as evidenced by the two Waterstalls results furnished by Captain Aitkin and Mr. Snoxell. Nothing else could be expected, when we consider the crude methods of the early workers, and make some allowance for improved skill, as time advanced ; for we have no proof that all the places named were in operation at the same time. There may also have been differences owing to the varying skill of the operators, and other conditions at identical times. Further, something in these variations may be accounted for by the different conditions to which the slags have been subjected during the subsequent centuries of their exposure to natural agencies. The Jackson's Rock site, for instance would be exposed to the wash of water draining a great area of peat, Waterstall would fare similarly though to a less extent, whilst the others would be largely free from this influence. Again the same two are each situated on the crest of a hill, where they are quite open and exposed to sun, wind and rain ; the other two have always been rather sheltered by the trees and profuse vegetation which surround them in their valley retreats.

This is the place perhaps to drive home one other point. The general question of the date when these crude methods of producing metallic iron were in operation at the places named, will be dealt with later. In the case of Cudworth, however, its situation within a mile or two of the Roman station at Castleshaw has given some apparent force to the usual habit of ascribing all such works—*i.e.* roads, manufactories and objects in general for which there does not appear to be an obvious and simple explanation at hand, to the Romans. If the imperial representatives at Castleshaw were engaged in making iron, a particularly unlikely event, seeing that they were in constant communication with much more suitable sources, there is no obvious reason why they should have carried the ore upwards to a place so far away from their own station. For this and other reasons

Mr. Wrigley concludes that the bloomeries of his locality are not of the Roman age ; a conclusion which the present writer would apply to all the works herein mentioned.

SOME FURTHER EXAMPLES OF PRIMITIVE IRONWORKS.

Mr. L. C. Miall [1] tells of a number of these primitive furnaces in the West Riding, with which he is personally acquainted. He names " Low Moor, in various parts of Hunsworth Wood, at Horsforth, in the neighbourhood of Barnsley (Worsboro' Dale), between Pately Bridge and Middlesmoor, and on the hillside near Holden Gill, about two miles from Steeton, I am further informed that they are known in the neighbourhood of Sheffield, Huddersfield and Wakefield." Some of these are approaching the kingdom to which the purview of the academic writer has extended, and may be included within his estimate of the extent of the mediæval and renaissance industry. Most of them, however, are beyond that range.

On the western side of the Pennine axis other remains are to be found which supplement those already given. In the Cliviger gorge between the West Riding and North-east Lancashire, near Holme, just past the apex of the anticline, is a farm-house known as Furness. Not far away within living memory, was a place where the coarse red pottery used for the larger dairy and kitchen utensils, was made. From this circumstance it has been inferred that the name was derived. But for all that, although, so far as the present writer is aware, no actual remains have ever been found near the place, possibly because they have never been sought for, there are what seem to be powerful reasons for believing that iron-working is the source from which the name has come. The place is not a mile distant from Ruddle Scout, where there is an ancient disused iron mine to be referred to later. The bareness of the district from timber, which is generally admitted to have been the case before the time of Dr. Whitaker the historian whose home was close by, may

[1] Ancient Bloomeries in Yorkshire.

217

reasonably be presumed to be the result of, or at least to have been helped by some such industry, which would consume very large quantities. It does seem certain that much of the ore was roasted just outside of the entrance to the mine. The name *Furness* itself, as we have seen, both locally and in at least one more widely known district is unquestionably associated with this industry in early times. Again there are in the neighbourhood two other places, where the same kind of earthenware was baked ; one of them singularly enough is only a few hundred yards away from the Walsden *Furness* already noted (p. 209). In both of these two latter cases the presence of the earthenware has fixed the name of " Pot Ovens " upon the spot. The word " furnace " except as applied to the modern blast furnace and as a place-name as indicated above, has no part in the local folk-speech.

Of bloomeries in the Forest of Rossendale, Mr. C. W. Partington [1] gives the following summary, while they have been treated of more in detail by the late James Kerr. " The chief furnaces were at (1) Cinder Hill, Redbrook, on the north-west side of Holcombe Hill, two miles from Rams-bottom and a like distance from Summerseat. (2) Priest Booth, three miles from Bacup, on the Todmorden Road, known as Saunderclough, from Cinder the name given by the peasantry to the scoriæ. (3) Smithy Croft, Rakehead, near Stacksteads. Smithy is the name still associated with the sites of old bloomeries in Coniston and Furness, which we also call *bloomsmithies.*" " These bloomeries were situated in wooded districts . . . . . It was less difficult to bring the compact ore from a distance than to transport for many miles a large quantity of bulky and cumbersome fuel, at a period when both had to be carried on the backs of pack-horses."

PROBABLE TIME WHEN THESE WORKS WERE IN OPERATION, AND SOURCES OF THE ORE.

As to fixing a date. when these blown-out furnaces were at work, there is not much evidence which will enable us

[1] *Manchester City News*, Agust, 5, 1916.

to speak with anything like certainty.   It has already been
observed (pp. 208-209), that in most cases little direct
association can be traced between most of the furnace remains
referred to above and the documentary allusions to be submitted later.   Most of the bloomeries already noted are on
the eastern side of the Pennines, while nearly all of the written
references relate to the western slope, though high up and
often near the top.   Before pursuing this phase of the subject
further, it may be useful to say something about the probable
sources of the ores used.   It is quite probable that in the case
of a few which are far removed from the principal known
iron-stone bands, local supplies which would never be considered as practicable in the modern era, were drawn upon.
Ruddle Scout already noted is a case in point.   The galleries
are over four feet in height, yet the several bands of clay
iron-stone nodules do not exceed a total thickness of six and
a half inches.   Considering the great value of the metal
when extracted, the convenience for fuel, and the cost and
difficulites of transport if the better and more distant supplies
were called upon, sparse and inferior local supplies would
offer compensating advantages.   Mr. Wrigley's opinion
respecting the origin of the material used in the Saddleworth
area has already been given (p. 214), and Mr. Partington
says, " The best quality of iron was produced in Furness, and
that district would therefore be supplied from thence.   That
this iron ore was smelted in Rossendale is proved by the
evidence of the red ore scoriæ from the old bloomeries, which
is found on comparison to be identical with that found on
the sites of Rossendale.   The richness of its ore, the character
and smallness of its bulk would also account for its use.
The yield of iron from the Furness ore would be at least
double that from the clay iron-stone of Yorkshire."   If the
use of the Furness ore be admitted, it proportionately increases
the magnitude of the industry in those districts whose remains
have been described above.   In some cases, e.g. Holden
Gill,[1] possibly Furness in Walsden, and certainly at Furnace
in Cliviger, if the foregoing contention (pp. 217-218) be

[1] L. C. Miall, *Ancient Bloomeries of Yorkshire.*

granted, the raw material was of home production. The Walsden workers may have got ore from the Coal Measures in the upper part of the Ramsden Valley : but do not seem to have left any surviving traces of such workings. There is a further possibility that the Lower Coal Measures, which crop out above Halifax, might also be drawn upon by the workers in iron in that district, and for some miles up Calderdale.

There is, however, one certain source of ore which was within a few miles of the bloomeries in the upper part of Calderdale, Rossendale, and which, as we shall see later from the De Lacy records, also sent supplies to the Clitheroe district. Captain Aitkin [1] explored and described this ancient mine, which had been worked on an extensive scale at a very remote period, and from whence a large quantity of ore must have been extracted ; for the date at which it was used is so distant that its entrances had become completely blocked up and concealed from view, and its very existence almost forgotten in the neighbourhood. " The situation of the mine is in Cliviger Valley (a deep rocky gorge . . . . . close to the summit, where the twin rivers Calder take their rise) in a steep escarpment, on the north-easterly side of the valley, known as Ruddle Scout."

" The workings . . . . consisting of a series of long drifts or chambers driven into the side of the hill, from whence other workings were set off . . . . large spoil-heaps opposite the several entrances . . . . . the furthest point reached being upwards of three hundred feet from the entrance, when further progress was arrested by standing water in one direction, and by a fall of roof in another." The height of the chambers is given at four feet one-and-a-half inches, and " the aggregate thickness of iron-stone only reached about six-and-a-half inches." The same De Lacy records which mention Cliviger iron ore also mention coal from the same locality. Mr. Aitkin calls attention to a bed of coal over the

[1] On the Discovery of an Ancient Iron Mine in Cliviger. Manchester Geological Society, Vol. XVI.

mine just described, which being near the surface has been at some time brought out by shallow surface sinkings. " Immediately overlying the coal is a bed of grey shale five feet in thickness, having a number of bands of ironstone running through it . . . . . If the coal were raised at the same time that the iron mining operations were being conducted, doubtless the iron-stone balls contained in the roof shale would be utilised, and that they were so is rendered probable from the fact that they appear now to be absent from the old spoil-heaps. If this assumption be correct, the aggregate quanity of iron-stone would receive a sensible increase." " It would appear, however, from the large accumulations of burnt shale of a brick-red colour, together with pieces of roasted ore which occur in close contiguity to the mine . . . . that the iron was calcined before removal—the body of burnt shale having been so considerable as to have given a character to the top of the escarpment so marked as to have earned for it the name of Ruddle Scout." To the foregoing the following footnote has been added :—" *Rud* being the Saxon for red, Ruddle being applied to red earth coloured with oxide of iron, and *Scout* being the Norman for a high rock."

Captain Aitkin's conclusion seems perfectly sound as to the main source of the ore which supplied many of the surrounding early iron-works. There is, however, one other source from which a supplementary supply may have been obtained ; " that [1] is the Glacial Drift of those districts where the ice in its journey had flowed over and beyond the outcrop of the Coal Measures and their accompanying iron-stone bands. Seldom would the ore be so thickly strewn in the drift as to make it worth being sought after alone. Yet . . . . . Ruddle Scout shows that the material sought must have been highly valued. There are places not many miles distant from the same spot, where Glacial Drift was worked by turning over and sorting for other purposes. In some of the valleys which creep up to the higher parts of the western slope of the Pennines, such as Shedden,

[1] Halifax Antiquarian Society, Proceedings, September, 1918 (p. 108).

Cantclough, Thorndean, Thursden, Wycoller Dean and others, an extensive system of sorting out the lime-stone was carried on during former times. It was burnt and made into quick-lime for building and agricultural purposes. Some of it also might be used as a flux for the iron-stone. In the same Drift is scattered a quantity of the clay iron-stone derived from the lower coal measures of the westerly portion of the neighbourhood. It is not altogether unreasonable to suggest that while the workers were sorting out limestone, and knowing the value of the iron-stone, it would be worth while keeping an eye open for the ore. Whether any was derived from the eastward . . . . I do not know, but seeing that the lower coal measures crop out again about Halifax it looks to me possible that there may be iron-stone bands in that locality."

It may also be useful to place upon record the fact, that in the immediate neighbourhood of the Waterstalls bloomeries there is a number of powerful springs of water, which on flowing over the surface deposit a brownish yellow substance. Mr. Philip Cockcroft, B.A., has shown his interest in such matters by kindly furnishing me with an analysis of the material. He writes thus :—" The ore contains 40.36% of metallic iron. I found no traces of phosphorus in the ore and only slight traces of sulphur." This shows an iron content of 1.17% higher than that of the clay iron-stone given above (p. 215). Whether its general condition as found, in the form of a fine powder is such that the material could be utilised by the early workers in iron is a matter which must be left to others to decide ; as also the point as to whether the streams had at that time flowed so long that there had accumulated a store sufficient to attract these old-time *entrepreneurs.*

The consideration of the problem of fixing an approximate date for the life of these furnaces may now be resumed. Of course in the complete absence of guiding testimony they might be fixed anywhere between primitive times and the seventeenth or eighteenth centuries, when the more modern

222

methods of working began to be developed. The materials
which indicate the existence of these bloomeries are of a very
durable nature, even though they are generally near the
surface. Except a few which are on a loose and steep hillside, when rolling fragments from above have accumulated
upon the little original flat surface, there is usually only a
layer of turf and a few inches of soil, seldom as much as a
foot covering the scoriæ, etc. Thus they are exposed to both
the mechanical and chemical disintegration of the atmosphere
and sometimes of adjoining streams. There is a remarkable
absence of traditional or legendary lore relating to them and
the conviction can hardly be escaped that if they had been
worked in the latter stages of the primitive system, some
memories would have lingered in connection with some of
them.   Mr. Wrigley's statement [1] that " no reference to
Saddleworth bloomery occurs in our local rolls," might be
applied to any of those described above.   As it frequently
happens that references are made in the *old wills* and *Parish
Registers* to the trade or calling of the parties concerned, a
total absence of any allusion therein to the industry, whether
direct or indirect, is equally remarkable.

This is all negative testimony, but as far as it goes
would appear to suggest the sixteenth century, when these
documents became numerous, as the period beyond which their
date must be placed.   This applies particularly to those
within the area of Halifax parish.   Of those within the
Lancashire border, where we know little of the contents of
the *wills* it is interesting to note that one of the extensively
worked bloomeries—that at Waterstalls, Walsden—is close by,
in fact part of, Bottomley.   Of the few Lancashire testaments
which have emerged from the general obscurity, there are
those of the Fieldens, a family which for centuries was located
at Bottomley.   Besides this are numerous allusions both to
this family and others of the district in the Rochdale parish
Records, as well as such fragments of the *Court Rolls
Subsidies, Surveys,* etc., as have been published.   Yet in

[1] *Songs of a Moorland Parish* (p. 165).

none of them is there the faintest hint of connection with, or knowledge of, the industry, of which the remains already described prove conclusively did at one time exist there.

Mr. Miall [1] is of opinion that many of the Yorkshire bloomeries " do not date back much beyond the Civil War. Up to the time of Elizabeth the iron trade was quite insignificant. During her reign the foundries of Sussex and Gloucestershire rose into importance, but we find no mention of Yorkshire. The West Riding, especially the iron district, was then thinly populated and possessed few facilities for manufacture and commerce." Here again comes out the dominating academic philosophy of history based solely, as has already been urged more than once, upon the accidents of official records and the prejudices of the dominant classes, accepted entirely and without question by one of the most distinguished of local students. Preceding pages at least show, that the local history of the area with which we are at present especially concerned, must be sought in other directions than those in which general historians have hitherto been content to roam, when the evidence thus acquired will modify our conclusions upon the general industrial development of the nation. But for all that has been quoted from him Mr. Miall [2] is still in a position to tell us that " Thoresby states that bloomeries existed at Kirkby Overblow, and the papers of the Wentworth family include a contract for supplying wood and iron *blomes* at Kirkshill, near Otley in the 14th century." The first mentioned of these places is an example of an early industry having determined its name, *Ore-blowers* having undergone " cultured " corruption into its present form.

With regard to the Saddleworth bloomeries, [3] Mr. Wrigley holds the opinion that " Old local slag-mounds are, I believe, due to an old industrial system which, during the sixteenth, seventeenth and eighteenth centuries was driven

[1] C. Miall, *Ancient Bloomeries of Yorkshire.*
[2] *Ancient Bloomeries of Yorkshire.* [3] *Songs of a Moorland Parish* (p. 174).

by prohibitive enactments into our isolated moorland hollows."
This seems to be nothing more than an inference drawn
from the well-known fact that in order to insure a supply of
timber for ship-building, smelting in the customary areas of
academic historians was forbidden.   One cannot help
wondering how the problem would have been viewed in the
absence of this convenient fact.   [1] The same writer affirms :—
" The atiquary Leland writing of Blackley about 1550 says,
' For lack of woods the blow shoppes decay there '."   Thus
it appears that the industry existed in the district to the north
of Manchester before the middle of the sixteenth century, and
that it had prevailed either over so long a period or on such a
large scale, that the fuel supply was nearing exhaustion.
Surely we may infer that the beginning of such work at that
place had been largely determined by the prospect of an
abundant supply of fuel, and a demand for the product.
It may also be fairly concluded that the restrictions upon
iron-working would have little effect outside of those areas
which were accessible for timber to the sea.   The northern
uplands have never grown much timber suitable for the
construction of " the wooden walls of old England," even if
we could admit its accessibility when grown to the places
where it would be employed for ship-building.   Moreover,
there does not appear to be a great probability that the limitation of iron-working—say, in Sussex or Gloucestershire
would materially affect the production of these remote places.
The growing textile industries and increasing population,
such as have been demonstrated in the previous pages, might
rather be expected to have given all along an impetus to the
production of iron and steel for the tools used in cloth-making
and for the implements of agriculture.

The furnaces of Sussex. Staffordshire and other
iron-stone bearing districts, continued to operate, though
probably limited by legislative enactments, and certainly
by lack of fuel in those districts which were within the reach
of the ship-building centres, until the newer methods settled
the difficulty with respect to fuel in the coal areas, and at the

[1] *Songs of a Moorland Parish* (p. 174).

same time killed the industry in others. This limitation of supplies from these districts which have received acknowledgment from the ordinary historian, was probably largely made up for by increased importation of foreign material, as well as from the more remote historical outlands ; and the quantities imported during this period may have tended to mislead students as to the extent of previous dependence upon outside sources. The vast majority of the manors, the farming accounts of which have hitherto been drawn upon for materials in compiling the Industrial History of England are situated outside of the iron-bearing districts ; these in their turn, with the exception of Kent and Sussex, are outside of the area which has come within the purview of academic writers. The necessary supplies of iron for the operations of husbandry and manufactures were perforce obtained from the great fairs and market-towns of the recognised area. Thus the iron obtained from these sources is the only supply which has come within the knowledge of these inquirers, and has therefore come to be recognised as the only supply available. Other supplies were as unknown as the districts from which' they emanated. One cannot help wondering whether the prejudices of early scribes, officials and owners, with their continental sympathies, as suggested later (pp. 240-241), in relation to English made cloth, extended to other native products, is reflected in their treatment of iron, and may have resulted in the palming off of some of that material as foreign, which was really native in origin.

Mr. Partington says [1] :—" as Rossendale was disforested in the reigns of Henry VII and VIII about the year 1500, at which time it contained a considerable extent of cultivated and pasture land, it seems likely that in the course of the next 100 years until 1600 the necessary wood for charcoal fuel would have become so diminished in quantity that this process of iron smelting could not have been profitably carried on much beyond that period." Unfortunately for us, the seventeenth century is the time when *Wills, Court*

[1] *Manchester City News*, August, 5th, 1916.

Rolls, and similar documents begin to fail us. Nay even where publication has been effected, they drop off about this time. There remains, however, the partial compensation that deeds relating to landed property often cover the blank, as do more or less completely the imperfect records of local public bodies, such as parish and township authorities, Quarter Sessions, and so forth. But so far as these documents have come under the eye of students and inquirers, there is very little, if any, matter at all pertaining to the subject before us. On the other hand it is to be borne in mind that we are now close upon, in fact actually within, the era of the great improvement brought about by the utilisation of pit coal as a fuel for smelting. Such localities as we have been specially concerned with, where the ore had to be fetched from comparatively long distances by primitive methods of transit, would first feel the effects of the competition achieved by greatly improved methods and increased means of production. The probable scarcity of fuel in Rossendale has already been alluded to as a reason for giving up the smelting of iron. The same consideration applies to some other localities where the remains of bloomeries exist. The principal one in upper Calderdale, Waterstalls, is surrounded by lean and barren slopes almost oppressive in their bare monotony. Others lower down the valley are on ground such as no one would ever attempt to cultivate, even as a permanent pasture, and have been left free to natural growth. In some cases where trees are present, there is reason to believe that most of the existing ones have been artificially planted. It would be a difficult task to find a single one in the neighbourhood of the slag-heaps, the life of which would cover a century. Before proceeding to give the documentary evidence which may have some bearing upon the age of these bloomery remains, it may be stated that the finding of cast iron at Ramsden in Walsden fixes the time when that one at least was in operation as subsequent to the discovery of that convenient form of iron, whenever that may have been. " It is . . . . . on record that a cast iron slab exists in Burwash Church, Sussex, belonging to the 14th century[1]."

Some of the available records may now be drawn upon for extracts relating to this industry. The following are from the *De Lacy Records* :—

	£	s.	d.
" Haslindene[2]. A forge for iron farmed out in Roscyndale	3	0	0"
N.B.—Compare this with " Rent of the Mill " ..		13	4
" Hoddesdene, old brushwood for a forge for 13 weeks		13	0
Akerington, brushwood and ore sold to a forge there for 27 weeks	1	14	0
Tottington, firewood sold for a forge for 16 weeks	1	16	6
Halton, Rent of Gilbert the Smith for a plot of waste at the forge, this year being the first ..		1	6
Clivachre, iron sold for 10 weeks		6	6
Sea Coal sold there			3
Cliderhowe, a plot for a forge under the Castle, this year being the first		1	0
Penhulton[3], the profit of the Iron Mine of Weal and the Woods raised and yearly sold in the the said Forests		ix	iiij "

Then in a more southerly portion of the same county borderland and nearly the same date it is stated :—[4] " A very interesting case was brought up at the York Assizes on 1st July, 1338, which proves not only that the inhabitants of this district knew that some of the shales overlying the coal measures contained iron ore, but that they actually smelted it on the spot ; and to this period may be attributed some of the ' bloomeries ' which are known to have been worked in the neighbourhood." From the preserved report of the case the author gives the following :—" John, son of

---

[1] Captain Aitkin, above. [2] Two " *Compoti* " of the Lancashire and Cheshire Manors of Henry de Lacy, Earl of Lincoln, XXIV and XXV, Edward I, Chetham Society, Vol. CXII (pp. 168, 142, 173, 188). [3] De Lacy Inquisition of 1311, Chetham Society, Vol. LXXIV. [4] Colonel Fishwicke, *History of the Parish of Rochdale* (p. 84).

Adam de Bukeleigh, William and Geoffrey, brothers of the said John are attached to answer to the Abbot of Whalley why with force and arms they took and carried away the goods and chattels of the said Abbot at Whyteworth, to the value of 100 shillings . . . to wit, three hundred pieces of iron (*pecias ferrie*), cloths-woolen and linens, whereby he is damaged to the amount of £20.

"The said William denies having done this. John and Geoffrey declare that they are not culpable in this matter . . . . . they say that the said John is Lord of the thirtieth part of the town of Whyteworth, that Geoffrey is Lord of the other thirtieth part of the town, and that the said Abbots and others are Lords of the residue of the said town, and that the Abbot, likewise John and Geoffrey, in the waste of the said town were wont to dig at an iron mine, and smelted from the mine aforesaid up to the iron." (The above references to cloth are of interest in connection with what has been said previously (pp. 208-210) with regard to the textile trades in Rochdale and the surrounding districts).

Again, "[1] In 1586 William Hallowes, a cutler, was settled in Rochdale and carried on his business. More than twenty years before this (in 1561) John Ashworth of Greene had a house in the northern end of Brandwood, and was described as a cutler, as was also his son. Near to Greene is a place still known as Cutler's Green, and tradition says that these Ashworths came from Sheffield in the fifteenth century. One of this family some fifteen years ago (he being then nearly eighty years of age) related that he well remembered the large amount of scoriæ to be found in the neighbourhood where the ancient ' bloomery ' was supposed to have been at work." The above William Hallowes would appear to have been a man of some substance, as he was [2] " sent to the Duchy Court with a petition of enquiry as to whether Shore Moor in Spotland was equally divided."

At the very beginning of the fouteenth century there was a forge at Rastrick near Halifax, for we have the record :—

[1] Ibid. (pp. 43-44).   [2] Fishwicke, *Rochdale* (p. 84).

[1] " The forge at Rastrick now lies waste which used to pay yearly 6d." Possibly this disuse came about through its nearness to the more plentiful supplies of Low Moor. The development of the industry at this more favourably placed centre, allied with specialisation and greater freedom of intercourse between the peoples of different localities might easily be responsible for those peoples drawing their supplies from that quarter. Again, under the heading of *Sowerby* two historians [2] give us the following information :—" There is in the forest an iron forge which may continue for ever, worth £9 12s. 0d. yearly." This extract would seem to indicate that the industry was of some magnitude. These quotations cannot be said to be associated definitely with the remains previously described, except in a very limited degree. Cliviger was supplying iron ore to Clitheroe on or before the close of the thirteenth century, and possibly Rossendale and some other places. They do, however, clearly prove that on both sides of the Pennine region iron was being extracted from the ore as early as the latter part of the same century. The Ramsden Clough (Walsden) case shows us that, whether working later or earlier, activity was there being displayed after the discovery of the making of cast iron, of which we have no evidence prior to the fifteenth century. But as to when the various sites described above were the scenes of active operations, there is little evidence available to help us to a positive conclusion. There appears to be no evidence, either documentary or otherwise later than the sixteenth century. The absence of later testimony, however, cannot be said to have more than a negative value. The whole result of our inquiry leaves us unable to make a definite pronouncement further than to say, that before that date iron smelting was far from being unknown in these upland regions in the earlier centuries.

[1] Extent (or Survey) of the Graveships of Rastrick, etc., 1319, Halifax Antiquarian Society (p. 17). [2] *Domesday Book of the Manor of Wakefield*, made in 1364, quoted in Watson's *History of Halifax*, also in Crabtree's *History of Halifax* (p. 408).

MEDIÆVAL LEAD WORKING.

The smelting of lead is not directly connected with the present subject ; but its association with the general question of the earlier developments of industry may justify a reference to it at this place.   Being less refractory, its extraction from the ore would be accompanied by fewer difficulties to the primitive workers than would be the case with the harder metal.   The Romans worked the mines of Derbyshire and some other places.

The *De Lacy Records,* already several times cited, contain a number of references to the sale of lead, its conveyance to other places, payment for ore, mining, fuel, etc. Hence it is quite evident that where the material existed our northern mediæval forebears were not unable to take advantage of its possibilities : *e.g.* in the year 1305,

	£	s.	d.
Cliderhowe [1], 2 cart loads and 36 stones of lead sold	18	18	0
Carrying 7 loads of lead from Baxenden to Bradford		12	2

---

[1] Two " *Compoti* " of the Lancashire and Cheshire Manors of the Earl of Lincoln (pp. 9, 183-185), Chetham Society.

CHAPTER XII.

THE INFLUENCE OF FLEMISH AND OTHER IMMIGRANTS UPON ENGLISH INDUSTRIAL DEVELOPMENT.

The Popularly Accepted Theory Relating to Early English Industry.

T has come to be one of the common-places of historical treatises, when dealing with the fourteenth century, to wax eloquent upon the supposed great impetus given to English manufacturing skill as the result of a considerable influx of Flemish craftsmen during that period. Emily Richings in *Chaucer's May Time* has epitomised the long prevailing historical conception of Edward III's commercial policy in relation to the cloth trade, and has incidentally reflected a too common literary facility for gratifying a popular appetite for easily acquired, because conspicuous, material for telling narative. It follows that disproportionately great effects have been credited as having sprung from what were in reality feeble causes, relatively to much greater but obscure ones, which were in fact the decisive operating factors. In the story the King enters the Queen's chamber and is greeted, " Thrice welcome, my Lord and King ; thou dost find me at a task congenial since Flemish weavers, now established at Norwich, entreat our employment of the Court requesting choice to be made of the samples wherewith their cloth is woven." The King replies, " The law hath been framed to compel wearing of cloth from looms of Norwich, and even at Court fur will be forbid save on Royal mantles." The writer goes on, " Edward's knowledge of the Flemish wool-trade was acquired from his Queen under whose protection the little foreign colony settled

232

on English shores.   Merchants were held in growing esteem, foreign traders being given safe-and-sure-conduct, exempting them from frontage, pavage and murages, the mediæval taxes for repairing houses, walls and streets.   Leading merchants entertained kings and princes, offering them costly gifts which gained the honour of ready acceptance."

The marriage of Edward III with Philippa of Hainault we can easily conceive may have stimulated intimacy between the two peoples, and resulted in an abnormal wave of migrations both ways.   The inward movement only would disturb the susceptibilities of native patriotic fervour, and force into prominence both the presence in England—possibly in unusual numbers—of foreigners, while the Queen and the anxiety of her countrymen to make the most of the alliance with England might well excite remark.   The preference now given by the English Court to Flemish craftsmen and dealers would necessarily excite jealousy and fierce opposition from those traders who had previously been accustomed to possession of the Royal ear.   The very station of the parties to these events, the Court and the privileged and organised trade Guilds were instrumental in securing the record of their actions, and the keeping of them in rememberance.   Consequently they have given them a prominence in historical writings which they could not have acquired otherwise.   In such wise can an event which both in itself and it's results is small, by the fortunate position of it's author, be magnified into the grandeur of a great determining factor in history, and a decisive force in national policy.

There was also another force at work helping to emphasise the prominence which has been given to Edward III's sanction to the settlement of Flemish weavers in England. At that time the Renaissance sentiment of sovereignty was being formed throughout Europe in the usual primitive manner, that is, by warlike opposition to " foreigners."   That prejudice had to be overcome, when the Queen wished to favour her countrymen.   The growing sentiment in high quarters could not neglect any opportunity of reflecting

233

itself. Whether students by confining their attention to particular districts and limited sources of information, have not allowed themselves to be misled, is open to doubt. Considering the exclusive spirit of political and social institutions, and the great distrust of " foreigners " at this time, the presence in a town of even a small number of aliens, though under definitely proved royal sanction, may quite easily have aroused a temper, the surviving evidence of which may easily have led to the exaggeration of its significance. The very fact of the presence of rivals, even in small groups here and there, was so far at variance with accepted traditions, that the whole affair must have loomed large in the mind, and excited the jealous imagination of the suspicious natives.

There were also other circumstances which students have failed adequately to realise, namely, that about the middle of the fourteenth century, when the Merchant and Crafts Guilds were in their youthful vigour, synchronised with the wave of immigration ; and that the movement itself elicited disproportionate attention from the fact that immediately these rivals showed their faces, the virile organised forces of both workmen and traders would be up in arms. They would make out what the public opinion of the time regarded as a very strong case for regulation, if royal and political forces were too strong for them, and could not be prevailed upon to prohibit the influx of aliens altogether. The official place put forth on behalf of a friendly reception to the royal *proteges*, that of extending native trade under strict regulations, and consequently the probability of future monopoly conditions, were just such as would be calculated to appeal, if anything could to the prejudices of these exclusive and privileged classes. Chroniclers and all interested in recording public affairs—of which records the annals of Trade Guilds form a considerable proportion of the sources from which students have drawn—moving almost exclusively amongst the classes which were fomenting the opposition, *i.e.* the craftsmen and traders of the towns, could not fail to be influenced by the manifestations of discontent which they saw around them. Add to this, that the finding of state and

Dyeing Supersedes Spinning (p. 254).

Photo. by W. Heard.

local documents relating to these incidents, and of course affecting only these districts to which it has been usual to look as the sole centres of activity and seats of manufactures, to say nothing of general historical movements, together with the prevailing idea amongst historical writers, that home manufactures were rather crude, and a distorted conception of the whole would very easily grow.

Professor Thorold Rogers [1] has put the effects of these migrations in the most definite and extreme form, thus :— " Now the history of Norfolk is peculiarly interesting. It has twice been made the seat of a weaving industry, and on both occasions by immigration from the same race, the Flemings, in the first instance by a kind of voluntary over-flow, in the second by the compulsory exile of the Flemish Calvinists, during the time that Alva's Council of Blood, Granville and Titelmaun were engaged in extirpating or expatriating Protestants." These two makings of any industry and both in the same place, would seem to imply that the locality has some special fitness for the purpose. The first of them has almost universally been credited with developing into a national supremacy. The second episode, however, implied that after a time the first round of prosperity waned, and the trade flitted. Why this should ensue, with a presumably favourable locality, especially skilful craftsmen, and enterprising traders, is a phenomenon which it would be very interesting to have explained. The similar desertion which has been alleged as result of the Industrial Revolution somehow comes into mind.

POLITICAL MOTIVES BEHIND THE KING'S ACTIONS.

What the Plantagenet Kings really did in relation to the Flemish immigrants was probably of a two-fold nature : they sought to allay the discontent of an assertive section of their subjects by giving official sanction and the colour of a desirable thing, to a policy which was trying the temper of the latter ; at the same time they made a political move to gain credit in those parts of the Continent where they

[1] *Industrial and Commercial History of England* (p. 299).

were anxious to cultivate friendly relations and thus secure some advantage to themselves. A shrewd political move may be discerned in the welcome given to the banished artisans from Ghent, Ypres and Bruges after the events in Flanders in the year 1328. War patriotism and the prospects of trade benefits would commend the move to native traders and craftsmen. The generally accepted idea of the social organisation and sentiment which prevailed at the time, as well as the exclusive trade policy attributed to the Guilds, imply the very great difficulty of strangers, and more especially those from a foreign land, settling in, or even approaching the confines of any community, where these authorities had any power or influence. This accepted shibboleth of all the exponents of the English character at this period implies the necessity of effective protection to every single newcomer. Indeed, in view of what has been stated already, and of the deficient force of the central administration—at least as the distance from its source increased—it is difficult to see how immigration and settlement could take place at all, especially in the towns, without strong encouragement and protection, not only from the King, but most important of all from a powerful local authority, all of which circumstances would force into undue prominence the events they related to. As we shall presently see, there was at even an earlier date, a widespread distribution of these aliens, which suggests that favourable local conditions were in the first place the active force which initiated and established the practice over a much more extended area than has been the custom to recognise ; and the later immigrations were but the extension to the privileged towns of a practice which had long been common elsewhere.

These considerations seem to drive to the conclusion that Edward III only gave sanction and regal authority, and possibly turned an existing custom which had long obtained in parts where interested privilege did not intervene, to his political advantage. In fact he simply legalised and turned to his own advantage a well established custom of his principal and most profitable subjects, present or prospective.

At this time the whole policy of the central administration towards traders and industrial centres was directed to make them into sources of royal revenue. The wealth already existing amongst the merchants, and the jealousy which it excited by its power amongst the older aristocracy, implies that there must have been for some time previously an extensive and profitable trade, in which the business capacities of the people had been displayed to advantage. Then again, does not the financial convenience which Edward III was able to make of wool imply that there was great competition for the available supplies? Not simply abroad, but that the possibilities of English consumption were so great that the risk of Flanders ceasing to take it was a neglible contingency ; and that if the effect of export taxes were to be to retain the wool in England, the only result would be to give a fillip to the home cloth-trade, and still be indirectly a profitable source of revenue. May we not find here the greatest service which this King rendered to the already exisiting English cloth-trade by affording means for its further development and striking a shrewd blow at the principal rival? It is also to be noted that it is not until many years after the great plague, when land-holders had sought to relieve their difficulties by converting great areas into sheep-walks, that we hear much of unemployment resulting from that cause in those parts of the country which have been in the habit of largely monopolising the attentions of historians.

If the King and his advisers are to be credited with any knowledge at all of the free industrial activities which have in preceding pages been shown to have existed at the time outside of the areas of the authority of the Guilds, and knowing the then tendency of close neighbouring traders and craftsmen—which these might become—to associate themselves into Guilds, which would very soon pray for a charter, and be prepared to pay for the privilege ; we may reasonably assume that he would see his interest in courting good relations with these scattered groups. The existing Guilds had already secured that end. The encouragement given to these

" pioneers " of the woollen industry has been dilated upon
as a splendid example of the statesmanship and commercial
sagacity of the English King.   The justice of this extreme
laudation may well be doubted.   One thing it does show,
it credits the royal patriot with a very imperfect knowledge
of the industrial capacity of his home dominions, and what
the people whom he took under his regal sway, had been
doing for many years.   If any credit is due to Edward, he
must also take a share of blame for having assisted in placing
on a larger and surer basis pure capitalistic enterprise.   For
certainly most of the foreigners we come across, are possessed
of some amount of wealth, are generally traders rather than
craftsmen, and often employers of numbers of men.   So
far as these settlers did come over here, it implies an already
existing industrial development sufficient to enable them to
prosper at least in an equal degree with the possibilities of
their own native land, which was reputed to be the world's
centre of trade and manufactures.   Exception of course
must always be made for those whose intense conscientious
scruples led to their being driven out by religious persecution,
and other less creditable causes.

FLEMINGS AND OTHER FOREIGNERS IN NORTHERN UPLANDS AT AN EARLY DATE.

The   generally   accepted   account   of   the   Flemish
immigration as given by historical writers, that is, as having
begun on an extensive scale during the reign of Edward,
does not find confirmation from the facts as they appear in
the north-central area of the country, and especially in the
old parish of Halifax.   In so far as the Flemings or other
foreigners did settle in this locality, it is very curious if they
first chose the most remote and uninviting regions of the
country for so doing.   Be it remembered too that at this time
at any rate they were not driven out of their native land, a
fact which may place the whole question in a new light.
Their arrival here was near upon a century before the reputed
invitation, migration and royal protection.   Moreover,

there is a curious absence of evidence of any having come into these parts as a result of Edward's policy. The presence of obvious foreigners in upper Calderdale long before Edward III's time would seem to suggest that the immigration from the Continent of people of some standing in the world may imply that such migration was a more common incident than has generally been supposed ; and that it was only in the more populous centres, where the organisation of traders and others had developed into strong and exclusive monopolies, that a voice sufficiently loud to be heard, could be raised and made effective in those high quarters, which have always held a disproportionate hold of scholars and inquirers.

Most of the names we find in the records, are probably of persons whose rank was above the common people ; else there would be little chance of their appearing there. The common and unorganised people especially in remote places, have always had the deaf ear turned to them. Moreover, it cannot by any stretch of the imagination or respect for a hoary tradition, be allowed that the mission of the immigrants was solely or even mainly, one of instructing the incompetent natives in a craft of which they had imperfect knowledge or only a clumsy facility. Some of those we find in the Calder Valley so early as the thirteenth century were almost certainly less industrial pioneers than military and agrarian adventurers, or the descendants of such. Their (perhaps necessary) association with the local governing class suggests that some were of the two last-named types. In other districts, where names of persons with a Flemish flavour have been found in the records of the fourteenth century, and in obedience to the accepted tradition have been gratuitously associated with the cloth trade, it would be interesting to have an investigation of the records of the previous century with a view of ascertaining whether Flemish or other foreign names occur. Of others it is difficult to say definitely to which class they primarily belonged, whether mere adventurers or craftsmen and traders, as it has previously been shown that there was here at that time some amount of cloth-working going on. But bearing mind what has been said previously (Chapter II and

IV) respecting the physcial features of the locality and the temperament of the people, it is very difficult to believe that they came so far into such a district to introduce the textile or any other craft. The very most that can be allowed is, that prospects were so good as to tempt a few hardy and courageous individuals to take advantage of possibilities already existing ; possibly some may have been associated with both trade and military, agrarian, or official interests. These and some others, particulars of whom will be given later, make it worthy of note that the mere presence of Flemish names in any given locality at any time subsequent to the fourteenth century, does not establish their bearers as descendants of England's reputed textile pioneers.

There is another point. Too much may very easily be made of the alleged practice of the better kinds of cloth at this time having to be brought here from abroad, before these foreign experts had diffused amongst English workers their secrets and skill. Perhaps we see here nothing more than the English manifestation of a generally prevailing idea amongst certain of the people in many countries, that a product of a foreign land, merely because it was different from native products, was attractive and therefore preferred. Assuming the fact to be as stated, namely, that much of the cloth used by the higher classes was imported, and the home demand therefore—as we shall see—reduced to quite small dimensions as a result of this prejudice, we have to remember that the users of such goods were a small minority of the population. By descent, training and prejudice they were associated with kindred, institutions and customs prevailing abroad and inclined to underrate the skill and capacity of the native boors whom they had always been accustomed to regard as inferiors and generally deficient ; for their military pride largely dominated their judgment. Those in the less accessible parts they knew little about, and were prone to look upon as " wild " and " uncivilised," because of their persistent refusal to acknowledge the decrees and authority of the self-constituted rulers. The superiors who lorded it over the lower ranks were, moreover, the class which formed and reflected the only sentiment which was in a position to make itself heard, acted upon and placed upon record, but was not necessarily the most general and widely spread sentiment. But for all that, even as early as 1258 there had been a baronial recommendation advising the use of English cloth in preference to foreign ; and in 1271, both the export of wools and the import of cloth had been forbidden for a time. The inspiring motive of these actions was in the main political ; but the facts may be taken as an indication that even amongst the naturally prejudiced higher social ranks, home-made fabrics were not so far behind in quality as has been commonly assumed. At the present time, however, a somewhat different sentiment prevails. To doubt native equality, if not superiority, to any other people in almost every respect insures the author of the flinging of a hard name at him, if not of more severe treatment.

The more pleasant and flattering view in relation to old-time skill, of Mr. Abram,[1] is not entirely without some show of reason in its favour. He says :—" The love of display and fine clothes which began in the court of Edward II and soon spread to all classes, may have been a curious mani-festation of the skill of native craftsmen in producing fabrics and manipulating them for effect. Certainly in all below the highest ranks the goods, the demand for which must have been considerable, would be the product of native talent. To assume otherwise is to ignore the proved capacity of the English workers ; and an import of such goods much greater than the most pessimistic view of native skill would admit . . . . . M. Jubinal tells us that among the items in an inventory of Charles V. of France, dated 1371, were ' *salles d' Angleterre,*' which he explains as ' *des tapis de pieces de drap* ' probably from this country. Hence it would appear that English workmen could make materials which commended themselves even to the highest of the land which has been thought to be greatly in advance of ours. It is generally said that the foreign craftsmen settled mainly about London and Norwich,

---

[1] *English Life and Manners in the Middle Ages* (p. 181).

and the fact of the nearness to and trading associations with the Continent of these two places gives the assumption some force. Possibly at the particular time under consideration these places may have possessed a special attraction for the immigrants.

But on the wider and more general question of the Flemish descent upon these shores, if the conventional sources of information are supplemented by inquiries into a hitherto little worked field, it will be found that this is an altogether defective account of the movement. These people are found to be much more widespread, and settled in their chosen habitats earlier than is usually assumed. If the easier access to, and more general acquanitance with, the south and the east as compared with the extreme North-West Riding of Yorkshire be admitted, the numbers that appear to have pushed their way into the latter area at an even earlier date, would seem to suggest that, accepting the academic assumption, the former localities in the middle of the fourteenth century must have experienced a notable incease of population. Such a great augmentation does not, however, appear to have attracted the attention of chroniclers or critics. Moreover, any very extraordinary influx at this particular time must have received its principal impetus from the confidence created and the prospects held out by the report of their own kindred already established here rather than from any promised protection of the King. It is not easy to conceive that in the social conditions which are generally held to have prevailed at this time, a large body of people would be prepared to leave home, kindred and familiar associations, to take up their abode amongst suspicious strangers and entirely new surroundings, unless they had some assurance from trusted acquaintances, that they would be safe and comfortable in doing so. Of course it would be folly to pretend that even a small number of specialists, nay even of others not particularly associated with the craft but accustomed to an atmosphere of trade and industry, when scattered amongst an interested community, did not influence the latter. These could not fail to pick up something of technical procedure, requirements and knowledge of markets from those whose experience had been different from their own insular opportunities. But is it too much to suggest that the continental craftsmen also profited by new ideas picked up from their acquaintances over here? It would be strange indeed if some mutual benefits did not accrue from an association even of a limited character and extent.

If names bearing a flavour of Flemish or other foreign origin are of any significance in this connection, we find some interesting facts in the higher portions of the Yorkshire Calderdale. Mr. John Lister [1] in the work already mentioned gives the following :—" In the year 1332, which is five years *before* the foreign cloth-workers were allowed to settle in England I find in the *Court Rolls* a Thomas Fleming mentioned as mortgagee of $5\frac{1}{2}$ acres of land in Hipperholme. The principal was 25s. and the sanction of the Hall Mote of Brighouse was required to enable Henry of the Broke to pledge his land . . . . to this apparently well-to-do foreigner. The Fleming pays five marks into Court as security for his performance of the contract." Again Sir John [2] Fleming (Flaundresi) was witness to a deed not later than 1257. About the middle of the next century Robert de Flaynsburg witnessed another. At the Wakefield Court [3] held at Michaelmas in the year 1308 amongst a number of others Reynold le Fleming pays 4s. (the highest of the lot, where fines are fixed in some relation to the means of the individual), and Robert de Fleming 2s. for respite to the next Court. At Rastrick *Tourn* [4] in December of the same year, a John le Fleming appears, and Henry le Frankisse serves as a juryman. At subsequent courts several persons of the last name are mentioned, some of them apparently of very doubtful repute. At earlier courts such non-indigenous names as " Norman " and " Westrene " are found, and though only a Christian name, " German " crops up. In all these cases the individuals

[1] H. Ling Roth and J. Lister, *The Yorkshire Coiners and Old Halifax* (p. 146). [2] *History of the Stansfield Family* (p. 109). [3] and [4] *Wakefield Manor Court Rolls*, Yorkshire Archæological and Topographical Society, Record Series.

are of such rank, position, or accepted standing in the community as to warrant the inference that they are of long residence and known character, sufficiently so at all events as to be allowed the ordinary political and social rights.

The most devoted adherents to the theory of Flemish influence upon the textile industries do, however, admit their presence in England before the fourteenth century, the latter half of which is reckoned as the special period of the immigration of the weavers. Thorold Rogers [1] tells us that " the names in the Southampton rental of the twelfth century imply a considerable population of foreigners especially of Flemings ; and it appears from documents that there was a constant immigration from North-west Germany into the Eastern Counties." Another writer [2] applying his researches to a more limited area finds ; " In the year 1331, John Kemp, a master manufacturer from Flanders, received protection to establish himself at York, with a number of dyers and fullers to carry on his trade, and in the following year several manufacturers came over from Brabant and Zealand." But as has already (Chapter IX) been shown, the settling of these dyers and fullers cannot be regarded either as introducing those crafts or contributing much to their improvement in this country.

It has already been shown (pp. 195-197) that there is a strong probability that in the sixteenth century and earlier there was a considerable cloth trade in the neighbourhood of Rochdale. The usual gratuitous assumption of an influx of Flemings has been made ; but to this Colonel Fishwicke [3] gives no countenance whatever. He says : " this is utterly without foundation, and that such was not the case is borne out by the names found in the records of that period, and by the fact that even so late as the beginning of the seventeenth century the Parish Registers show an almost entire absence of foreign names." But for all that he mentions the name of William Mercator, a name with a distinctly foreign flavour, and

[1] *Work and Wages,* 1894 (pp. 9-1v).
[2] Crabtree's *History of the Parish of Halifax* (p. 300).   [3] *History of Rochdale* (pp. 10, 33).

in any case the circumstances in which it is mentioned suggests a position of wealth and authority. This man, he says, about the year 1238, granted certain lands in Wardle to the Abbot and Monastery of Stanlawe. The extreme north-west of Lancashire [1] in the year 1346, affords us the following example :—" Fourneuxe in the Wapentake of Lonsdale . . . . . The Abbot of Fourneux holds the Manor of Aldingham in Fourneux late of Michael Fleming, for the sixteenth part of a knight's fee as aforesaid, paying yearly at Michaelmas 10 li. and other foreign rent as is understood." Michael was evidently a person of some consequence in this part of the world long before the encouragement of an English woollen industry appears to have entered into a royal mind.

There is, however, another name, and that a local one, which will bear mention in this connection, and is interesting if only from the link which it shows may have once existed between the Yorkshire Calderdale parts and the low countries. It is also a case which has sometimes been advanced to support the Flemish origin of the English cloth industry. Throughout the higher part of the Calder watershed and in some adjoining places, the name of " Sutcliffe " is one of the commonest, and in its earlier forms is mentioned in the *Court Rolls* as far back as the year 1296. In the neighbourhood of Hipperholme there is a place called " Suthcliffe " or " Southclif " mentioned in the early records, and there can be little doubt that here is one origin of this particular clan. As is the case with most names, either personal or territorial, the spelling of this one is given in various forms until recent times ; but the origin is quite clear, and its growth into the present form equally so. If the contention submitted below can be substantiated (which is inserted here rather in the interests of fairness than acceptance) we are not without reason for believing that in this particular instance we have the case of a double origin for a territorial surname. Even so the number of surviving descendants is so great that one or both lines must have been very prolific. There is a possibility

[1] Three Lancashire Documents, etc., Chetham Society, Vol. LXXIV (p. 75).

that the second line is of Flemish descent, as has sometimes been claimed for the whole family, and what is more to our present purpose, it was at the earliest time at which we can trace it, interested in the cloth trade. In a work written by Lieutenant Colonel Thomas Sutcliffe, who was at one time in the Chilian service as Governor of the island of Juan Fernandez, entitled *The Rise and Progress of the Woollen, Linen and Cotton Manufacture from 1337 to 1738*, it is stated that, " Jans de Zoetcliffe (savouring of the Low Countries) who had settled near Bolton-le-Moors, Lancashire . . . . . . and his brother Gamel de Zoetcliffe, married a sister of —— Radcliffe the founder of the Todmorden family in the year 1339." It appears that this gentleman came into the Heptonstall district, established a fulling mill in Wadsworth, and sold the cloth in the Heptonstall market. The name " Gamel " in its Scriptural form " Gamaliel " appears to have been a favourite one in this family throughout the generations, and persists in its present representative at Stonesheygate. A tradition is told in the neighbourhood that certain of the Sutcliffes are of Dutch descent. Whether this tradition in its present specific form has managed to survive the usage of six centuries may be doubtful, but it cannot be denied. There is, however, the possibility that it is a lingering memory derived from the above now scarce work. The information just supplied is more directly interesting in relation to the task now before us in two respects. (1) As confirming the contention of a widespread distribution of Flemings before the time of Edward III, and (2) the fact that Bolton-le-Moors, situated in the very heart of mediæval darkest industrial England, was, in spite of all that has been said in that respect, of sufficient repute and activity in the cloth trade, to attract to it at least one commercial representative from the world's principal industrial and trading centre. There is another possible explanation of the origin of this de Zoetcliffe name and family. It is significant that by the year 1337 the Southcliffe family had dropped entirely from the Hipperholme records. By the year 1311 a member of it, Peter, was settled as a fuller in

Rastrick, and before 1379, Adam was in Wadsworth, which is about half-a-dozen miles distant.   Possibly one of the original members interested in textiles had migrated to the Low Countries ; then he or a descendant returned via Bolton-le-Moors to Wadsworth.

Motives Which Influenced the Migrants.

Having dealt, though by no means exhaustively, with the distribution both in time and space of these immigrats to our island, brief attention may now be given to the question of the motives which induced them to take up residence here.   The religious aspect of the question, which, in connection with the later migrations plays so large a part in the generally received explanation, can only have operated at that one definite and limited period, when the flame of persecuting zeal was being especially fanned.   That the reports sent back by the earlier emigrants of their experiences in the new home, may have decided both the fact and locality to the victims of clerical or political intolerance on the Continent, is very probable.   Reciprocally, the good fortune found by the exiles may have stimulated movement of that part of relatives and acquaintances, whose consciences were less sensitive.   But obviously these considerations could only apply to the later wave ; there must be some other reason for all of the earlier migrations, and also for a portion of those during the period of great persecution.   We may safely assume that native overcrowding was not a potent factor in the case.   That not special affection existed for the English and their country, impelling the adventurers to sacrifice themselves and their prospects in the interests of a benighted and less progressive people, is almost certain.   Nor is it likely that funds were available to compensate the craftsmen who spent their time in instructing their new neighbours for the sacrifices thus made.   Masters who brought servants with them, in so far as the servants were utilised for that purpose, most likely looked for some solid advantage therefrom.

It is not unlikely that this influx of foreigners to our shores had much in it of an anticipation of a modern practice, namely, that of captains of industry seeking promising opportunities for extending business, and relief from various disadvantages real or imaginary of their own country or locality by setting up in a new one. And in the non-guild areas the number of immigrants we have seen were present may have found the motive of escape from the harrasing of the continental trade organisations. For such a policy to be successful a combination of favourable circumstances is necessary, amongst others, an adequate supply of suitable workers. If the operations of the industry are simple, the ordinary unskilled person, even without knowledge or experience, may be easily trained, but if intricate and requiring skill some amount of previous experience is essential. Now the whole force of the assumed great advantage derived by English industry from the settlement of the Flemings here is based upon the premises that the latter established and taught the manufacture, weaving, dyeing and finishing of a much superior class of fabric to that to which the English had previously been accustomed. To have effected this implies that the native born operatives themselves were already possessed of considerable knowledge and skill. The most that could be required in order to secure some advance in trading operations, was organisation and judicious direction of existing talents. For the successful establishment of old industries in new situations, the presence of qualified workers, either actual or potential, is a necessary condition. In mediæval times, when all was hand labour, and the different branches of a craft not so specialised—to say nothing of the general principles of industrial organisation being less understood and developed than is the case in modern times—this condition would be especially necessary.

It is quite evident that apart from the compulsory or obligatory exiles, some strong material motive must have operated to have caused these adventurers to leave home, kindred and old associations, at a time when these ties were closer and less easily broken than modern conditions permit.

To have chosen such comparatively out of the way and uninviting regions, as we have already seen that many of them did, emphasises the point. Interests in the rewards of military and political services may have been, almost certainly were, the incentive with some of the earlier arrivals. Amongst the earliest we have seen would be included the near descendants of some of the first Norman adventurers. Possibly some others may have been their relatives and friends invited over to share and assist in securing the spoils of the great victory. With some others, these influences do not seem so obvious ; and in such cases as the Zoetcliffes alluded to previously, it was certainly not so, but rather the possibilities of a trade with which they were already familiar, and for which the resources of their chosen home afforded scope. None of those with whom we have become acquainted appear to have been of the rank simply of skilled operatives, whose mission was to teach their craft to the less expert natives. All were of a higher social standing, apparently fairly rich, and with the exception of military and official personages, either employers or dealers, or both. Or, possibly they were agents, whose office was to buy up the products of the island industry for shipment to their employers or acquaintances on the Continent.

It was probably by such means as this last that the great reputation of such places as Flanders and Norwich as manufacturing industrial centres were enhanced. Whilst being the seats of actual production themselves, they also drew to themselves as a commercial headquarters a large volume of goods from outside sources. The object of these enterprisers must have had a fair prospect of fulfilment, and promised encouraging profits, to have induced their directors to take the risks and shortcomings of residence in a land far from home, and amid strange surroundings. The difficulties would be increased by the attitude of the jealous and exclusive people around them, which would be especially great in the northern regions ; unless indeed these also saw an advantage in the presence of the strangers, a contingency which prevailing habits of thought would not readily engender.

All of these conditions argue the existence of a trade of sufficient magnitude and prospects, and in need of an outlet, to benefit both parties. This conclusion is confirmed by Thorold Rogers [1] with regard to the second wave of immigration, namely, " I make no doubt that there was during Elizabeth's reign a considerable immigration of Flemings, chiefly traders, occasionally manufacturers." That something partaking strongly of this nature was the animating force of all the alien movements, other than those promoted by military, agrarian and official adventure, is the only conceivable explanation suggested by pure reasoning, and is confirmed by the facts at our disposal.

---

[1] *Industrial and Commercial History* (p. 49).

An Early Spinning Mill (p. 256).

Photo. by H. Hardaker.

CHAPTER XIII.

THE INDUSTRIAL REVOLUTION.

THE GENERALLY ACCEPTED CONCEPTION.

THE evidence which we have already seen existing of the prevalence of a widespread and early established textile industry within some of even the upper reaches of the north-central mountainous districts of England, will have prepared us for a somewhat modified conception of what took place at the time of, and subsequent to, the consummation of the Industrial Revolution. It has also been seen that the smelting of iron, the manufacture of salt, and possibly some other industries were by no means unknown in the northern highlands and central plains, centuries before the time at which it has been the custom to credit these parts with entering upon their manufacturing career. The idea has been general, that the industrial activity existing in the north before the period which we have now reached, was very limited in amount, and confined to the coarser kinds of cloth. Professor Thorold Rogers, whom many writers have been content to repeat and amplify in a way of which he would probably not entirely approve,[1] says :— " Many small and obscure villages in the South of England had flourishing manufactures of textile fabrics, at a period long preceding the migration of the Norfolk industries to the West of England, from whence, in comparatively *recent times*, they have travelled to the North." J. R. Green[2] speaks far more definitely and has probably given a wider prevalence to the generally accepted idea. He says of the Elizabethan period :—" The South and West of England still remained the great seats of industry and wealth, for they

[1] *Work and Wages*, (p. 47). [2] *Short History of the English People* (p. 394). 1902 Edition.

251

were the homes of mining and manufacturing activity . . . . We see the *first signs* of the Revolution which has transferred English manufactures and English wealth to the North of the Mersey and Humber in the mention which now meets us of the friezes of Manchester, the coverlets of York, the cutlery of Sheffield, and the cloth trade of Halifax." De Gibbens [1] speaks of the " great Eastern and Western centres of industry, which before 1760 had excelled the other centre, the West Riding, in prosperity." Toynbee [2] and others speak in similar strains, and the impression one gets from these writers is, that after the invention of natural power driven machinery there was an almost bodily and sudden migration of a great trade from its old home to a comparatively new and strange abode. At this time according to them, the woollen and worsted industries established themselves mainly in the West Riding of Yorkshire, and the cotton trade became permanently planted as a flourishing organism in Lancashire, where it had effected its birth a few years previously. It should, however, be noted in passing that some attempts had previously been made to establish the last-named industry in the South.

In this statement of the case as usually presented, we have at least an incomplete account of what happened. What actually did take place was, not so much a bodily migration, as a concentration of these industries in districts where all the conditions necessary for their successful working under the new order existed more completely than anywhere else. Not only the new conditions which the circumstances of the immediate times demanded were met, but as has already been shown in the preceding pages, and will be further demonstrated in those to come, old established practical acquaintance was already firmly rooted. Here practically the whole population were steeped in the traditions, and technically expert in all the operations of the particular trade. Here too were organisers and leaders, who were familiar with both the sources of the raw materials and the

---

[1] *Industrial History of England*, 1890 (p. 162).   [2] *Industrial Revolution*, Chaps. ii, iv. and xiii.

avenues through which the finished product could be disposed of advantageously.   Both were absolutely free from those estrictions, either of class convention or unconsciously acquired habits of thought, which had elsewhere paralysed energy and cramped initiative.   Most important of all, it was here also where the new machines were invented, and the power for driving them was available.   In short, here not one or two, but a combination of all the conditions essential for a new order presented themselves.   In the early days of machinery, when the only existing source of mechanical power in any magnitude or regularity was water having some fall, before the days of the steam engine, the industry was of necessity confined to the hilly districts, where water power could be utilised—that is, the narrow valleys which score the hillsides—or where the uplands lent themselves to the collection of the rainfall and springs, the waters of which could then be conducted to their destined end potential with mechanical energy.   This energy only required tapping and conducting on to the water-wheels suitably placed for its utilisation.   Reservoirs for storage of water were a necessity, and to the construction of these the valleys naturally lent themselves.

Fitness of the Northern Uplands for the New Conditions.

Abundant evidence of these old mills and their " dams " and " goits " still exists in many of the deep narrow valleys which drain the Pennines.   The upper dozen miles of the Yorkshire Calder will serve as an example.   The tributary branches of the main stream naturally attracted the attention of the first mill-builders, partly because of the people living mainly on the upper slopes, so that they were thus placed near the labour supply, but chiefly because in these side cloughs the fall is more rapid than in the main stream, and consequently the water power is more effective and less difficult to store ; thus the earlier hold of the water could be secured with less restrictions upon the freedom of its use and liability to customary or prescriptive rights. The Ryeburn, Luddenden, Cragg, Colden and Dulesgate valleys have each their series of from six to twelve of these one-time busy hives of industry now entirely derelict so far as concerns their original purpose. Some have almost disappeared, others as a consequence of their valuable water rights and position have been transformed into dye or bleach works, or some other industry in which water is an important adjunct. Above each are to be found their old " dams " and " goits " leading on to the water-wheel race, and the " tail-goit " below. Above all right up in the moorlands were often constructed by the joint effort of the various users of the water larger storage reservoirs to be drawn upon as occasion required. Luddenden Valley had its Fly Flats Reservoir, Colden its Nodale Dam, Burnely Valley its Redmires Dam, and there were others. Very few indeed of these hillside cloughs were without their water-driven mills. Even the hillsides themselves as at Acre and Boston Hill in Wadsworth, Lumbutts in Langfield, and Eastwood and Cowhirst in Stansfield, had the drainage of the upper moorlands or surface springs collected and conducted to a convenient site for a mill or a small domestic enterprise.

When improved roads and canals had given the main valleys an advantage in transit arrangements, mills became more numerous there ; and in order to get the benefit of the water with the maximum of fall, it was impounded from the more sluggish main stream a considerable distance up. Ridgefoot Mill, Todmorden, takes in its supply over half-a-mile distant, the conveying " goit " constituting virtually also a reservoir. Moreover, in hilly districts the rainfall is usually greater, and, what is more important, more continuous than in low-lying districts, thus helping regularity of the supply of energy, upon which all relied at the time of which we are speaking. Each valley receives and concentrates the drainage of a large area above, and conducts the water down steep beds, and its stored up energy only requires tapping.

WHY THE NORTH PREVAILED OVER OTHER DISTRICTS.

But in connection with this question of the migration of the industries it is well to bear in mind that the uplands of the north are not the only portions of Britain, where these physical conditions prevail. Why, for instance, did they not serve the textile trade of the West, and with its associated old traditions place that district before all rivals ? In this connection another consideration presents itself regarding the alleged migration to the coal areas of the North. Why should the cloth trade move to this particular area and jump over the equally rich carboniferous deposits of the Midlands ? The old textile areas of the West of England are only just across the Bristol Channel from the South Wales coal-field. The West is also the district where the earlier, although crude, steam engines originated ; and we might have expected that the comparatively earlier and more general acquaintance with that class of motive power might have led more quickly to the adoption there, for the benefit of the lingering cloth trade, of the improved engine of Watt. Herein that locality would have another advantage, the abundant water power of the North tending to retard the free adoption of the newer motor in the latter district.

Although the West of England may not be as favour-able a place for the development and utilisation of water power as the Pennine regions of the North, the period of dependence upon water power alone was a short one ; and the old hand system did not die out immediately, but maintained a lingering, though possibly a sickly existence for many years. In that it was sustained by old association, prestige, and the natural conservatism both of the producers and the consumers. This period of transition and consequent depression was not so long that local skill and interest in the trade could have become extinct, or anywhere near that point, when the steam engine appeared. Consequently, had other conditions been equal, we might have expected that when the improvements in the steam engine and the new machinery became known, they would have been introduced and saved the situation, as they did on a small scale at a later period, as at Bradford-on-Avon.

The answer to the questions propounded in the last paragraph is to be found in the fact that none of the places named, or indeed any other, possessed in so complete a degree a combination of *all* the circumstances necessary for permanent success in the new order then opening out. In considering such a question as the one immediately before us, it must be borne in mind that a complicated industry cannot be suddenly established in a new district, nor be transferred from an old established one to another, unless the chosen place be possessed of very decided advantages, sufficient to countervail the inherent skill of the operatives, associations, and interests of the one that has previously held it. In the case now before us such special advantages did exist, but were of a different order from those which have been customarily recognised. The chief of these which operated are the following —(1) A real widespread living interest in machinery and mechanical devices, as well as means for economising labour and increasing production generally. (2) Power at hand for driving the machines, both in the early stages of machine production, when water was the motive power, and later when steam became the effective agent. (3) All the past history of the northern upland natives had tended towards the development in them of resource, energy, enterprise and freedom from the restraints of harassing or limiting restrictions, which it is generally agreed had often been imposed by custom or orgainised interests operating in other parts of the country. (4) A universally diffused technical skill born of centuries of occupation in all the processes of the trade, together with interest and enterprise in seeking out and catering for markets far and near. Of these points 1, 4 and 3, so far as relates to hereditary influence upon character, are those upon which the emphasis of the present work rests, as in the past they have been most inadequately, if at all, recognised.

Why the Recognised Manufacturing Areas Failed to Maintain Their Position.

The Eastern Counties and the West of England failed so largely in adapting themselves to modern requirements, because, besides being subject to the blighting effects of inopportune Guild restrictions, injudicious notions of monopoly and privilege, they under-estimated the probable consequences of the natural sources of power and the widespread skill possessed by their rivals. The Midlands never had the widely spread interest in textile work and water power resources which other localities had. Possibly also they had felt the unfortunate effects of Guild influence. The " backbone of England " combined not only the physical resources of the new order, the manipulative skill, the freedom from limitations upon resource, but its people also displayed that adaptability to the needs of the consumers, which will always be a powerful element of success. Mr. H. P. Kendall [1] in his paper on the *Hill Family of Soyland* in the middle of the eighteenth century says :—" would it had been possible to describe this old pattern book more fully, but it is utterly beyond my powers . . . . . It sets forth in the actual cloth the great variety of our local manufacturers and the excellent workmanship of local dyers, and it speaks to me from out the years of the toilers of Sowerby and Soyland whose untiring efforts in the wool trade for centuries previously had made the compilation of such a book possible. And in this 20th century, we, with all our science and complicated machinery, can show nothing better finished or better dyed than is contained in this book of 160 years ago, whilst as to the quality of the goods, we have all kinds from the cheapest to the most expensive." The same writer also says :—" Samuel Hill's capacity for fitting in with his customers' needs is well shown in a letter of this period to Mr. Abraham Van Broyes, where he says, ' I am sorry you will not make any further tryall in Broad Shaloons, because I think I could do something better . . . . . provided that I make constantly, but going from one

[1] Halifax Antiquarian Society, 1916.

sort to another spoils all the weavers as I have experienced all my life in what manufacturing I have been concerned in. And there is another thing you will do well to teach me, viz., if ye Broads must be sold in imitation of those made in other parts of England, as you formerly mentioned to me ; then I think you should have the Lists and Head End made as like them as possible, which, if you describe, I shall imitate as near as I can, but if you cannot describe them right you had best send a pattern of the Head End and List to Mr. Wm. Mowld, of Hull, from whom I shall have it with a small charge."

The distinction just drawn between the two peoples referred to, illustrates one aspect of the broad differences in the mental make-up, and in this case with a very striking result, of the these two races composing the English population already referred to (Chapter IV). The one were the descendants of conquering settlers and their vanquished and obedient victims, inheriting the conception that their mission in life was to direct the destinies and provide according to their own ideas for the needs and desires of those with whom they came into contact, and for which services the function of the latter was to pay tribute directly or indirectly. (In this case the tribute was indirect, when it took the shape of a liberal payment for the goods with which their masters thought fit to supply them). The other race consisted of the descendants of the refugees together with adventuring settlers who always refusing to surrender their personal and political liberty, recognised that their own prosperity depended upon their own efforts and largely involved the adaptation of their products to the needs or maybe the whims of those whose trading relations they wished to cultivate.

There is another point which may be briefly alluded to here, although more concerned with a general economic history, and not of particular local significance, has yet an interesting bearing upon the matter immediately before us ; namely, the privileged position of the commercialists who have in former times received the most exclusive attention of historians, national legislators and administrators, as showing another of the effects which may be expected to result from a class being surrounded by an atmosphere of privilege. Rogers [1] tells us :—" For a hundred years from the Battle of Bosworth to the days of Drake a strange languor came over Commercial England." Now this is just the period when the trading monopolists were lending themselves to the first of the schemes of the militarists and other adventurers to secure the conquest of Ireland by starving into submission or extir-pating the natives by the means of destroying their industries and educational facilities. Such a policy may also be looked upon as a corollary to the sole market idea which prevailed at the time and for long afterwards. It is not strange that this " languor " should have been seen to exist during the time that commercial activities were devoted to such an end. It may also be noted that since that date until recent years the general prejudice relating to everything Irish which has resulted from six-and-a-half centuries of arrogance, distrust and strife, has prevented both the Irish people and ourselves, as well as the rest of the world, from knowing the real state of affairs and course of events which have happened there.

Conditions Tending to the Origin and Development of New Methods.

Generally speaking new processess are invented and improvements in method establish themselves, where familiarity with the purposes to which they are to be put, and the demand for increasing or cheapening production exist. In such places they succeed, because there is a wide and well established interest and experience in the matters concerned. Of the great number of inventions of textile machinery, it is remarkable how few have emanated from the reputed ancient seats of the industry, the Eastern Counties and the West of England. It can scarcely be without significance that nearly all the mechanical inventions which initiated the revolution in the textile industries originated or were mainly

---

[1] *Commercial and Industrial History of England* (p. 400).

developed within the area, which it has been the custom to regard as a somewhat backward and desolate one, even in that county of Lancaster which has been generally looked upon as being previous to the Industrial Revolution, the most backward of all. It will not be out of place to restate them in their order and place of birth.

1733, Kay of Bury (Lancashire) invented the flying shuttle. He also effected other improvements.

1738.—Paul, a native of London, patented an apparatus for spinning by means of rollers. He lived part of his life in Birmingham, where the invention was carried through. Both these places are outside of the reputed home of the textile industry.

1748.—The same individual invented a machine for carding cotton, the principle of which was embodied in future machines.

1760.—Robert Kay (son of the above) invented the drop box for use in looms where it was necessary to use several shuttles.

1764.—Hargreaves of Blackburn invented the Spinning Jenny.

1771.—Arkwright, a native of Preston, at Cromford (Derby) established spinning by means of rollers.

1779.—Crompton of Bolton (Lancashire) invented the mule.

Soon afterwards the process of cloth printing by the use of cylinders was invented; again outside of the area where, on the assumption to which we have been accustomed we might have expected to find it. For it was Bell, a Scotchman, to whom we are indebted for this means of a great increase in productivity upon the old method.

Even the power loom, although some time elapsed before it became a practical success, did not originate in the East, West or South, where, as we are told, all the energy, enterprise and skill in cloth-making existed. The principle of it was conceived by Dr. Cartwright, who patented the "power loom" in 1785 ; though a southerner but from outside of the academic textile domain, his inspiration was derived from a conversation with a party of Lancashire and other northern manufacturers.

It is the same in this, as in many other cases ; the determination of who really was the first inventor of the power loom may be a disputed point. The honour has been claimed for others not named here, and as will be seen later, there is no intention in this place of definitely deciding the issue on behalf of any one of them, but merely of stating what is known of one whose case has hitherto received the most general acceptance. It may be noted in passing that the same remarks apply to the reputed inventors of the rest of the numerous contrivances which have been applied to the prep- aration and spinning of fibres mentioned above. Be that as it may, whether we take the first discovery of a principle or method, which, crudely conceived and worked out as it may be, and is therefore not a practical success, but which contains the germ which later workers more fortunately situated are able to develope and perfect ; whichever of these is entitled to the honour of having conferred the greatest benefit on mankind, apart from purely ethical considerations, is a fruitless discussion. In some cases, if not all, those later developments which are crowned with success—possibly owing as much to the peculiar circumstances of the immediate present as to the merits of the invention itself—are suggested and could not have come about without the stimulation and direction of thought by the earlier attempts. Seldom indeed is it that an entirely new principle or method is fully conceived and worked out in all its details by one mind. Step by step evolution is here as in most other cases the natural order of progress.

An early attempt to apply power other than that derived from the human muscle to the weaving of cloth was made by Robert Kay, who in the year 1748 patented a power loom. What was the source of the power intended to be used is not a principal point. Water power and wind power must have been familiar to all, as they had for centuries been in use for several purposes, *e.g.* the simple processes involved in grinding corn, and the fulling of cloth. Horses had also been employed for driving various sorts of contrivances used in the mechanical arts. Heptonstall has its tradition that there was once a horse-jinny at work in the Weaver's Square of that old town. Not much has been heard of the success of Kay's invention ; one possible contributary cause to that result may have been the fact that there was already a difficulty in supplying sufficient warp and weft to keep the existing hand-looms in full work, while the new invention threatened a still greater scarcity, as it would result in all the more rapidly using up the existing short supply. There is a great probability that these causes together with the generally prevailing prejudice against the monopoly conferred by a patent, and some others, deterred progress in this line at a time when the real and presssing want was an increased supply of yarn.

" In [1] the year 1748, John Kay .... and Joseph Stel^l patented improvements on the Dutch engine loom, which they said may go or be worked by hands, water, or other force." It may be useful to explain that " the first loom in which all the motions in weaving were connected and controlled by one motive power was the ribbon loom. A machine in which four to six pieces could be woven simultaneously is recorded to have been in existence in Dantzic in the last quarter of the sixteenth century." The date of this invention is interesting, as it is very early, or perhaps prior to any record of the Dutch loom in Lancashire. It also indicates the facility with which the local wealth of inventive genius as applied to the textile trades seized upon the many opportunities of activity, which the circumstances of the times and situation afforded. A few years later it was freely asserted that there were in Lancashire three times as many Dutch looms as there ever had been of any other kind, and that the number of

[1] *Encyclopedia Brittancica*, Ed. Nine, Vol. XXIV. (p. 465).

pieces woven in each of them as given above had considerably increased. These facts would seem to suggest a very great probability that the loom had been familiar in that district some time before the recorded date as given above. Otherwise we must assume a most unusually rapid development of this particular industry, and an adaptability to new conditions upon the part, both of merchants and weavers, which has seldom been paralleled.

We may now return to the statement of Dr. Cartwright's connection with the power loom. The quotations given below show that the evidence on his behalf has impressed some usually reliable authorities. The Cartwright Hall at Bradford, built by the first Lord Masham, denotes the strength with which the case appealed to at least one great figure in the textile world. At the time of his invention the Rev. Edmund Cartwright, D.D., lived at Hollander House in Kent. He was born at Marnham, Notts., and was educated at Wakefield Grammar School and Cambridge. At the latter place for some years afterwards he followed a scholastic career. In 1779 he was presented to the rectory of Goadby Marwood, Leicestershire. These details show that though the Doctor had but a very slight and indirect connection with the northern industrial area, he was equally remote from the better known cloth-making district of early times. His attention was accidentally turned to the possibility of applying power to weaving, which, together with its results, may best be given in his own words. He says [1] :—" Happening to be at Matlock in the summer of 1784, I fell in company with some gentlemen of Manchester . . . . . One of the company observed that as soon as Arkwright's patent expired so many mills would be erected, and so much cotton spun, that hands never could be found to weave it. To this observation I replied that Arkwright must then set his wits to work and invent a weaving mill . . . . The Manchester gentlemen unanimously agreed that the thing was impracticable."

" Some little time afterwards, a particular circumstance recalling this conversation . . . . I immediately employed a

[1] *Encyclopeia Brittanica*, Ed. Nine, Vol. VI. (p. 500).

carpenter and smith . . . As soon as the machine was finished I got a weaver to put in the warp . . . To my delight a piece of cloth such as it was, was the produce, as I had never before turned my thoughts to anything mechanical . . nor had seen a loom at work, or knew anything of its construction . . . My first loom must have been a most rude piece of machinery . . . . I then secured what I thought a most valuable property by a patent, 4th April, 1785 . . . I then condescended to see how other people wove."

" His [1] first power loom was a rude contrivance, but he afterwards greatly improved it, and made it an almost perfect machine. The first mill on his plan, that of Messrs. Grimshaw of Manchester, was wilfully destroyed in 1791. In spite, however, of the opposition of the hand loom weavers, the use of the power loom increased." In addition to the power loom Cartwright invented machines for combing wool and making ropes. He also tells us :—" I took out my last weaving patent [2] August 1st of that year."

The romantic circumstances attending Dr. Cartwright's entry into, and activities in, the field of textile invention may have unduly attracted the attention of writers ; and his ability to place on record his own experiences, may have helped to obscure the achievements of other workers in the same field, who were less fortunately situated and devoid of the powers of exposition. But it is fairly apparent that the gentleman did contribute something real to the solution of a difficult problem. For these reasons we are likely to know much more about him and this part of his work than any other individual, to one or more of whom we may be in reality indebted, unless in the future some at present altogether unknown sources of information be revealed.

" Weaving by power could never have succeeded but for the discovery by Mr. Radcliffe of Stockport of a process for dressing the web before it was put into the loom." " Peter Marsland [3] of Stockport . . . was the inventor of an

[1] *Encyclopedia Brittancica*, Ed. Nine, Vol. VI. (p. 500). [2] Ibid. Vol. V. (p. 166). [3] *Encyclopedia Brittanica*, Ed. Nine, Vol. VI. (p. 500).

improvement upon the power loom by means of the double crank, for which about the year 1807 he obtained a patent. The operation of the crank is to make the lathe give a quick blow to the cloth on coming in contact with it, and by that means render it more stout and even." Of course this brief and general statement does not include all the individuals who have taken a part in devising mechanical contrivances which have led to the greatly enhanced productivity of textile manipulation, they are but the chief incidents, the application of a new principle or the contrivance of methods for making practically and commercially successful ideas at which others had laboured with less tangible and fortunate results in overcoming difficulties and prejudices. In effect they are the outcome, the culminating points in a series of efforts made by various workers to meet a prevailing want. But the essential point for the present is that these great developments took place amongst a people who have been considered to be rather outside of the sphere, and until a later time comparatively little interested in the industrial and commercial affairs directly concerned. Possibly cotton was more amenable to the applications of mechanical devices in the earlier stages of the devlopment of the industry than some other fibres : but it must be remembered that the new fibre had come into use as a supplement to, and a substitute for, others which had already been long and extensively worked in Lancashire and adjoining parts.

WERE THE RECORDED NEW MACHINES ACTUALLY THE FIRST ?

It would seem that there is almost a doubt as to whether the machines alluded to above were in all cases really the earliest that were applied to the making of weft and warp. References in some local writings [1] certainly suggest that there were in fact some earlier ones. Our author says, " During the

[1] John Travis, *Fielden Families of Walsden and Stansfield*, 1903 (p. 11). Mr. Travis published several booklets which prove him to have been a diligent collector of local, family, trade and general lore, derived from his own recollections and a wide circle of personal acquaintances.

lifetime of the late Abraham Fielden of Swineshead, a small mill was built in the clough below the farm where there was a more regular supply of *water power for turning the machines* then in use by these people, for the purposes of producing yarns for warp and ' wough,' for their trade in making stuff or Russell pieces. . . . Such small places for carding and spinning wool by power were a great help to the home manufacturing trade of those days ; but later, even these were pushed aside by other improved methods of working the fibre, until at length the old ways were completely driven out in the race and competition of the times." Now what is here related must have transpired many years prior to the earliest inventions we usually find related ; for on the page before the one from which we have quoted is given the will of the said Abraham Fielden, which is dated December 13th, 1681. Of the nature or style of the machines no indication is given further than appears above ; but it is certain that Mr. Travis was acquainted with the style and date of the later inventions. On page 20 he relates the building of another place by a descendant of the aforesaid Abraham Fielden, in the year 1786, and states :—" The Crompton methods of making warps and weft being adopted, etc."

Again on February 19th, 1785, Thomas Eastwood is party to an indenture, by which amongst other things he conveys " one twining mill." Now there is every reason to believe, both from the name given to this implement, and from the fact that Thomas Eastwood and many others in the immediate neighbourhood were engaged in the cloth trade, that we have an allusion to some kind of a spinning machine. The name of " twining mill " as applied to a machine for spinning still survives in the neighbourhood of Halifax. In the district of Todmorden, of which Eastwood—the place of the original reference—forms a part, wool has now been entirely superseded by cotton. Of course the " twining mill " may be one form or development of one of the inventions named above ; but within twenty years of the earliest of them we have here a reference to a quite familiar object. It had most probably been in use some time at the date given (1785) :

in any case it shows that the men of this upland and remote district were alive to the best means available for the pursuit of their business.

LATER DEVELOPMENTS OF THE REVOLUTION.

The earlier mills of the water power districts retained their advantages over the classical manufacturing areas, until the improved steam engine appeared, which possessed the additional advantage over the preceding system of enabling mills to be placed in those positions, where all other conditions were most favourably combined. This brought about another partial migration, but neither so great nor so sudden as the previous one. The steam engine was introduced to most of the water power mills in order to supplement and regularise the supply of energy, which depending as it did largely upon the weather was limited and somewhat intermittent. Eventually the greater possibilities of steam power—unlimited in amount—favouring larger scale working and regular in operation, together with advantages of position —such as transit facilities and opportunities of providing for a more abundant supply of labour—resulted greatly to the disadvantage of these first mills. To begin with the smaller and more remote ones found it impossible to continue working; then these were followed by others nearer placed to the new conditions. Finally, those of the lower and more open parts of the tributary and the main valleys, together with those of the open country, dominated the situation. In some of the older established mills still surviving there has been effected a reversal of the former conditions. Instead of water as the sole motive power, or the principal one with steam as supplementary, steam is now most decidedly the principal, while water is a small supplementary agent.

RESTRICTIVE EFFECTS OF GUILD POLICY NOT SPECIAL TO THIS ERA.

It has been usual to associate the decay of the " old centres of industry," and the rise of the " new," with the hampering effects of the ancient merchant and craft Guilds, as a result of which the " new " being free from the restrictions to which the " old " were subject, were in the enjoyment of a considerable advantage. It should, however, be borne in mind that this was no new feature, or in any way special to that particular epoch, except that, as suggested a little later, the adverse conditions had become somewhat accentuated. It was a relation which had existed for centuries. Still, we must admit that some influence such as has been indicated would accrue ; indeed, so far the influence wielded by the Guilds and the results which they undesignedly achieved, are a striking example of the injudicious and excessive use of the powers of privilege and monopoly. The authors wrought their own destruction. It was not alone that short-sighted restriction and narrow regulation in the interests of a class, may hamper a trade when conditions are normal ; but during a period of upheaval and great change fixed habits and inelastic rules, clung to when there is also displayed in another part of the same field perfect freedom and great energy. may do much to paralyse the efforts of those who are subject to their hindering influence. The power of initiative and the desire for adaptability are deadened just at the time when it is most necessary that they should be alert and active.

In this repsect the character and powers of the mediæval Guilds are fairly well known. When at the height of their influence and before their ultimate decay, their guiding spirit, so far as it had effected the course of the industry, had been one mainly of unrestrained monopoly, directed solely to the immediate interests of the members, while the trade was limited to those who were members, and its whole policy was subject to restrictions directed by a social and economic outlook which to a great extent had already become obsolete. But whatever these institutions may have been in earlier times, by the sixteenth and especially the seventeenth centuries— probably influenced by the infamous conduct of Henry VIII towards their wealth—those in the trades of the Guild districts had become self-seeking closed corporations, unadaptive to progress or to any changed conditions ; without vision, with no conception of any interest but that of the immediate material benefit and ease of their own set, and with no means of securing that but at the expense of others.   Quite probably, however, the Guildsmen as a rule were perfectly unconscious that these effects would be achieved, thanks to the conservative outlook engendered by privilege, and the prevailing habit of thought, which the mentality of the times and situation nurtured.

GREATLY ENHANCED PRODUCTIVITY.

With the advent of the new machinery, operating only where natural power was available, and the whole population steeped in the newer conceptions and industrial traditions generally, the productivity of the northern textile centres soon exceeded the previous total for all England.   Statistics for the whole country and different parts of it, giving detailed and accurate figures in the respective areas for successive periods, on which reliable comparisons can be based, are very difficult to obtain, it may be do not exist.   But sufficient evidence of a character not so direct and precise exists to justify the presumption already put forward. Evidence has already been given (Chapters IX and X) which clearly establishes the fact that long before the date usually fixed as the beginning of the Industrial Revolution, a much greater share of the total productivity of the country was being effected in a limited portion of the hitherto overlooked area than had at one time been suspected.   It has been shown (pp. 190, 257) that a single firm carrying on its operations under most disadvantageous conditions as to situation, was at one time doing nearly one per cent. in value of the total officially recognised export trade.   Abundant evidence exists in the shape of buildings of the seventeenth and early eighteenth centuries, both business premises and residences of workpeople and employers, *wills*, business and property documents, public and private records and experiences of various kinds, to prove that the case just cited was but one amongst a large number of many great and innumerable small ones, which existed in the particular area, which we have under review, on both sides of the Pennines.   Indeed, in the light of the evidence already submitted, which by no means exhausts the sources, it cannot be regarded as an unreasonable inference to conclude that even before the great change began, quite half of the manufactures of the nation had their origin outside of the usually recognised regions.

The same evidence points to a strong probability that the free region was worked to its full extent before the era of the revolution, and only required the devising of increased means of production to trench effectively upon the market supplied by their enervated competitors. The greater freedom from regulation and tradition enabled the northern manufacturers to make a fuller use of new fibres, and by that means to outrival their competitors in the Eastern counties and the West of England. This fact may help to explain why some Acts of Parliament were passed, laying down the sizes, materials, etc., of cloths, which applied particularly to northern goods. They reflected largely the feeling which prevailed generally in the privileged districts, and were probably instigated from those quarters by the monopolists. The acknowledged increased production which the new machinery brought about, could not fail to increase the produce even with a stationary number of workers, which, however, was probably always greater than has been previously realised. But the rapid increase in population of the towns and villages affected, and the number of weavers' and other workmens' cottages evidently built about this date—they can be identified by their style alone—testify to a considerable increase in population, a corresponding industrial activity, and probably also improvement in material resources.

At first these growing places became the acknowledged centres of the trade, not so much by acquiring that of the reputed older centres, as by discovering and adapting themselves to the requirements of the new markets which were revealed to indomitable energy coincident with large means of supply and cheapened production. The remark attributed to the merchant by Dr. Cartwright, that " as soon as Arkwright's patent expire . . . so much cotton would be spun, that hands never could be found to weave it," implies that there was prevailing at the time an idea that there existed a considerable unsatisfied demand for cloth. The Eastern counties, the West, and South, were not immediately displaced, but lost their ground gradually. Some small quantity still survives in certain parts, but only by virtue of the adoption of the modern methods of the north. The larger operations of a new centre, even though it may have originally catered for quite a new market, tend to a concentration there of the whole. A great part of the increased trade of the modern centres came in the first place in response to the enterprise and adaptability shown in more promptly meeting the rapidly growing demands, which arose through a combination of causes :—*e.g.* increased opportunities by rapid production and improved transit facilities, of meeting an existing, but hitherto imperfectly known or supplied demand, and the cheapening of goods relative to greater and more constant real wages, which arose out of the more rapid production and a greater use of substitutes such as cotton in place of the older fibres. The conservatism of prejudice had acted against cotton as it does against all innovations : it is a human failing which the older interests had exploited for their own advantage, but which now began to retire before the generally recognised advantages of the new drapery.

The development of the cotton industry in the districts around Manchester affords a good illustration of the growth of a new industry, where inherent skill and local natural advantages can successfully utilise unfamiliar raw materials, realise new opportunities and cope with old prejudices. To have been so immediately successful the natives must have been familiar with and expert in textile pursuits, while the commercial and industrial leaders must have been alive to the demands of the world markets, and the new means of supplying their needs. They must also have had the sagacity to realise the possibilities of a new material for that end, and enterprise enough to seize upon its possibilities and adapt their labours to its supply.

CONCENTRATION OF THE IRON INDUSTRY IN THE NORTH.

Previous to the eighteenth century the iron industry was not so exclusively confined to the Southern counties as it has been the fashion to assert. Like the textile trade, there was much of this work scattered over many parts of the country, which, though small in amount in most places, was in the aggregate quite a considerable proportion of the whole. Two factors contributed to its necessary migration from its early principal seat, namely :—(1) The fuel used in the old process of working was rapidly becoming exhausted, and must before long have necessitated the removal of much of the iron working to other areas. Either great quantities of fuel must have been brought into the old area, or the ore must have been transferred to the localities where fuel could be had. Moreover, the strictly limited supply of fuel, if confined to wood, must have prevented the iron industry from ever achieving either its later efficiency, or a tithe of its amount. Another effect of the new methods of iron-working was to set free the available timber supplies for other purposes. The compact ore would be most likely to lend itself to travel. When the new process of utilising coal for fuel was perfected, the available supplies were a long way off from the southern area, but in association with or near to deposits of ore which would equally fulfil the required purpose. (2) The manufactured iron would in the southern area be very far from the places—the industrial centres—where most of the home consumption would be required. This circumstance would apply more exactly at the period of which we are speaking than to-day, when the modern facilities for carriage had not been so fully developed. Thus for both of the foregoing reasons the southern iron industry must in any case very soon have waned in its old home. Like the textile industry it was not so much a migration to the new centres where power was available, as a concentration in those parts where all the necessary conditions for success under the new order existed, namely, skill, organising ability, adaptability, raw materials, and natural sources of power.

INDEX.

INDEX.

Abodes of Early Natives :—9, 22, 62-3.
Abel Cross :—45.
Academic :—Histories, 3, 5, 6, 8, 13, 143-4 ; Training, 60, 63, 76, 224 ;
    Deficiencies, 143-7, 166, 207-8, 224, 234-5 ; Error in Transcription,
    87.
Agriculture :—In the Pennines, 24, 84-106, 123-6, 159-63 ; Combined with
    Manufactures, 84-5, 167.
Anabaptists :—56-7.
Analyses :—Ore and Scoria, 213-6, 222.
Anglo-Saxons :—66.
Armour, chain :—210.
Ashton-under-Lyne :—Cloth Trade and Corn, 197-9.
Autumnal Slaughter :—87-8, 101-10, 142.

Backwardness of North :—What it really is, 30, 77-8, 124-5.
Baptists :—57-8.
Barrow :—Sepulchral, 32-3.
Beasts, Wild :—22-3, 94, 121, 129.
Beaumont Clough :—Bloomery, 211.
Blackley :—Early Iron-working, 225.
Blackstone Edge :—Roman Road, 66.
Bolton :—Early Cloth Trade :—201-2, 246.
Bride Stones :—Rock Scenery, 19 ; Cross under, 49.
British Church :—29, 30, 49 ; late Survival, 31.
Boundary Stones :—36-8, 43.
Bronze Age :—Barrow, 32 ; In Hill Country, 29, 61-2.
Brunanburh :—Site, 13.
Burnley :—Church, 31 ; Associations with Yorks. Borderland, 48 ; Fulling
    Mill, 204.

Calders :—Sources of, 20-2 ; Diversions, 19-20.
Claderdale :—Upper, a type of Hill Country, 15, 22, 94 ; Opened to World
    15-16 ; Ironworking, 208-12 ; Water Power, 253-4.
Catholes Cross :—45-6.
Cattle :—Breeding, 23, 92, 121-6, 141 ; Winter Feeding, 86-92, 115-42 ;
    Autumnal Slaughter, 101-5, 142 ; Human Food, 84-5, 104-6 ; Hides
    and Carcases, 200 ; Wandering, 94.
Celtic Church :—See British.
Christianity :—Introduction, 29-31 ; Early remains, 38-50.

Churches :—Celtic, 29-31, 49 ; Romish, 29-30 ; Burnley, 31, Cross Stone,
40-1, 53 ; Heptonstall, 53 ; Halifax, 31 ; Todmorden, 53 ; Neglect
of Hill Country, 31, 39-40, 53 ; Lands, 55.
Churchmen :—Activities, 52-4 ; Secular Duties, 53, 55 ; Bribes, 53.
Civil Wars :—8.
Classes dominating Policy and Records, 5-6, 29, 52, 143, 186, 233-4, 240-1.
Climate :—16, 26-7, 114, 130, 161, 164-5, 254.
Cliviger :—Iron, 215, 217-8, 220-1, 228-30 ; E. and W. Calders, 20-2 ;
Dr. Whitaker, 60-1 ; " Mill " and " Walk Mill," 204.
Clothiers :—Interests and Energies, 176-90, 256-8 ; Houses, 188 ; Wills,
177-80, 184-5.
Cloth Trade :—Early, 147-51, 164-7, 199 ; Poll Tax Returns, Government
Documents and Wills, 170-7 ; Ashton, 192 ; Burnley, Colne and
Walfreden, 204 ; Rochdale, 195-7 ; Whitworth, 229 ; Halifax and
Colchester, 173-5 ; Monopolists, 186, 189, 257, 259, 267-8 ; Quality
of Goods, 177, 240-1 ; Exports, 148-50, 190-1.
Clerics :—Part in Records, 52 ; Relations to Ecclesastics, 55.
Colne :—Highway to, 45 ; Cloth Trade, 204.
Communications :—Difficulties in Hilly Districts, 15-6, 48, 193, 198.
Conquerors :—Get the ear of World, 12 ; Limited success in N. Hills, 66-72,
155-7.
Corn :—Growing and Grinding, 89, 93-9, 109-10, 123-7 ; Imports, 93,
159-61, 198-9 ; Oats and Wheat, 95-100, 127.
Cotton :—199, 201-2.
Cromlech at-Walshaw Dean :—33.
Crosses :—38-51.
Cross Stone :—40-1.
Cross Lee :—Old Settlement, 43.
Cumbria :—48.

Day Labourers :—128-9.
Day Work :—A Measure of Land, 117.
Dissenting Conventicles :—Situations, 40 ; Licensed Meeting Places, 57.
Doomsday Book :—Places not mentioned, 67-8, 155.
Dove Keeping :—109-10, 123, 128.
Dues, Manorial :—Easier in Upper Calderdale, 69-71, 139-41.
Dyes and Dyeing :—190, 257.

Ecclesiastics :—Relations with Natives, 10-1, 52 ; Relations with Clerics, 55 ;
Nearest Establishments, 10 ; Distant Authorities, 73 ; Earliest Buil-
dings, 39, 58 ; Act Book of Whalley, 54.
Exports :—Corn and Wool, 149 ; Cloth, 148-50, 190-1.

Fawcett, Rev. T. :—Cross Stone, 40.
Flemings :—Migration of, 235-6 ; In North, 238-43 ; Rogers on Early, 244 ;
Edward III, 235-8 ; N.W. Lancashire, 245 ; Sutcliffes, 245-7 ;
Motives, 247-50.
Flint Implements :—19.

Pennine Hills :—Unrecognised by Historians, 1, 5 ; Unsuited to Mediæval Ambitions, 7, 67-8, 145 ; Occupied since Stone Age, 61-2 ; Physical Conditions, 15-24, 151-2 ; Tendency to Manufacturing, 163-5 ; Early Manufacturing, 152, 181-2 ; Less Obscure, 188 ; Ironworking, 207-30.
Pilgrimages :—44, 55-6.
Poaching :—107-8.
Poll Tax :—Trades in W. Riding, 170-1 ; Rochdale, 195-6 ; Names, 55.
Population :—Rural and Urban, 148 ; Outlands, 152-6, 158, 160, 163.
Poultry and Eggs :—112.
Pre-Christian Relics :—31-6.
Presbyterianism :—56.
Puritans :—Favourable Soil, 56 ; Symbolism, 38.

Quakers :—56-7.
Querns :—98-9.

Rattonstall :—Manor, 37 ; Bloomery, 211.
Ramsden :—Bloomeries, 209-10.
Reformation :—Its Appeal, 39, 56.
Religious Houses :—Absence, 10 ; Pilgrimages, 55-6.
Rochdale :—Poll Tax, 195-6 ; Cloth Trade, 195-7 ; Ironworking, 229.
Romans :—Influence, 10, 66 ; Church, 29-30 ; Roads, 66 ; Things Old or Uncommon ascribed to, 215.
Rossendale :—Highway to Halifax, 43 ; Vaccaries, 23, 121 ; Wolves, 23 ; Bloomeries, 218-9, 226.
Ruddle Scout :—Iron Mine, 215, 217, 220-1.
Rural Industries :—147-51, 165-7.

Saddleworth :—Bloomeries, 212-4, 223-5.
Saltworks :—123, 127-8.
Saunderclough :—Bloomery, 210.
Saxons :—62.
Saxifield :—Site of Brunanburh, 13
Scandinavians :—62, 66.
Scotch Wars and Raids :—76-7.
Serfdom :—71-2.
Settlers :—Early, 144-5.
Sheep :—52, 110-4 ; Number of, 161-4.
Smithycliffe :—Bloomery, 212.
Soil :—5, 92, 135, 154, 160-2.
Soyland :—Cloth Making, 190, 257-8.
Specialisation :—Tendency to, 151-2, 154.
Stansfield :—Township, 37, 43 ; Family, 93-4 ; Menhir, 35-6 ; Baptists, 57.
Status of Hill People :—11, 60.
Steam Power :—255-7, 267.
Stiperden :—Cross, 47-51.
Stones :—Menhir, 34-5.

INDEX -- PLATES.

281